# ZERO BREAK

# ZERO BREAK

EDITED BY

## MATT WARSHAW

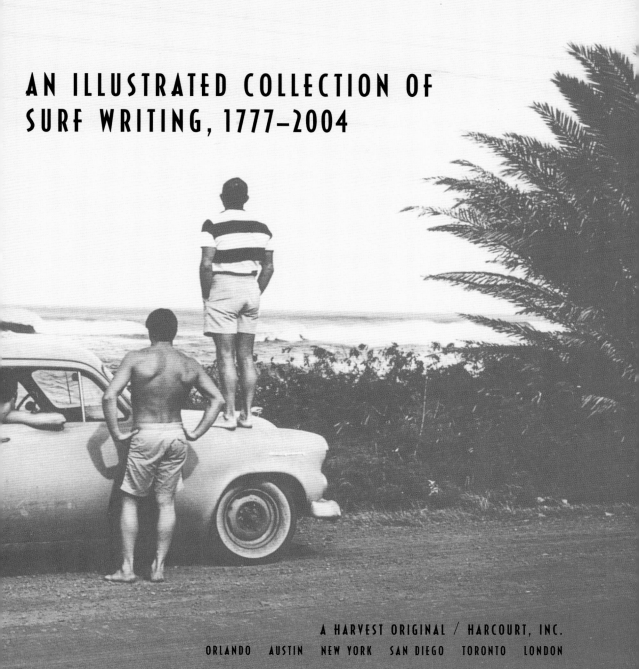

# AN ILLUSTRATED COLLECTION OF
# SURF WRITING, 1777–2004

A HARVEST ORIGINAL / HARCOURT, INC.

ORLANDO   AUSTIN   NEW YORK   SAN DIEGO   TORONTO   LONDON

Requests for permission to make copies of any part of the work should be mailed to the following address: Permissions Department, Harcourt, Inc., 6277 Sea Harbor Drive, Orlando, Florida 32887-6777.

www.HarcourtBooks.com

Library of Congress Cataloging-in-Publication Data
Zero break: an illustrated collection of surf writing, 1777–2004/edited and with an introduction by Matt Warshaw.—1st ed.
p.   cm.
"A Harvest original."
ISBN 0-15-602953-7
1. Surfing—Anecdotes.   I. Warshaw, Matt, 1960–
GV840.S8Z47 2004
797.3'2—dc22   2004010668

Text set in Adobe Garamond
Designed by Linda Lockowitz

Manufactured in China
First edition
K J I H G F E D C B A

Permissions Acknowledgments begin on page 356 and constitute a continuation of the copyright page.

*Dedicated to Sarah Malarkey,*
*Dan Duane, Liz Weil, August Hidalgo, Stasia Lord, the*
*Eisenmanns, Kelly Duane, Steve Helig, Lili Malabed, Kevin Starr,*
*Mark Renneker, and the rest of my spracked-up San Francisco set.*
*I bring a ten-dollar bottle of wine, you guys give me dinner,*
*movie reviews, dirty jokes, love advice, and surf talk.*
*We stay 'til we die. Nobody leaves!*

**zero break** General expression for any rarely seen big-wave break located well offshore. "First break" is the place where medium to large swells normally crest; "second break" is where the same wave either re-forms and crests again, or where smaller waves initially break. Zero break waves are the biggest in any particular area, and are usually thought of as being dangerous and somewhat mysterious.

—from *The Encyclopedia of Surfing*

# CONTENTS

# INTRODUCTION

Captain James Cook, celebrated master and commander of the *Resolution,* in the service of God, King, and the British Navy, dropped anchor at Tahiti's Matavai Bay in late 1777 and rowed ashore for a quick surf check. A single canoe-paddling native was riding the small waves along the northern point. Cook was impressed—not just by the strange new "amusement" itself, but in the near-rapturous state it seemed to produce, to the point that the surfer showed no interest in the sunburned visitors, or their impossible three-masted vessels floating in the waters nearby. "I could not help concluding," Cook wrote in *A Voyage to the Pacific Ocean,* the wildly popular multivolume account of his third and final venture, "that this man felt the most supreme pleasure while he was driven on so fast and smoothly by the sea." First written account of surfing. Bull's-eye.

Having spent way too much time slogging through the millions of banal, overwrought, mistaken, or otherwise stoke-sucking words published on surfing over the past two-hundred-plus years, I now find myself veering pretty regularly into the near reaches of surf world burnout and cynicism. Follow your passion diligently enough and it often becomes... a job. Yet I still marvel at Cook's "supreme pleasure" sentence, at its compact elegance, and how the wonder and simplicity of his words mirror the wonder and simplicity of wave-riding itself. The opening paragraph of Genesis ends with "and the Spirit of God was moving over the face of the waters," and I don't think it's too ridiculous, and maybe only a *little* imperialist, to say Cook's passage gives surfing its own creation moment. (Staying with the religious analogy for a moment, I'm happy to credit Cook alone for the first surfing reference—just as Genesis is credited to Moses and not to unknown author J or whoever—even though scholars agree that it was likely written by the surgeon of Cook's consort ship, *Discovery,* and further ghosted by a London editor.) Cook is an antidote for surf world burnout and cynicism. The day I read his stoked little dispatch and don't feel cheered is the day I throw the boards and wetsuits on the curb and drive east to begin a new life somewhere in the foothills.

Cook is also the obvious starting point for a surfing anthology. Where it goes from there, after the rest of the small but reputable surf-lit canon is accounted for (Mark Twain, Jack London, Tom Wolfe, and a few others), is pretty subjective. Glancing at the *Zero Break* table of contents, it looks as if I've favored either darker pieces or comedy. Other editors would probably select differently: more travel-adventure pieces, for example, or more surfer profiles. But I've always thought the mother lode of surf-writing material, fiction and nonfiction, is located along the seam between the surfing and nonsurfing worlds, and that this material is best processed as comedy or tragedy. (Two of my favorite pieces are missing from this collection: the Jeff Spicoli sections of Cameron Crowe's *Fast Times at Ridgemont High,* and William Finnegan's 1992 *New Yorker* essay "Playing Doc's Games." Crowe has never granted excerpt rights for *Fast Times,* and, in fact, has never allowed the book itself to be reprinted. Finnegan is saving "Games" for his own surfing book.)

Not counting the six excerpts that make up *Zero Break*'s opening section, all but one of the pieces included in this anthology were published within the past forty years. This is partly a function of supply, as the number of surf-themed essays, articles, and books shot way up in the early '60s.

But it's also a matter of quality. Surf writing, in general, has improved steadily over time. It's also worth noting that all but five of *Zero Break*'s pieces were written by nonsurfers, or surfers writing for the nonsurfing reader. Surfer-to-surfer text is arcane and insider, encoded with first names (Andy, Kelly, Corky, Lisa), unlocated places (Bells, the Bay, the 'Bu), and slang that can be fun or indecipherable or both ("Bru, that sunset is *mental!*"). None of the pieces included here demand any real surf knowledge on the part of the reader. Then again, a little context and perspective never hurt, and the evolution of surf writing is a worthwhile story itself.

Nearly all post-Cook surf writers remarked on the sport's beauty and grace, but for a long time there was an ocean of difference between those doing the writing (missionaries, sea captains, and first-generation travel writers, mostly American, all white, none comfortable in the wave zone) and those doing the surfing (dark-skinned Polynesians who could swim before they could walk). So more than anything it was the oddity of the sport that connected the handful of nineteenth-century surf-related monographs, travelogue excerpts, book chapters, magazine features, and newspaper articles. The physics of balancing atop a floating wood plank was strange enough, but mostly it was the astonishing notion of play in an element that to the Western mind was just slightly safer than fire. The division between surfer and surf watcher was always made clear. To see a native "riding on an immense billow, half-immersed in spray and foam," missionary William Ellis noted in his 1831 book *Polynesian Researches,* "is one of the most novel and interesting sports a foreigner can witness in the islands." Or as Mark Twain wrote thirty-five years later, after a game but futile attempt at surfing, "None but natives ever master the art of surf-bathing thoroughly."

Christian missionaries arrived in Hawaii in 1820, and the natives who survived the ensuing plague of Western-borne disease for the most part were remade into modest, obedient, busy-handed Calvinists. Surfing, meanwhile, withered and nearly died under what a visiting writer archly described as "the touch of civilization." The revival began at the turn of the century, following Hawaii's annexation by the United States. Waikiki was the most popular surfing area, and the sport was buoyed by the islands' rising tourist economy and the public's appetite for travel writing, both of which portrayed wave-riding as exotic, colorful, and romantic. Newspapers and magazines rushed to correct the long-standing idea that there was a race-connected knack to surfing: "The Daring Sport of the Pacific Islands," a *Collier's* headline read, "In Which Both Natives and Whites Become Adept at Triumphing Over the Beach-Combers."

Two big surf world events took place in 1907: *Woman's Home Companion* published Jack London's feature article on his Hawaiian surfing experience, and Honolulu's George Freeth—the Irish-Hawaiian surfer described by London as "a sea-god . . . calm and superb"—moved to Los Angeles and introduced the sport to Southern California. Freeth became California's first professional lifeguard, and this, along with mainland visits by Hawaiian surfing master and Olympic gold medalist Duke Kahanamoku, made the sport even more dashing and gallant—the recreation of choice among a new set of bronzed beachside heroes.

Surfing's peril and risk were a source of ongoing fascination to writers. London, who, as one biographer put it, aspired to be "a great writer with biceps to match," set metaphors off like cannon-shot, making the very act of entering the ocean sound like nothing short of a death sentence. "Thousand-ton" waves roll forth as "white battalions of the infinite army of the sea," while London himself is nothing more than "a finite speck of pulsating jelly . . . soft and tender, susceptible to hurt, fallible and frail." The common man, London says, wouldn't stand a chance. But as he watches this "kingly species" of surfers, barreling toward shore in spray-flecked magnificence, he rises from the beach to "bit the sea's breakers, master them, and ride upon their backs as a king should."

The sport grew. By the beginning of the Depression, surf colonies were established in Australia and New Zealand, as well as on the East, West, and Gulf coasts of America. In 1931 California bodysurfer Ron Drummond self-published five hundred copies of a twenty-six-page soft-cover primer titled *The Art of Wave Riding*; four years later Wisconsin-born surfing champion Tom Blake published a similar number of his *Hawaiian Surfboard,* a hardcover book with chapters on surf history, board construction, competition, and wave-riding technique.

Modern surfing was forty years old when America entered World War II, and its gathered collection of writing, small but growing, carried on for the most part in the same enthusiastic and reverent tone used by London. Nobody mentioned the punch-outs between Hawaiians and Californians. Nothing about the special "surf lessons" offered by the Waikiki beachboys to officers' wives and University of Hawaii coeds that ended with furtive half-submerged couplings fifty yards beyond the wave zone. Nothing about tedious flat spells, nasty rivalries between top surfers, or boozy weekend surf club get-togethers. This filtering-out process wasn't so much a failure on the part of those who wrote about surfing as it was the style of the times, when sports and leisure were relegated to a little sun-room in the house of literature, well removed from heavyweight topics like race and class, Communism and Fascism, war and Depression. Just as beery philistine Babe Ruth was presented exclusively as a big, lovable, good-hearted slugger, wave-riding was shown as thrilling and heroic, with surfers referred to as "aquatic artists," and surf stories wandering freely between truth and myth. "The ocean was like glass, except for the swells [which] were running about 30 feet high," Duke Kahanamoku tells Tom Blake in *Hawaiian Surfriders,* recalling a gigantic summer swell from 1917. "We were so far out, we recognized the captain on the bridge of a passing steamer." Kahanamoku was an Olympic hero who golfed with Douglas Fairbanks, taught FDR's sons how to surf, drew a paycheck as sheriff of Honolulu, and made headlines in California for daring rescues as a lifeguard. If he told Blake he'd ridden a fifty-footer across the bow of a passing steamer and done a reverse kickout onto the lido deck, nobody was going to call him out.

Surfing went through a decade-long overhaul after the war, marked by streamlined balsa-core boards, a new set of turns and cutbacks, and the founding of a niche industry.

As Southern California replaced Waikiki as the sport's hub, the surfer image was also transformed: Duke Kahanamoku, the sport's archetypical figure for decades, dark-haired and soft-spoken, gave way to the peroxide blond suburban teenager barreling down Pacific Coast Highway in a $25 woody wagon. Surfing continued for the most part to baffle the general public. It looked fun and exciting, but somewhat pointless. Paddle out, ride, repeat. It couldn't be a *sport,* really; nobody kept score. Yet it seemed oddly addictive. As the surfing population began to shoot up in the mid-'50s, California beach community conservatives snapped to attention in the face of what appeared to be a youth-culture pincer movement, with Brando and Elvis sweeping down from the inland valleys, and these new surfing hooligans massing along the shore. Antisurfing measures were passed, while county lifeguards were told to monitor surfers, creating a permanent rift in what had once been a unified beachfront bloc.

Viewed from the outside, surfing had gone from strange and exotic to strange and menacing, and the change was reflected in surf literature, including 1957's *Gidget,* the first popular work of surf fiction and the opening shot in a ten-year commercial surf boom. Frederick Kohner, a Viennese-educated scholar and playwright, wrote *Gidget* in six weeks. His affection for surfers is obvious, but librarians and PTA members across America paged through the book and red-flagged dozens of passages: the Malibu gang bantering over the latest issue of *Playboy,* Moondoggie responding to an insult from another surfer with "Ah—blow yourself!," a tiki torch beach party that sets off a fire in the nearby hills. In this context, D. S. Halacy's young-adult novel *Surfer!* (1965) can be read as a beach city elders' revenge fantasy. After a gang of switchblade-carrying surf punks damage public property, the city plows over the local break with a sand dredger, and surfers are told that from now on they'll only be able to ride on weekends, within the confines of a nearby Marine base.

The predictable next step was to cross surfing with pulp fiction, and five-and-dime paperback racks were soon stocked with titles like *Hang Dead Hawaiian Style, Scarlet Surf at Makaha,* and *Cute and Deadly Surf Twins.* (Meanwhile, the surf press, founded in 1960 with the creation of *Surfer* magazine and backed mainly by eager young surfboard manufacturers with a vested interest in "cleaning up" the sport, spoke in a conformist, even reactionary, voice. "The Surfer's Creed," a four-point loyalty oath published in a 1963 issue of *Petersen's Surfing,* reads in part as follows: "Surfing is our hobby and our recreation. We will not allow it as such to interfere with any of the duties we owe to our home, our job, our school or community.")

Not everyone viewed the sport with tight-jawed disapproval. A congratulatory *New Yorker* review described Bruce Brown's 1966 crossover hit *The Endless Summer* as a "brilliant documentary about surfing as a sport rather than as a fad or gimmick," and *Life* ran a warm profile on John Severson, *Surfer'*s thirty-two-year-old founder and publisher. The first surfing biographies also appeared in the mid-'60s: *This Surfing Life,* a humorless but sincere effort by world champion Bernard "Midget" Farrelly of Australia, and the easygoing *You Should Have Been Here an Hour Ago,* by American favorite Phil Edwards. *Surf's Up! An Anthology of Surfing* was published in 1966, three years after *Surfing Guide to Southern California,* the sport's first guidebook. Peter Dixon's *The Complete Book of Surfing,* released in 1965, sold over 300,000 copies before the decade's end.

New Journalism pioneer Tom Wolfe meanwhile seemed to split the difference between the surfing scolds and admirers in his 1966 essay "The Pump House Gang." Rank-and-file teenage surfers, as observed by Wolfe during his brief visit to the beaches of La Jolla, are dead-enders who smoke and drink and steal car parts. He seems both delighted and disgusted when recounting how the La Jolla surfers, after seeing headlines about the Watts riots, decide to drive into Los Angeles and check things out; one surfer brings a tape recorder and says he's going to make a record called "Random Sounds from the Watts Riots." But there's also an older and much smaller group of surfers, mostly captains of surf industry, Bruce Brown among them, that the Yale-educated Wolfe admires as happy escapees from the workaday world. "Brown has the money and *The Life,*" Wolfe writes in his hyperitalicized style, before speed-shifting into a riff that careens from descriptive to mocking to something close to wistful. "[Brown] has a great house on a cliff about 60 feet above the beach. He is married and has two children, but it is not that hubby-mommy you're-breaking-my-gourd scene. God, if only everybody could grow up like these guys and know that crossing the horror dividing line, 25 years old, won't be the end of everything."

While surf magazines in the late '60s jumped into the deep end of the counterculture, mainstream surf writing generally continued as a kind of sociological treasure hunt for the lurid, the violent, and the prurient. *Life Australia* speculated that big-wave surfers were "latent homosexuals," while *Time* noted that "Riding a board through the surf is a little like going on hashish." A *Sports Illustrated* feature story on a pro contest in Santa Cruz seemed to take quiet delight in the anticontest guerrilla tactics of local surfers, who stole boards from visiting pros and at night pushed the empty judges' scaffolding off the beachfront cliffs. (James Michener's *Hawaii* brought the reverence back to surfing, just for a moment, as a wool-clad freshman missionary sees natives riding waves for the first time. "Apparently," he says in a hushed voice to his wife, "there are many who can walk upon the waters.")

Surf writing fell out of fashion during the 1970s. The shortboard revolution at the end of the previous decade had brought radical changes not only to surfboards, but to the way surfers viewed themselves and their sport. Hanging ten, *Gidget, Endless Summer,* the Beach Boys—surfing's cultural touchstones from just a few years earlier—now seemed hopelessly dated. As the surf press earnestly tried to redefine surfing ("sport" was far too Establishment), variously describing it as "a dance on a liquid stage," "a mystical experience," "a way to humble ourselves before God," mainstream writers lost interest. The early and mid-'60s "surf craze," for one thing, had clearly run its course. And maybe they just didn't know what to make of surfing's new pose—a Charlie Quiznel Surfboards ad in *Surfer,* for example, showed Quiznel standing nude and long-haired in a forest, arms spread, face to the heavens. No product shots; no mention that it's even an ad for surfboards. Just a naked hippy and a quote: "I had a vision." Maybe so. But Tom Wolfe and the rest of the American pop culture literati didn't want to know about it.


Jump ahead thirty years, to the early '00s. Surf-themed museum exhibits are reviewed in the *New York Times,* surfing documentaries air on PBS, and surfer models are featured in ad campaigns for life insurance and bath towels. Latent homosexuals are off the surf world radar. Latent free market surf capitalists—a queerer breed in many respects, given the righteous nonmaterialistic pieties mouthed by surfers through the decades—have turned the sport into a red-hot lifestyle commodity: Surf companies are listed on the NYSE, department stores put surfers on billboards, top pros sign million-dollar contracts, beach city toy stores double-order the new surfing edition of Monopoly.

Surf writing played a role in this latest image makeover. In 1982 *Sports Illustrated* ran a well-researched cover story on Pipeline, the fabled Hawaiian surf break, while *California* magazine published a feature on Malibu legend Mickey Dora. Even the perpetually stoned Jeff Spicoli, introduced in Cameron Crowe's 1981 book *Fast Times at Ridgemont High,* was a funnier, better-drawn, far more believable surfing miscreant than his '60s predecessors. (Sean Penn did a pitch-perfect job with Spicoli in the *Fast Times* movie, and his drawling voice and mannerisms—but none of the red-eyed soul—have been recycled continuously for more than twenty years, from *Bill and Ted's Excellent Adventure* to *Dude, Where's My Car?* and *Finding Nemo.*) Surf fiction also took a step forward with Kem Nunn's *Tapping the Source,* a ghoulish 1984 noir thriller set in Huntington Beach. Surf magazine writing improved as well, led by the efforts of Nick Carroll, Derek Hynd, Phil Jarratt, Sam and Matt George.

Surf lit continued to flourish in the '90s, highlighted by William Finnegan's magisterial "Playing Doc's Games," published as a two-part *New Yorker* article in 1992, and Daniel Duane's 1996 memoir *Caught Inside.* Finnegan and Duane take a similar approach to an inherent surf narrative problem: that the sport doesn't easily lend itself to a customary setup/conflict/resolution plot structure, but instead fits into most surfers' lives as a familiar and indispensable routine, like running, or church, or therapy. In "Doc's Games," Finnegan recalls his decision to give up life as a full-time surfer—a pursuit that had taken him on surf junkets to Hawaii, Indonesia, Fiji, and beyond, and landed him in a beachfront home in San Francisco—in order to become a career writer in New York. Duane's *Caught Inside* transformation comes at the other end of the surf experience, from neophyte to full-timer, but he has reservations about the commitment required, and the way in which the sport can at times appear to be utterly pointless. "One thing seems weird about it," Duane's wave-riding mentor, Vince, says near the end of the book, "is that to anybody who's inside surfing, you know it doesn't mean shit." Startled, Duane looks at Vince and wonders to himself: "All those years given to such a beautiful pursuit, and still so much doubt. I didn't agree, didn't even believe he meant it, but perhaps only because the price had, as yet, been so much lower for me."

More often than not the sport is still written about in trite, dull, ineffective, or bombastic prose. Surf violence remains a favorite angle for the unimaginative journalist: A 1982 *Esquire* feature managed to group surfing territorialism with drive-by shootings and gay rape-murders, and a flood of "surf rage" articles appeared as recently as the early '00s. (Anecdotal evidence was the rule here, even with the venerable *New York Times*. Surfing lineups can be tense and unpleasant, but fights in the water are a lot rarer than they are on playground basketball courts and soccer fields, and if the easygoing surfing brotherhood has always been a bit of a hoax, so is the idea of widespread surfing thuggery as reported in dozens of magazine and newspaper articles.) Surf world titillation—updated versions of '60s articles describing "sexy twist parties" where "bikinis come off easy"—remains a common surf-writing trope, but again writers and editors seem poised to amplify events, or invent them outright, in service of the story. The last photo in "Big Blue," a long 2002 *Vanity Fair* article, features six of the world's best big-wave riders posed on the beach, facing away from the camera, trunks dropped to their ankles, and you can imagine the overseeing editor back in New York bending the page back and thinking how *edgy* it is. Surfers themselves certainly aren't above manipulating the media. The six nude *Vanity Fair* surfers all have boards planted in the sand in front of them, angled so that the surf-company logos are as clearly visible as their milky-white behinds.

But if it's true that surf writing is packed with average or below-average work, it's also true that good pieces—serious to satirical; essays, articles, novels, even poems—appear more often and in more places than ever before. Former *Surfing* editor Nick Carroll once said that he "didn't want to intellectualize surfing," and I suppose on some level I understand the idea that the sport's purity is somehow lessened by thinking about it and writing about it. I cherish the quote from the anonymous Malibu surfer who told a *Life* reporter just after *Gidget* was published in 1957, "If I had a couple bucks to buy a book, I wouldn't. I'd buy some beer." But looking at the *Zero Break* table of contents gives me a mild euphoric rush. Maybe, like Dan Duane, I'm still looking for validation for all those hours, days, years spent in the water, and this book answers that need, at least in part. I love how surfing is elevated and honored by the writers in *Zero Break.* I love just as much how the featured writers are energized and inspired by surfing, and how adept they are at passing the feeling on to the reader. Surf journalist Mike McGinty described in 1993 how difficult the surf-writing task can be. "I don't need paper and ink, I need 24-karat gold monster-cable speaker wire with one end plugged into Backdoor Pipeline and the other soldered into your adrenal gland. I need elongated vowel sounds and exaggerated hand movements. Can you feel it? Did it work? Do you have any idea what surfing is really like? Sure. But only because you're a surfer. Not because I said so."

Great image, wrong conclusion. Yes, as a surfer I understand surfing. But that understanding is deeper, finer, and better contoured for the efforts of Mark Twain, William Finnegan, Susan Orlean, and the rest of the 24-karat-gold writers, nonsurfers and well as surfers, who've examined the sport. And if I do at times feel as if I'm a member of a kingly species, it's partly because I surf, and partly because Jack London said so.

NATIVE
SURF RIDER.

# ONE

# THE MOST SUPREME PLEASURE: SURFING INTRODUCED

Surfing bibliophiles are at this very moment lining bookshelves with protective sheets of plasticizer-free polyester, trolling online for first editions of *Hawaiian Surfboard* and *You Should Have Been Here an Hour Ago,* and gently sniff-testing the pages of old favorites for cursed mildew. Happy on the beach, happy in the library. This is a different breed of surfer. But even the most devoted surf-world bookworm will admit that the sport is shown to best effect in visual form. "Surfing is so photogenic," wrote *New York Times* film critic Elvis Mitchell in 2003, "it's hard to believe that film wasn't invented just to capture it." True. The sport's emotional range, and much of its history, can be easily arranged into a chronological pastiche of images, from black-and-white *National Geographic* plates to Kodachrome *Surfer* magazine covers, vast IMAX panoramas, and downloaded QuickTime video clips.

But surfing also had a long precelluloid history, followed by a much shorter period where photography wasn't yet the sport's equal, mechanically or artistically. In the late eighteenth century, the politely amazed surf-related entries from CAPTAIN JAMES COOK's seafaring voyages were published without illustration, as was HERMAN MELVILLE's brief but captivated take on the sport in 1849's *Mardi*. MARK TWAIN's self-deprecating paragraph on surfing, from 1872's *Roughing It,* is accompanied by a pair of line drawings, but the real attraction is Twain's sauntering wordplay. All three pieces are short—surfing before the twentieth century was never more than a curiosity to nonsurfers. But notes of color and feeling did get transmitted and they arrived in well-crafted words, phrases, and sentences, not photographs or film clips.

JACK LONDON was the first well-known writer to really take surfing on as a literary assignment, after he tried "surf-riding" while visiting Waikiki in 1907. "A Royal Sport," London's 4,000-word essay, was illustrated with surfing action photographs, but the waves shown are small and gentle, and the images are reproduced on the page as near miniatures. London's prose is meanwhile nothing but oversize as he trumpets the sport's thrills and dangers, adjectives landing like cymbal shots, with waves variously described as "mighty monsters," "bull-mouth breakers," and "great smoking combers."

London's voice echoed across the next forty years of surf writing, while the sport was exported from Hawaii to the Americas and Australia, and presented as an attractive new form of daredevilry. A surfing philosophy of sorts emerged after World War II as surfers turned their sunburned backs on the hardworking postwar prosperity, and instead put value on time spent in the water or lounging on the beach. The new surfers were younger and more insolent than those of the prewar generation, and by the time Czech-born screenwriter FREDERICK KOHNER reintroduced the sport to the reading public in 1957 with his debut novel *Gidget,* beachfront city councils were moving against "surfing hooliganism" with no-surf zones, surfboard licensing fees, and other small but annoying legislative acts. Kohner also thought surfers were coarse and reckless, but he dug their easy-rolling style, and honored the magnetic attraction of a warm beach met by a pulsing summer swell. *Gidget* has no shortage of babble and froth. But that's not a bad thing if you've set out to capture the rampantly stoked voice of a fifteen-year-old girl "in love with a surfboard," and this slender book holds up nicely as the first modern piece of surf fiction.

### EXCERPT FROM
# A VOYAGE TO THE PACIFIC OCEAN

The first published accounts of surfing are found in *A Voyage to the Pacific Ocean,* a popular four-volume set of books originally published in 1784 that describe the final voyage of celebrated British sea captain and navigator James Cook (1728–79). Cook himself has long been credited as the author of the original description of wave-riding—a short but enthusiastic report of a canoe-surfer at Tahiti's Matavai Point—but researchers now believe the passage was taken from notes made by one of Cook's lieutenants. A longer description of board-riding, in Hawaii, was developed from notes written by James King, who became captain of the voyage following Cook's death. Both entries are presented here.

### DECEMBER, 1777, MATAVAI BAY, TAHITI

NEITHER ARE THEY [the Tahitians] strangers to the soothing effects produced by particular sorts of motion, which in some cases seem to allay any perturbation of mind with as much success as music. Of this, I met with a remarkable instance. For on walking one day about Matavai Point, where our tents were erected, I saw a man paddling in a small canoe so quickly, and looking about him with such eagerness on each side, as to command my attention. At first I imagined that he had stolen something from one of the ships, and was pursued; but, on waiting patiently, saw him repeat his amusement. He went out from the shore till he was near the place where the swell begins to take its rise; and, watching its first motion very attentively, paddled before it with great quickness, till he found that it overlooked him, and had acquired sufficient force to carry his canoe before it without passing underneath. He then sat motionless, and was carried along at the same swift rate as the wave, till it landed him upon the beach. Then he started out, emptied his canoe, and went in search of another swell. I could not help concluding that this man felt the most supreme pleasure while he was driven on so fast and so smoothly by the sea; especially as, though the tents and ships were so near, he did not seem in the least to envy or even to take any notice of the crowds of his countrymen collected to view them as objects which were rare and curious. During my stay, two or three of the natives came up, who seemed to share his felicity, and always called out when there was an appearance of a favorable swell, as he sometimes missed it by his back being turned, and looking about for it. By then I understood that this exercise...was frequent among them; and they have probably more amusements of this sort which afford them at least as much pleasure as skating, which is the only of ours with whose effects I could compare it.

## MARCH, 1779, KEALAKEKUA BAY, HAWAII

The surf, which breaks on the coast round the bay, extends to the distance of about one hundred and fifty yards from the shore, within which space the surges of the sea, accumulating from the shallowness of the water, and dashed against the beach with prodigious violence. Whenever, from stormy weather, or any extraordinary swell at sea, the impetuosity of the surf is increased to its utmost height, they choose that time for this amusement, which is performed in the following manner: Twenty or thirty of the natives, taking each a long narrow board, rounded at the ends, set out together from the shore. The first wave they meet, they plunge under, and suffering it to roll over them, rise again beyond it, and make the best of their way...out into the sea. The second wave is encountered in the same manner with the first; the great difficulty consisting in seizing the proper moment of diving under it, which, if missed, the person is caught by the surf, and driven back again with great violence; and all his dexterity is then required to prevent himself from being dashed against the rocks. As soon as they have gained by these repeated efforts, the smooth water beyond the surf, they lay themselves at length on their board, and prepare for their return. As the surf consists of a number of waves, of which every third is remarked to be always much larger than the others...their first object is to place themselves on the summit of the largest surge, by which they are driven along with amazing rapidity toward the shore. If by mistake they should place themselves on one of the smaller waves, which breaks before they reach the land, or should not be able to keep their plank in a proper direction on the top of the swell, they are left exposed to the fury of the next, and, to avoid it, are obliged to dive and regain their place, from which they set out. Those who succeed in their object of reaching shore, have still the greatest danger to encounter. The coast being guarded by a chain of rocks, with, here and there, a small opening between them, they are obliged to steer their boards through one of these, or, in case of failure, to quit it, before they reach the rocks, and, plunging under the wave, make the best of their way back again. This is reckoned very disgraceful, and is also attended with the loss of the board, which I have often seen, with great horror, dashed to pieces, at the very moment the islander quitted it. The boldness and address with which we saw them perform these difficult and dangerous maneuvers, was altogether astonishing, and is scarcely to be credited.

# MARK TWAIN

## EXCERPT FROM
## *ROUGHING IT*

The Civil War had just ended when fledgling writer and humorist Mark Twain (1835–1910) arrived in Hawaii as a travel correspondent for the *Sacramento Union* newspaper. Dozens of his travel essays were later collected and published in the 1872 travelogue *Roughing It;* Twain's brief but wry look at surfing—long thought to have been included in the original *Union* articles—was in fact written especially for the book.

A T NOON, we hired a Kanaka [native Hawaiian] to take us down to the ancient ruins at Honaunau in his canoe—price two dollars—reasonable enough, for a sea voyage of eight miles, counting both ways.

The native canoe is an irresponsible looking contrivance. I cannot think of anything to liken it to but a boy's sled runner hollowed out, and that does not quite convey the correct idea. It is about fifteen feet long, high and pointed at both ends, is a foot and a half or two feet deep, and so narrow that if you wedged a fat man into it you might not get him out again. It sits on top of the water like a duck, but it has an outrigger and does not upset easily, if you keep still. This outrigger is formed of two long bent sticks like plow handles, which project from one side, and to their outer ends is bound a curved beam composed of an extremely light wood, which skims along the surface of the water and thus saves you from an upset on that side, while the outrigger's weight is not so easily lifted as to make an upset on the other side a thing to be greatly feared. Still, until one gets used to sitting perched upon this knifeblade, he is apt to reason within himself that it would be more comfortable if there were just an outrigger or so on the other side also.

I had the bow seat . . . and faced the Kanaka, who occupied the stern of the craft and did the paddling. With the first stroke the trim shell of a thing shot out from the shore like an arrow. There was not much to see. While we were on the shallow water of the reef, it was pastime to look down into the limpid depths at the large bunches of branching coral—the unique shrubbery of the sea. We lost that, though, when we got out into the dead blue water of the deep. But we had the picture of the surf, then, dashing angrily against the crag-bound shore and sending a foaming spray high into the air. There was interest in this beetling border, too, for it was honey-combed with quaint caves and arches and tunnels, and had a rude semblance of the dilapidated architecture of ruined keeps and castles rising out of the restless sea. When this novelty ceased to be a novelty, we turned our eyes shoreward and gazed at the long mountain with its rich green forests stretching up into the curtaining clouds, and at the specks of houses in the rearward distance and the diminished schooner riding sleepily at anchor. And when these grew tiresome we dashed boldly into the midst of a school of huge, beastly porpoises engaged at their eternal game of arching over a wave and disappearing, and then doing it over again and keeping it up—always circling over, in that way, like so many well-submerged wheels. But the porpoises wheeled themselves away, and then we were thrown upon our own

resources. It did not take many minutes to discover that the sun was blazing like a bonfire, and that the weather was of a melting temperature. It had a drowsing effect, too.

In one place we came upon a large company of naked natives, of both sexes and all ages, amusing themselves with the national pastime of surf-bathing. Each heathen would paddle three or four hundred yards out to sea (taking a short board with him), then face the shore and wait for a particularly prodigious billow to come along; at the right moment he would fling his board upon its foamy crest and himself upon the board, and here he would come whizzing by like a bombshell! It did not seem that a lightning express train could shoot along at a more hair-lifting speed. I tried surf-bathing once, subsequently, but made a failure of it. I got the board placed right, and at the right moment, too; but missed the connection myself.—The board struck the shore in three quarters of a second, without any cargo, and I struck the bottom about the same time, with a couple of barrels of water in me. None but natives ever master the art of surf-bathing thoroughly.

## "RARE SPORT AT OHONOO"
### EXCERPT FROM *MARDI*

American novelist Herman Melville (1819–91) went to sea at age eighteen as a merchant marine, worked on a whaler, served with the U.S. Navy, lived with a native tribe in the Marquesas, and was jailed in Tahiti as a mutineer. He began writing after his return to New York. *Mardi: and a Voyage Thither* was published in 1849, two years before *Moby-Dick,* his seafaring masterpiece. *Mardi* sold poorly and got mostly negative reviews, although one critic lauded the book for its "fanciful descriptions of nature amid all her variations." Chapter 90, "Rare Sport at Ohonoo," opens with the book's narrator aboard a whaler as it approaches a verdant South Seas island, along with shipmate Braid-Beard, and Media, king of the Mardi island chain.

APPROACHED FROM the northward, Ohonoo, midway cloven down to the sea, one half a level plain; the other, three mountain terraces— Ohonoo looks like the first steps of a gigantic way to the sun. And such, if Braid-Beard spoke truth, it had formerly been.

"Ere Mardi was made," said that true old chronicler, "Vivo, one of the genii, built a ladder of mountains whereby to go up and go down. And of this ladder, the island of Ohonoo was the base. But wandering here and there, incognito in a vapor, so much wickedness did Vivo spy out, that in high dudgeon he hurried up his ladder, knocking the mountains from under him as he went. These here and there fell into the lagoon, forming many isles, now green and luxuriant; which, with those sprouting from seeds dropped by a bird from the moon, comprise all the groups in the reef."

Surely, oh, surely, if I live till Mardi be forgotten by Mardi, I shall not forget the sight that greeted us, as we drew nigh the shores of this same island of Ohonoo; for was not all Ohonoo bathing in the surf of the sea?

But let the picture be painted.

Where eastward the ocean rolls surging against the outer reef of Mardi, there, facing a flood-gate in the barrier, stands cloven Ohonoo; her plains sloping outward to the sea, her mountains a bulwark behind. As at Juam, where the wild billows from seaward roll in upon its cliffs; much more at Ohonoo, in billowy battalions charge they hotly into the lagoon, and fall on the isle like an army from the deep. But charge they never so boldly, and charge they forever, old Ohonoo gallantly throws them back till all before her is one scud and rack. So charged the bright billows of cuirassiers at Waterloo: so hurled them off the long line of living walls, whose base was as the sea-beach, wreck-strown, in a gale.

Without the break in the reef, wide banks of coral shelve off, creating the bar, where the waves muster for the onset, thundering in water-bolts, that shake the whole reef, till its very spray trembles. And then is it, that the swimmers of Ohonoo most delight to gambol in the surf.

For this sport, a surf-board is indispensable: some five feet in length; the width of a man's body; convex on both sides; highly polished; and rounded at the ends. It is held in high estimation; invariably oiled after use; and hung up conspicuously in the dwelling of the owner.

Ranged on the beach, the bathers, by hundreds dash in; and diving under the swells, make straight for the outer sea, pausing not till the comparatively smooth expanse beyond has been gained. Here, throwing themselves upon their boards, tranquilly they wait for a billow that suits. Snatching them up, it hurries them landward, volume and speed both increasing, till it races along a watery wall, like the smooth, awful verge of Niagara. Hanging over this scroll, looking down from it as from a precipice, the bathers halloo; every limb in motion to preserve their place on the very crest of the wave. Should they fall behind, the squadrons that follow would whelm them; dismounted, and thrown forward, as certainly would they be run over by the steed they ride. 'Tis like charging at the head of cavalry: you must on.

An expert swimmer shifts his position on his plank; now half striding it; and anon, like a rider in the ring, poising himself upright in the scud, coming on like a man in the air.

At last all is lost in scud and vapor, as the overgrown billow bursts like a bomb. Adroitly emerging, the swimmers thread their way out; and like seals at the Orkneys, stand dripping upon the shore.

Landing in smooth water, some distance from the scene, we strolled forward; and meeting a group resting, inquired for Uhia, their king. He was pointed out in the foam. But presently drawing nigh, he embraced Media, bidding all welcome.

The bathing over, and evening at hand, Uhia and his subjects repaired to their canoes; and we to ours.

Landing at another quarter of the island, we journeyed up a valley called Monlova, and were soon housed in a very pleasant retreat of our host.

Soon supper was spread. But though the viands were rare, and the red wine went round and round like a foaming bay horse in the ring; yet we marked, that despite the stimulus of his day's good sport, and the stimulus of his brave good cheer, Uhia our host was moody and still.

Said Babbalanja, "My lord, he fills wine cups for others to quaff."

But whispered King Media, "Though Uhia be sad, be we merry, merry men."

And merry some were, and merrily went to their mats.

# JACK LONDON

## "A ROYAL SPORT"
### EXCERPT FROM *THE CRUISE OF THE SNARK*

Jack London (1876–1916) was one of America's most popular authors in 1907 when he sailed from San Francisco to Honolulu aboard his homemade schooner, the *Snark*. "A Royal Sport," London's 4,000-word surfing essay—by far the most detailed and enthusiastic report on an activity that would soon cross the Pacific and take root in Southern California—first appeared in the *Woman's Home Companion;* it was later published as a chapter in his 1911 travelogue, *The Cruise of the Snark*.

THAT IS what it is, a royal sport for the natural kings of earth. The grass grows right down to the water at Waikiki Beach, and within fifty feet of the everlasting sea. The trees also grow down to the salty edge of things, and one sits in their shade and looks seaward at a majestic surf thundering in on the beach to one's very feet. Half a mile out, where is the reef, the white-headed combers thrust suddenly skyward out of the placid turquoise-blue and come rolling in to shore. One after another they come, a mile long, with smoking crests, the white battalions of the infinite army of the sea. And one sits and listens to the perpetual roar, and watches the unending procession, and feels tiny and fragile before this tremendous force expressing itself in fury and foam and sound. Indeed, one feels microscopically small, and the thought that one may wrestle with this sea raises in one's imagination a thrill of apprehension, almost of fear. Why, they are a mile long, these bull-mouthed monsters, and they weigh a thousand tons, and they charge in to shore faster than a man can run. What chance? No chance at all, is the verdict of the shrinking ego; and one sits, and looks, and listens, and thinks the grass and the shade are a pretty good place in which to be.

And suddenly, out there where a big smoker lifts skyward, rising like a sea-god from out of the welter of spume and churning white, on the giddy, toppling, overhanging and downfalling, precarious crest appears the dark head of a man. Swiftly he rises through the rushing white. His black shoulders, his chest, his loins, his limbs—all is abruptly projected on one's vision. Where but the moment before was only the wide desolation and invincible roar, is now a man, erect, full-statured, not struggling frantically in that wild movement, not buried and crushed and buffeted by those mighty monsters, but standing above them all, calm and superb, poised on the giddy summit, his feet buried in the churning foam, the salt smoke rising to his knees, and all the rest of him in the free air and flashing sunlight, and he is flying through the air, flying forward, flying fast as the surge on which he stands. He is a Mercury—a brown Mercury. His heels are winged, and in them is the swiftness of the sea. In truth, from out of the sea he has leaped upon the back of the sea, and he is riding the sea that roars and bellows and cannot shake him from its back. But no frantic outreaching and balancing is his. He is impassive, motionless as a statue carved suddenly by some miracle out of the sea's depth from which he rose. And straight on toward shore he flies on his winged heels and the white crest of the breaker. There is a wild burst of foam, a long tumultuous rushing sound as the breaker falls futile and spent on the beach at your feet; and there, at your feet steps calmly ashore a Kanaka, burnt golden and brown by the tropic sun. Several minutes ago he was a speck a quarter of a mile away. He has "bitted the bull-mouthed breaker" and ridden it in, and the pride in the feat shows in the carriage of his magnificent body as he glances for a moment carelessly at you who sit in the shade of the shore. He is a Kanaka— and more, he is a man, a member of the kingly species that has mastered matter and the brutes and lorded it over creation.

And one sits and thinks of Tristram's last wrestle with the sea on that fatal morning; and one thinks further, to the fact that Kanaka has done what Tristram never did, and that he knows a joy of the sea that Tristram never knew. And still further one thinks. It is all very well, sitting here in cool shade of the beach, but you are a man, one of the kingly species, and what that Kanaka can do, you can do yourself. Go to. Strip off your clothes that are a nuisance in this mellow clime. Get in and wrestle with the sea; wing your heels with the skill and power that reside in you; bit the sea's breakers, master them, and ride upon their backs as a king should.

And that is how it came about that I tackled surf-riding. And now that I have tackled it, more than ever do I hold it to be a royal sport. But first let me explain the physics of it. A wave is a communicated agitation. The water that composes the body of a wave does not move. If it did, when a stone is thrown into a pond and the ripples spread away in an ever widening circle, there would appear at the centre an ever increasing hole. No, the water that composes the body of a wave is stationary. Thus, you may watch a particular portion of the ocean's surface and you will see the same water rise and fall a thousand times to the agitation communicated by a thousand successive waves. Now imagine this communicated agitation moving shoreward. As the bottom shoals, the lower portion of the wave strikes land first and is stopped. But water is fluid, and the upper portion has not struck anything, wherefore it keeps on communicating its agitation, keeps on going. And when the top of the wave keeps on going, while the bottom of it lags behind, something is bound to happen. The bottom of the wave drops out from under and the top of the wave falls over, forward, and down, curling and cresting and roaring as it does so. It is the bottom of a wave striking against the top of the land that is the cause of all surfs.

But the transformation from a smooth undulation to a breaker is not abrupt except where the bottom shoals abruptly. Say the bottom shoals gradually for from a quarter of a mile to a mile, then an equal distance will be occupied by the transformation. Such a bottom is that off the beach of Waikiki, and it produces a splendid surf-riding surf. One leaps upon the back of a breaker just as it begins to break, and stays on it as it continues to break all the way in to shore.

And now to the particular physics of surf-riding. Get out on a flat board, six feet long, two feet wide, and roughly oval in shape. Lie down upon it like a small boy on a coaster and paddle with your hands out to deep water, where the waves begin to crest. Lie out there quietly on the board. Sea after sea breaks before, behind, and under and over you, and rushes in to shore, leaving you behind. When a wave crests, it gets steeper. Imagine yourself, on your board, on the face of that steep slope. If it stood still, you would slide down just as a boy slides down a hill on his coaster. "But," you object, "the wave doesn't stand still." Very true, but the water composing the wave stands still, and there you have the secret. If ever you start sliding down the face of that wave, you'll keep on sliding and you'll never reach the bottom. Please don't laugh. The face of that wave may be only six feet, yet you can slide down it a quarter of a mile, or half a mile, and not reach the bottom. For, see, since a wave is only a communicated agitation or impetus, and since the water that composes a wave is changing every instant, new water is rising into the wave as fast as the wave travels. You slide down this new water, and yet remain in your old position on the wave, sliding down the still newer water that is rising and forming the wave. You slide precisely as fast as the wave travels. If it travels fifteen miles an hour, you slide fifteen miles an hour. Between you and shore stretches a quarter mile of water. As the wave travels, this water obligingly heaps itself into the wave, gravity does the rest, and down you go, sliding the whole length of it. If you still cherish the notion, while sliding, that the water is moving with you, thrust your arms into it and attempt to paddle; you will find that you have to be remarkably quick to get a stroke, for that water is dropping astern just as fast as you are rushing ahead.

And now for another phase of the physics of surf-riding. All rules have their exceptions. It is true that the water in a wave does not travel forward. But there is what may be called the send of the sea. The water in the overtoppling crest does move forward, as you will speedily realize if you are slapped in the face by it, or if you are caught under it and are pounded by one mighty blow down under the surface panting and gasping for half a minute. The water in the top of a wave rests upon the water in the bottom of the wave. But when the bottom of the wave strikes the land, it stops, while the top goes on. It no longer has the bottom of the wave to hold it up. Where was solid water beneath it, is now air, and for the first time it feels the grip of gravity, and down it falls, at the same time being torn asunder from the lagging bottom of the wave and flung forward. And it is because of this that riding a surf-board is something more than a mere placid sliding down a hill. In truth, one is caught up and hurled shoreward as by some Titan's hand.

I deserted the cool shade, put on a swimming suit, and got hold of a surf-board. It was too small a board. But I didn't know, and nobody told me. I joined some little Kanaka boys in shallow water, where the breakers were well spent and small—a regular kindergarten school. I watched the little Kanaka boys. When a likely-looking breaker came along, they flopped upon their stomachs on their boards, kicked like mad with their feet, and rode the breaker in to the beach. I tried to emulate them. I watched them, tried to do everything that they did, and failed utterly. The breaker swept past, and I was not on it. I tried again and again. I kicked twice as madly as they did, and failed. Half a dozen would be around. We would all leap on our boards in front of a good breaker. Away our feet would churn like the sternwheels of river steamboats, and away the little rascals would scoot while I remained in disgrace behind.

I tried for a solid hour, and not one wave could I persuade to boost me shoreward. And then arrived a friend, Alexander Hume Ford, a globe trotter by profession, bent ever on the pursuit of sensation. And he had found it at Waikiki. Heading for Australia, he had stopped off for a week to find out if there were any thrills in surf-riding, and he had become wedded to it. He had been at it every day for a month and could not yet see any symptoms of the fascination lessening on him. He spoke with authority.

"Get off that board," he said. "Chuck it away at once. Look at the way you're trying to ride it. If ever the nose of that board hits bottom, you'll be disembowelled. Here, take my board. It's a man's size."

I am always humble when confronted by knowledge. Ford knew. He showed me how properly to mount his board. Then he waited for a good breaker, gave me a shove at the right moment, and started me in. Ah, delicious moment when I felt that breaker grip and fling me. On I dashed, a hundred and fifty feet, and subsided with the breaker on the sand. From that moment I was lost. I waded back to Ford with his board. It was a large one, several inches thick, and weighed all of seventy-five pounds. He gave me advice, much of it. He had had no one to teach him, and all that he had laboriously learned in several weeks he communicated to me in half an hour. I really learned by proxy. And inside of half an hour I was able to start myself and ride in. I did it time after time, and Ford applauded and advised. For instance, he told me to get just so far forward on the board and no farther. But I must have got some farther, for as I came charging in to land, that miserable board poked its nose down to bottom, stopped abruptly, and turned a somersault, at the same time violently severing our relations. I was tossed through the air like a chip and buried ignominiously under the downfalling breaker. And I realized that if it hadn't been for Ford, I'd have been disembowelled. That particular risk is part of the sport, Ford says. Maybe he'll have it happen to him before he leaves Waikiki, and then, I feel confident, his yearning for sensation will be satisfied for a time.

When all is said and done, it is my steadfast belief that homicide is worse than suicide, especially if, in the former case, it is a woman. Ford saved me from being a homicide. "Imagine your legs are a rudder," he said. "Hold them close together, and steer with them." A few minutes later I came charging in on a comber. As I neared the beach, there, in the water, up to her waist, dead in front of me, appeared a woman. How was I to stop that comber on whose back I was? It looked like a dead woman. The board weighed seventy-five pounds, I weighed a hundred and sixty-five. The added weight had a velocity of fifteen miles per hour. The board and I constituted a projectile. I leave it to the physicists to figure out the force of the impact upon that poor, tender woman. And then I remembered my guardian angel, Ford. "Steer with your legs!" rang through my brain. I steered with my legs, I steered sharply, abruptly, with all my legs and with all my might. The board sheered around broadside on the crest. Many things happened simultaneously. The wave gave me a passing buffet, a light tap as the taps of waves go, but a tap sufficient to knock me off the board and smash me down through the rushing water to the bottom, with which I came in violent collision and upon which I was rolled over and over. I got my head out for a breath of air and then gained my feet. There stood the woman before me. I felt like a hero. I had saved her life. And she laughed at me. It was not hysteria. She had never dreamed of her danger. Anyway, I solaced myself, it was not I but Ford that saved her, and I didn't have to feel like a hero. And besides, that leg-steering was great. In a few minutes more of practice I was able to thread my way in and out past several bathers and to remain on top of my breaker instead of going under it.

"To-morrow," Ford said, "I am going to take you out into the blue water."

I looked seaward where he pointed, and saw the great smoking combers that made the breakers I had been riding look like ripples. I don't know what I might have said had I not recollected just then that I was one

LORD BYRON
Excerpt from "Childe Harold"

*And I have loved thee, Ocean! and my joy*
*Of youthful sports was on thy breast to be*
*Borne, like thy bubbles onward; from a boy*
*I wanton'd with thy breakers—they to me*
*Were a delight; and if the freshening sea*
*Made them a terror—'twas a pleasing fear,*
*For I was as it were a child of thee,*
*And trusted to thy billows far and near,*
*And laid my hand upon thy mane—as I do here.*

of a kingly species. So all that I did say was, "All right, I'll tackle them to-morrow."

The water that rolls in on Waikiki Beach is just the same as the water that laves the shores of all the Hawaiian Islands; and in ways, especially from the swimmer's standpoint, it is wonderful water. It is cool enough to be comfortable, while it is warm enough to permit a swimmer to stay in all day without experiencing a chill. Under the sun or the stars, at high noon or at midnight, in midwinter or in midsummer, it does not matter when, it is always the same temperature—not too warm, not too cold, just right. It is wonderful water, salt as old ocean itself, pure and crystal-clear. When the nature of the water is considered, it is not so remarkable after all that the Kanakas are one of the most expert of swimming races.

So it was, next morning, when Ford came along, that I plunged into the wonderful water for a swim of indeterminate length. Astride of our surf-boards, or, rather, flat down upon them on our stomachs, we paddled out through the kindergarten where the little Kanaka boys were at play. Soon we were out in deep water where the big smokers came roaring in. The mere struggle with them, facing them and paddling seaward over them and through them, was sport enough in itself. One had to have his wits about him, for it was a battle in which mighty blows were struck, on one side, and in which cunning was used on the other side—a struggle between insensate force and intelligence. I soon learned a bit. When a breaker curled over my head, for a swift instant I could see the light of day through its emerald body; then down would go my head, and I would clutch the board with all my strength. Then would come the blow, and to the onlooker on shore I would be blotted out. In reality the board and I have passed through the crest and emerged in the respite of the other side. I should not recommend those smashing blows to an invalid or delicate person. There is weight behind them, and the impact of the driven water is like a sand-blast. Sometimes one passes through half a dozen combers in quick succession, and it is just about that time that he is liable to discover new merits in the stable land and new reasons for being on shore.

Out there in the midst of such a succession of big smoky ones, a third man was added to our party, one Freeth. Shaking the water from my eyes as I emerged from one wave and peered ahead to see what the next one looked like, I saw him tearing in on the back of it, standing upright on his board, carelessly poised, a young god bronzed with sunburn. We went through the wave on the back of which he rode. Ford called to him. He turned an airspring from his wave, rescued his board from its maw, paddled over to us and joined Ford in showing me things. One thing in particular I learned from Freeth, namely, how to encounter the occasional breaker of exceptional size that rolled in. Such breakers were really ferocious, and it was unsafe to meet them on top of the board. But Freeth showed me, so that whenever I saw one of that caliber rolling down on me, I slid off the rear end of the board and dropped down beneath the surface, my arms over my head and holding the board. Thus, if the wave ripped the board out of my hands and tried to strike me with it (a common trick of such waves), there would be a cushion of water a foot or more in depth, between my head and the blow. When the wave passed, I climbed upon the board and paddled on. Many men have been terribly injured, I learn, by being struck by their boards.

The whole method of surf-riding and surf-fighting, I learned, is one of non-resistance. Dodge the blow that is struck at you. Dive through the wave that is trying to slap you in the face. Sink down, feet first, deep under the surface, and let the big smoker that is trying to smash you go by far overhead. Never be rigid. Relax. Yield yourself to the waters that are ripping and tearing at you. When the undertow catches you and drags you seaward along the bottom, don't struggle against it. If you do, you are liable to be drowned, for it is stronger than you. Yield yourself to that undertow. Swim with it, not against it, and you will find the pressure removed. And, swimming with it, fooling it so that it does not hold you, swim upward at the same time. It will be no trouble at all to reach the surface.

The man who wants to learn surf-riding must be a strong swimmer, and he must be used to going under the water. After that, fair strength and common-sense are all that is required. The force of the big comber is rather unexpected. There are mix-ups in which board and rider are torn apart and separated by several hundred feet. The surf-rider must take care of himself. No matter how many riders swim out with him, he cannot depend upon any of them for aid. The fancied security I had in the presence of Ford and Freeth made me forget that it was my first swim out in deep water among the big ones. I recollected, however, and rather suddenly, for a big wave came in, and away went the two men on its back all the way to shore. I could have been drowned a dozen different ways before they got back to me.

One slides down the face of a breaker on his surf-board, but he has to get started to sliding. Board and rider must be moving shoreward at a good rate before the wave overtakes them. When you see the wave coming that you want to ride in, you turn tail to it and paddle shoreward with all your strength, using what is called the windmill stroke. This is a sort of spurt performed immediately in front of the wave. If the board is going fast enough, the wave accelerates it, and the board begins its quarter-of-a-mile slide.

I shall never forget the first big wave I caught out there in the deep water. I saw it coming, turned my back on it and paddled for dear life. Faster and faster my board went, till it seemed my arms would drop off. What was happening behind me I could not tell. One cannot look behind and paddle the windmill stroke. I heard the crest of the wave hissing and churning, and then my board was lifted and flung forward. I scarcely knew what happened the first half-minute. Though I kept my eyes open, I could not see anything, for I was buried in the rushing white of the crest.

But I did not mind. I was chiefly conscious of ecstatic bliss at having caught the wave. At the end of the half-minute, however, I began to see things, and to breathe. I saw that three feet of the nose of my board was clear out of water and riding on the air. I shifted my weight forward, and made the nose come down. Then I lay, quite at rest in the midst of the wild movement, and watched the shore and the bathers on the beach grow distinct. I didn't cover quite a quarter of a mile on that wave, because, to prevent the board from diving, I shifted my weight back, but shifted it too far and fell down the rear slope of the wave.

It was my second day at surf-riding, and I was quite proud of myself. I stayed out there four hours, and when it was over, I was resolved that on the morrow I'd come in standing up. But that resolution paved a distant place. On the morrow I was in bed. I was not sick, but I was very unhappy, and I was in bed. When describing the wonderful water of Hawaii I forgot to describe the wonderful sun of Hawaii. It is a tropic sun, and, furthermore, in the first part of June, it is an overhead sun. It is also an insidious, deceitful sun. For the first time in my life I was sunburned unawares. My arms, shoulders, and back had been burned many times in the past and were tough; but not so my legs. And for four hours I had exposed the tender backs of my legs, at right-angles, to that perpendicular Hawaiian sun. It was not until after I got ashore that I discovered the sun had touched me. Sunburn at first is merely warm; after that it grows intense and the blisters come out. Also, the joints, where the skin wrinkles, refuse to bend. That is why I spent the next day in bed. I couldn't walk. And that is why, to-day, I am writing this in bed. It is easier to than not to. But to-morrow, ah, to-morrow, I shall be out in that wonderful water, and I shall come in standing up, even as Ford and Freeth. And if I fail to-morrow, I shall do it the next day, or the next. Upon one thing I am resolved: the *Snark* shall not sail from Honolulu until I, too, wing my heels with the swiftness of the sea, and become a sunburned, skin-peeling Mercury.

## EXCERPT FROM
# *GIDGET*

Frederick Kohner (1905–86) studied at the Sorbonne and received a Ph.D. in psychology from the University of Vienna, then fled Czechoslovakia just ahead of the Nazi occupation. He arrived in Southern California and immediately began working in Hollywood; his screenplay for 1938's *Mad About Music* was nominated for an Academy Award. *Gidget,* his 1957 debut novel, written in just six weeks, was based on the stories told by his fifteen-year-old daughter about learning to surf at Malibu. Kohner went on to write the script for the 1959 screen version of *Gidget,* as well as a number of sequel books. He also wrote Broadway plays and taught film classes at the University of Southern California.

### EARLY SUMMER

I'M JUST CRAZY about swimming. I really am. I must have been thrown into some Southern California swimming pool when I was six months old...and I've been in the water ever since.

Pools are not the real thing of course. But give me a mountain lake (like the one on the Brenner Pass I swam in last year in Europe) or the Garda Lake or that bitchen Mondsee in Austria—even Lake Arrowhead. Boy, they're doing it to me.

But the real thing is the ocean. And I don't mean that crummy Adriatic Ocean and I don't mean the Atlantic either (I tried them all out). I mean the Pacific. I've been in and out of that bitchen Pacific from Carmel down to Coronado and there's no water around the world that can beat it.

That's what Rachel Carson says too, and she ought to know having written that terrific book *The Sea Around Us.*

I guess the whole thing started because I'm so short. I'm not quite five feet but if it hadn't been for that year-round swimming I'd probably stayed a dwarf. My mother had this crazy idea that I'd grow if I'd only stretch my body as much and long as possible and that's why she made me swim from the time I can remember. She took a boat up at Arrowhead Lake and I had to swim close to her as she rowed and rowed—for hours. Turned out to be not such a crazy idea after all. Most of her friends laughed at it and so did Dr. Rossman who is our family doctor, but—lo and behold—what started out as a dwarf grew into an almost five-footer. When someone asks me about my height I always say five foot, naturally, like when someone wants to know my age I say going on seventeen.

I was sixteen last month.

I'm really quite cute. I've real blond hair and wear it in a horsetail. My two big canines protrude a little which worries my parents a great deal. They urge me to have my teeth pushed back with the help of some crummy piece of hardware, but I've been resisting any attempt to tamper with my personality. The only thing that worries me is my bosom. It's there all right and it sure looks good when I'm undressed, but I have a hard time making it count in a sweater or such. Most of those kids in Franklin High are a lot taller and have a lot more to show—but most of them wear those damn falsies that stick out all over the place and I'd rather be caught dead than be a phony about a thing like your bosom. Imagine what a boy thinks of you once he finds out. And he finds out sure as hell the first time he takes you to a show.

It's different in a bathing suit of course. Nothing helps there—no falsies or such phony stuff.

I've got a couple of real sexy-looking bathing suits that're pretty low-cut and have a skin-tight fit. When Jeff saw me the first time, I was wearing the pink one and that's why he called me Pinky—real corny.

Now that I mentioned his name I better stick with him for it's Jeff's story as well as mine and when I think back of that summer and all those things that happened it'll be Jeff first and then a long, long stretch of nothing and then Cass, the great Kahoona, or maybe it will be Cass first and Cass last—who knows what comes first to your mind once you sport a lot of bags under your eyes?

Well, that day—it was the Fourth of July—I went with my parents to good old Malibu. They go there all year long—on account of me liking to swim and then on account of *them* being sort of nuts about sun and fresh air and a lot of running around to "keep fit." They always meet with a bunch of other fresh-air fiends and loll around and talk a lot of boring stuff, intellectual and such, my old man being a professor of German Literature at U.S.C.

Most of the time I take a girl friend along when I ride out to the beach with them—Mai Mai or Poppy or Barbara—but this Fourth of July I was alone. Everyone was afraid of traffic and accidents and sunstroke (we had some two hundred degrees of heat that day)—so I was good and stuck with the old lady and the old man. I took my portable radio along though and heaps of peanut butter sandwiches and *Love Is Eternal* which I have been reading on and off for a year. I'm really horrible about reading. It's embarrassing, especially for my old man who is a Doctor of Literature, but it just seems impossible for me to concentrate. To be honest I'd rather write a book than read it. I once discussed this problem with Larry who is my sister's husband and a professional headshrinker. The way he explained it to me is that I'm suffering from an inferiority complex on account of my old man having zillions of books around the house and reading like a maniac. Could be—but I'm not worrying about it. I sort of feel that living life is better than reading about it in books.

I always like to get out for a real long swimming binge before I eat my sandwiches, so that Sunday I put on a pair of fins that belonged to

Billy who is a deep-sea-diving enthusiast. Billy comes down to the beach with more stuff than Cousteau took to inspect the *Silent World:* tattered overalls, face plates, oxygen masks, barbed spears with a line on them, old tire tubes, and other spooky equipment. Billy's a great expert on inspecting the lower depths of Rancho Malibu and a cunning killer of perch, bass, octopus and abalone. Once he plucked a lobster weighing ten pounds.

Personally I don't care for all this underwater crap but I do get a kick out of putting on the fins and a face plate and observing the love life of the abalone—which is quite fascinating, believe me—and that's exactly what I did on that fabulous Fourth of July day.

The coast was flat and even when I started out—hardly a ripple in sight. I headed out for the wide open spaces which is a cinch with those fins—if they fit over your feet.

A diver can kick a couple of times and—smack!—he's fifty feet under water. Besides, you can streak through the choppiest waves with them like a bitchen rocket ship. Little did I know that day what I was in for.

I was out there for about ten minutes slipping in and out the waves, diving down to look around occasionally in some corridors of kelp, coming up for some drags of air again, when this huge thing came from nowhere. A wave as big as a house rose suddenly out of the smooth surface feathering with foam on the top—and crashing down at me. Boy, it sure knocked me silly.

When I came up again—and just in time to get a fresh drag—another one came, big and green and swelling, sucking up all the water in front of me. I dove quickly the way I had learned it and let it pass—and came up again. Only now I noticed that I was far out—almost at the end of the pier. The place I had started from was nowhere in sight and one tremendous wave after another came rolling in towards the shoal water. The tide was coming in and I was caught in it!

Boy, it nearly choked me. I'd never get back. I realized that I had been swept towards the cove side of the beach. The waves broke here and rolled like a long, incredibly powerful cylinder towards the shore.

I dove, came up again, saw another wave skyhigh zooming towards me, dove again, came up—caught air—and screamed.

While I screamed I realized that it was stupid, the noise of the crashing wave almost blasting my eardrums. Who would hear me? Even under the surface it was gurgling and churning by now and green and red specks danced up and down before my eyes.

Once more I made a lunge towards the surface, stuck my head out and opened my mouth to suck for fresh air.

That's when I saw them.

Half a dozen boys squatting barely a hundred feet away from me on their surfboards…waiting for the big hump. It was such a funny sight, like a goddamn Fata Morgana. I wasn't alone any more. I would be saved.

Again I screamed. No one heard me. Another wave came pounding along. I ducked it. By now the salt water was biting my eyes. I began to struggle blindly—trying desperately to get to the surface again. I mechanically treaded with my fins, rose up, fought for air—and was all of a sudden lifted to the surface. A pair of powerful arms were around my neck, almost strangling me.

The next moment I felt some hard board under my body and struggled out of the grip that held me.

"Hey—you're choking me!"

"Want a lift?"

I was sitting on a surfboard in the clear water beyond the surfline and the guy who had fished me out of the water had a grin on his face as wide as Joe E. Brown's. I was glad I was saved but I sure didn't care for that smile on his face. He felt pretty big.

"Hey, Shorty—what're you doing out here?"

He griped me.

"What do you think I'm doing," I said, "looking for some seagull eggs?"

He laughed. "Find any?"

"Sure," I retorted, "I've tucked them under my fins."

That smug grin got smugger—if that was possible.

"Ahhh—that's why you got lost, Pinky." He looked down at my fins as if they were a couple of toilet seats.

"What's wrong with it?"

"What's right with it," he said drily.

Dammit, I felt like spitting in his face.

Meanwhile the other guys on the boards came to life.

"Olé Moondoggie!" someone yelled.

Moondoggie! Some name!

"Who's that fine-looking coozy?" hollered another one. He wore a straw hat as big as a cartwheel.

"Is she for real, Moondoggie?" another surfer called over.

My lifesaver screwed up his face.

"Bite the rag, you guys," he snorted. Then he turned around—I was dangling at the tail end of the board—and said evenly: "Okay—to the nose, Pinky!"

I hadn't the faintest notion what he meant. All I knew was that he had a lousy personality.

"It so happens my name isn't Pinky," I said.

"Getting mad, little girl?"

"Will you please take me to the shore," I said haughtily.

"You hear this, men?" he hollered. "She wants to go to the shore."

"My folks will be worried," I said. "I've been out here for some time."

"Okay, Kiddo," said the character they called Moondoggie. "Slide on your tummy up front—I'll get you back to Mamaville."

He sure was playing the hot shot.

I didn't say anything and just did as he told me. He, too, slid down, turned his head to look back towards the onrushing waves, dropped his hands into the water and began to paddle.

I began to paddle with my arms the way I saw the others doing it . . . then a big wave came moving in with a rush. I could feel the water fall underneath me as it rose. It was a smooth and pure wave, not a trace of foam in it. Moondoggie and I tandemed forward with a couple of strokes and the board began to move ahead. I could feel the board being lifted upwards as we cut the water with our bands. The speed increased. I got a tremendous kick out of it. "Watch out, Pinky!" he yelled.

The wave was now at its highest peak. For a moment I had this ear-splitting buzz in my head, and then—zoom—we went down, the board almost dropped away under our stomachs, the water hissed and roared, foam tossed over my shoulder. Then the noise was dying down and the board chittered and came to a crunching halt in a few inches of water.

We were in the cove.

I looked around. Only two other guys had made it. The others had gotten the ax.

I felt so jazzed up about this ride I could have yelled. Moondoggie swung his long legs around and dragged the board ashore. He was tall, I could see it now, all of his gorgeous six-foot-two. "Well, Pinky," he said, "how was that for a pull-out?"

"Great," I said.

"Anytime."

He went down and lifted the board up, swung the thirty-five pounds over his head as if it were a pair of skis and walked away. I stood there like a dope, with those crummy fins still on my feet.

"Hey," I yelled after him, "thanks for the ride."

He didn't even turn his head. A real freep—if you ask me. He wore tight blue jeans that had those phony fringes but he had a damn good build—I must admit.

About two hundred feet offshore stood this old Quonset hut made from bamboo sticks and palmettos and odd pieces of driftwood. There was a crude fence built around it and in the enclosure some of the surfers were squatting in the sand, their knees drawn under their body. When Moondoggie came up to the fence they called out.

"Hey, Jeff—some coozy?"

"It's me—and I'm in love again," someone started on a uke.

"Sharp—real sharp!"

"Ah—blow yourself!" was all my lifesaver said. He wasn't mad or anything. Jeff Moondoggie. Funny name. I yanked the fins off my feet and started back towards the bay where my parents sat. I figured they must have had a dozen hemorrhages by now, with me gone for an hour and all. I was impatient to get back to them—but not *too* impatient. I was thinking of the ride on that board with Jeff and I was terribly proud of myself. I wondered whether I would be able to lift that board the way he did and carry it up the beach over my head. Boy, to be able to ride this—all by yourself!

Boards were nothing new to me. I've been skiing for years and I've done some waterskiing too. This was different. I don't want to sound corny but my heart went flippity-flop and I got all hot inside just thinking of it.

Then I saw this grubby-looking guy with these pants that looked like male frenchies working away with a wood plane on an unfinished surfboard. He had a regular workshop made up on the beach and a sign said WANT BOARDS—ASK STINKY. A few boards—one with a nude girl à la Monroe painted on it—leaned against the fence.

I forgot about my old lady and old man and all and watched the guy. The shavings were flying around as he planed away like a madman.

"Hi," I said.

He said "Hi" too but gave me a big freeze otherwise—just polishing away on that damn board. I wondered whether all surfers were like him and Moondoggie—snooty bastards.

"Who's Stinky?" I asked.

"Me," he said . . . just ignoring me.

"How much is such a board?"

That made him look up. He wasn't exactly friendly as he gave me the once-over.

"For yourself?"

"No—for my Aunt Hester," I said . . . trying to be funny.

"This is seventy-five bucks," Stinky said, not moving a muscle, "but you couldn't handle it, little one."

I was peeved. "Why not?"

"How much you weigh?"

"Ninety-five pounds."

He screwed up his face and shook his head.

"Can't carry it," he said.

"How about a lighter one?"

He scanned around his workshop, dropped the plane, reached for an old beaten-up thing with a lot of notches in it and lifted it up with one hand.

"What about this abortion?"

"Huh?"

"Twenty-five bucks," he said. "Weighs only twenty pounds. A Wili Wili. Lift it!"

I lifted it. It felt like a sack of pebbles. "I'll put some fiberglass on," Stinky said. "Look like new."

"You'll be here tomorrow?" I asked.

"Sure thing."

"Okay—make it look like new. I'll pick it up at ten."

It usually takes me years to make up my mind.

Also I had exactly three dollars and eighty-five cents to my name.

Further: I knew my old man would raise a horrible stink on account of being a non-swimmer and getting stomach spasms already when I do a little bodysurfing.

But I also knew that the most desperate thing I wanted on that fatal day in July was a surfboard of my own.

I had already decided what to call it: *Moondoggie.*

## MIDSUMMER

Thinking back now I can't tell honestly what got me more jazzed up: the thrill to paddle out on the board and get initiated into the art of surfing— or the fact that those guys made me a member of the crew.

I was "The Gidget" but then they all had their funny names and by the time I could manage a belly slide past the first waves out beyond the surfline I had forgotten that they had other names and sometimes I forgot even that my name was Franzie and that's no joke.

"Olé—here comes the Gidget!"

"Hey, Gidget, when do we get another leg of lamb?"

"Got some booze, Gidget?"

"Let's drag the Gidget in the hut and teach her some technique."

Boy, I sure felt right at home with the crew. They were regular guys—none of those fumbling high school jerks who tackle a girl like a football dummy. No sweaty hands and struggles on slippery leather seats of hot rods. The bums of Malibu knew how to talk to a girl, how to handle her, make her feel grown up.

Every day—and I managed to come out to the cove almost every day—someone else let me have a board to practice. On Don Pepe's board I learned how to keep in the center and paddle evenly—on Hot Shot

Harrison's how to control the direction you're taking with your feet—on Malibu Mac's how to get out of a "bone yard" when you're caught in the middle of a set of breakers—and on Scooterboy Miller's hot rod I learned how to avoid a pearl dive.

The great Kahoona showed me the first time how to get on my knees, to push the shoulders up and slide the body back—to spring to your feet quickly, putting them a foot apart and under you in one motion. That's quite tricky. But then, surf-riding is not playing monopoly and the more I got the knack of it, the more I was crazy about it and the more I was crazy about it, the harder I worked at it.

Meanwhile home life became one big jigsaw puzzle. First I figured I'd clue my old lady in on the whole operation but Larue talked me out of it. As far as grownups are concerned she wasn't harboring any foolish illusions. "Listen, Jazz-bo," she said, "I know your mom a lot better than you do. She might even let you go out there and wheedle the old man, but you can bet your shaggy fins she's going to mess it up for you. She'll be sitting home worrying and the next thing, she'll be snooping around and she'll be out there in Malibu in the flesh *and the next thing,* she'll try one of those boards herself and, being the athletic type, she might get a kick out of it and before you know it *she's* going tandem with you and that's the end of the whole blast. Forget it, Jazz-bo, will you?"

Larue's got lots of pimples but she makes up for them with a sound working brain. So I decided to muddle along.

Well, you know how it is when you start with one little old hairy lie—you think you get away with it and then the little old hairy lie becomes one *big* old hairy lie.

Of course I was telling the truth when I said that I was going out to old Malibu and sometimes one of the girls who picked me up—Mai Mai or Barbara (whenever Larue's car was unavailable)—really came along, but I never took them to the cove, or even near it. They were sort of curious about the surfing crowd but I managed to keep them at a safe distance. They really had no idea what was coming off—even though Barbara had a couple of fangled chassis that would put Jayne Mansfield to shame.

Then there was the problem of the produce.

You've heard of icebox raids but the way I went gallivanting off with the whole legs of lamb, kegs of cheese, heaps of peanut-butter sandwiches, tons of bananas, was freakishly reckless, to say the least. "Are you feeding the seals?" my mother ventured surreptitiously one day when she caught me stowing away a whole package of wieners in my beach bag.

"Ha-ha." What a laugh. "We're having a wienie roast."

"Who's we?"

"Barbara and I. You know she feeds her tapeworm—and he's nuts about wieners."

My old lady gave me a queer look that spoke volumes. I guess this was the first time she caught on to my horseplay.

However, what I scrounged in the kitchen kept me in good stead with the Go-Heads of Malibu.

Their appetite was monstrous.

They fell over the contents of my beach bag like a pack of hound dogs.

They never had anything edible along and when they got hungry they all chipped in and got some hamburger over at Johnny Frenchman's joint, and a few bottles of coke and beer. Mostly beer. They could skoal two cases of beer in no time flat. What puzzled me most at the beginning was the great Kahoona. How did he keep himself supplied? There were always some cans of beans standing around in his shack, and coffee and sugar, but it wasn't exactly what you might call a well-balanced diet.

The great Kahoona! I had to think of him all the time. I had seen bums up in the skiing country, like Warren Miller, and then I saw a lot of other ski-bums at Aspen, Colorado, and everywhere my old lady took me in winter. I even once saw a *beach-bum* in some corny T.V. show with

## THE NEW TOM BLAKE, STREAMLINED, AIR-CHAMBER HAWAIIAN HOLLOW SURFBOARD

WITH THE INVENTION of the new Air-Chamber Streamlined Hollow Surfboard by Tom Blake (surfboard expert of Waikiki Beach, Honolulu), and its introduction into the United States, the millions of swimmers and bathers of this country have available a sport which has always been considered exclusive to the Hawaiian Islands.

The Tom Blake Air-Chamber Hollow Surfboard has been approved by Hawaii's greatest surf riders, and by America's greatest aquatic stars.

At Waikiki Beach, the Great Duke Kahanamoku rides nothing but a Hollow Surfboard. Miss Beatrice Newport, of Honolulu, world's best girl surf rider, says: "The Hollow Board is delightful, fast, light and sporty to ride."

Helene Madison and Johnny Weissmuller, world's champion swimmers, are enthusiastic users of the Hollow Surfboard.

A small sail can be rigged on the Board. Rapids shooting on small rivers is a highly exciting sport. With a fast boat to tow you, aqua-planing is the thing. The Hollow Surfboard is a great aid to the lifeguard on a rescue.

Lovers of water sports everywhere agree that Waikiki has given the United States a great new sport, new pleasure, and a splendid life-saving device in this Streamlined Hollow Surfboard.

SPECIFICATIONS: Length, 12 feet, 10 inches. Maximum breadth, 21½ inches. Maximum depth, 5½ inches. Weight, 44 pounds. Delivered ready for the water. Made of genuine African Mahogany, finest materials, finest workmanship, by the oldest woodworking manufacturer in the United States. Only brass screws and waterproof marine glue used throughout. Three coats spar varnish; beautiful two-tone finish.

Irene Dunne. He had a shaggy beard a *mile long* and he was always whit-tling away at some driftwood. But before you knew it he had this beard shaved off and it turned out he wasn't a bum at all but some hack writer who had been disappointed in his love life and stuff.

Well, Cass wasn't that kind of a phony character.

It was Lord Gallo who gave me the scoop one afternoon as I was sit-ting out in the surf with him waiting for a halfway decent wave to take us in. Lord Gallo's real name is Stan Buckley and he goes to Pomona College and he was the most educated of the guys even though he had this fatal craving for Gallo wine that made him sometimes doddering like a bowl-ing pin undecided whether to stand up or fall down.

"I'll clue you in on that guy, Gidget," said the Lord. "We are all sort of seasonal surf-bums—but Cass is the real article. He's been around from Peru to Nanakuli. This here is bathtub stuff for him. Do you know that he's the only guy besides Duke Kahanamoku who came in on Zero break without spilling?"

I had heard about the Duke because Scooterboy had his name on his board and Duke Kahanamoku is to surfing what the Babe is to baseball bugs. But Zero break was Hawaiian to me.

"Zero break comes up only once a year, during storm surf or when there's an earthquake or some ground disturbances undersea," explained the Lord. "Now with all those H-bomb blasts you get them more often. But only in the islands. The waves get up to thirty feet and they come in on a thirty-miles-an-hour speed. Man!"

I was duly impressed. Still, what do you do the rest of the year? I haven't got too good a thinking brain but right off the elbow I know you've got to have money—*l'argent*—geld—and you can't travel around the world on a surfboard.

The way Lord Gallo put it, though, the great Kahoona had made the amazing discovery that you could.

"You may not dig this, Gidget," said the wise man from Pomona, "but for Cass this bumming around the beaches is a way of life...as the man said. Like another guy goes and sells vacuum cleaners, bumming is his stock in trade. And believe me, it takes as much know-how and talent and brains. He never loses a season on stupid things like trying to make a living or get a job."

"What's he feeding off?" I asked.

"The sea, bird-brain," said his Lordship. "He broils himself some abalone steak or lobster, the kind you can't order at Jack's or King's. Sometimes some buttermouth or perch. Or he scoots up to Pismo for some of those giant clams that you can bake in the ground. Maybe we'll let you come to our next luau, Gnomie...then you'll get a taste of it."

Well, that cleared up a few points. It's a monotonous diet, the way I see it, but it can keep a fellow going a long way. I could understand now how much he appreciated my peanut-butter sandwiches for a change.

"The guys are sponsoring him. Ever heard of the great Aga Khan?" he went on. "Well, he's a small operator compared to the great Kahoona."

I ventured one more conventional question: "What's a guy like him going to do when he gets older?"

"He's got a theory on that," confided the Lord among the Go-Heads. "He once told me: the only way to get economic independence is to be independent of economics. The more money you make, the less independent you are of it. And once you make a lot of dough, you're more dependent than when you're broke."

The Lord concluded his profile of the great Kahoona: "Believe me, Kiddo, this guy's got something. He's found the answer to a lot of things that bother us. The time to start making dough is when you get old and creaky. While you're young, you got to take a holiday. And he's taken one long hell of a holiday—ever since he was born."

There were some more questions on my mind like why Cass had never been married or if he had been, what happened to it, and also why there was never a girl around the place—and how he built his shack—and if it was always the same shack—and how he transported it—and where he went when the season folded in October—and how it felt when he rode the waves of Makaha at Zero break, but just then his Lordship had turned his head and saw a bitchen set of waves coming up fast and he yelled, "Shoot it!" which means the wave is breaking behind you, and I got in position and we both missed it and *Fiasco*—that is the Lord's board—went into a terrible pearl dive and jackknifed back at us and we both dove fast and when we came up *Fiasco* was miles away from us.

And the next thing I know was that some hands grabbed me and lifted me out of the tide—and if it wasn't again Moondoggie, giving me this smug, big grin as if he had just been standing by to fish me out.

I wanted to get off the board—trying to help Lord Gallo retrieve *Fiasco.* But he had a firm grip on me.

"Don't fidget—Gidget."

"Oh—go to Gunneriff!" I told him. It was part of the monkey-talk I had picked up from the boys. I didn't know exactly what it meant.

"Take it slow, Joe."

"Turn deaf, Jeff."

That chopped him royal.


## LATE SUMMER

I must have been sleeping way into the morning because when I opened my eyes the sun was filtering into the hut and I heard a roar from the outside as if all hell was loose.

The great Kahoona was nowhere in sight.

My blouse and skirt looked a mess, all wrinkled up, and I decided to go out and have a morning swim before breakfast.

I slipped out of my clothes and threw them on the cot and just as I was about to head out, the door to the hut opened.

The sudden impact of the sun blinded me for a moment.

"Morning, Cass," I called out.

Anybody could have made that crazy mistake. The guy who stood in the door frame was almost as tall as Cass and he wore jeans and a T-shirt like him.

It wasn't the great operator, however. It was one of his sponsors. It was no other than Moondoggie.

"Gidget," he said flatly. "What in hell . . ."

My mind was jumping around so quickly—I hardly could keep track of it. Has he been looking for me? Did he think I had been sleeping with the great Kahoona? And if so—what would I tell him? I didn't know what to say so I just gave a fine imitation of a deaf mute and tried to brush past him and get outside.

"Hey, wait a moment . . ." He had grabbed me by the wrist.

Well, here it comes, I thought.

"I want you to answer me . . ."

"Why should I?" I said. "You didn't even talk to me last night."

"But now, *now* I want you to tell me . . ."

For a moment I felt an impulse to call for help, when I spotted the great Kahoona. He had just come out of the surf which was something tremendous. Waves about twenty feet high. That's the way it must look at Makaha or Zero break, I thought. I wished I could have seen him coming riding in. I had never seen them that bitchen, on my word of honor.

Jeff still had me by the wrist when the Kahoona came towards us, his board shouldered.

"Hi, man," he said quite calmly. "What a surf!"

Only then he noticed the way Jeff was almost crushing my wrist. He didn't say anything. He put the board down and leaned it against the hut. Then of all things he started to whistle.

I guess it was the whistling that brought out the beast in Geoffrey Griffin. He released the grip on my wrist. I noticed that all the tan had faded from his face. It was real white now. He made a couple of steps towards Cass. His right fist traveled in a short arc and he hit the great Kahoona solidly on the chin.

"Jeff!" I yelled.

"Shut up," he yelled back.

Cass had stumbled, but it seemed as if the jab had merely shook him up a little. It also had cleared his head.

There was a moment of silence as those two giants faced each other. Then the Kahoona's face spread out like an accordion; he really laughed, and at the same time he hit back at Jeff with a haymaker that sent him backwards, ricocheting into the wall of the hut. The Kahoona's surfboard started to sway and it would have crashed right down on Moondoggie if I hadn't had the presence of mind to hold out my hands and catch it at the last second.

Jeff stared up at the Kahoona. He was panting. And the Kahoona looked down at him and he kept smiling. And I stood there, gripping the surfboard in my hands, just staring.

Suddenly it hit me. I guess "like lightning" is too corny to write down but, Jeez, it fits to a T. It hit me that this wasn't a crummy movie I was watching. Two grown-up men had almost killed each other on account of little me—the gnomie—the shortie—the gidget!

I noticed some blood trickling from Jeff's nose as he lay stymied and bleary-eyed against the wall of the hut but instead of feeling compassion nothing but a pang of joy went through me. This was the pinnacle, this was the most. Surely nothing more wonderful would ever happen to me, ever.

Had I shouted they would certainly have thought I had gone crazy. So I did the next best thing to give vent to my soaring spirits. I lifted the board in my hands over my head and ran down to the water.

The board felt like feathers, all twenty-five pounds of it. The waves smashed against the dunes like one long, noisy, mad steam roller. I slid on the board and dug my hands into the water and shot over the foam like a speedboat. The water tingled about me—sharp and like cold fire. A wave and another wave, high as houses, but I didn't care. Once I glanced back over my shoulder and saw Cass and Jeff. They had obviously run after me and they yelled something I couldn't hear and they waved their arms crazily, urging me to come back.

No, I wouldn't go back. Not for the life of me. The scenery had been all set up for me like an opening performance. This was the final testing ground I had picked for myself.

A few more strokes and I was beyond the surfline. I couldn't see the coast any more, so high rose the wall of waves before me. I whirled around and brought the board in position. There was no waiting. I shot towards the first set of forming waves and rose.

I stood it. I have to come in standing, I told myself. I gritted my teeth.

"Shoot it," I yelled.

I was lifted up, sky high...and went down. But I stood it. One wave, another one.

"Olé!" I yelled. "Olé!"

Up I was—and down I went.

And still standing.

I was so jazzed up I didn't care whether I would break my neck or ever see Jeff again—or the great Kahoona.

I stood, high like on a mountain peak and dove down, but I stood it.

The only sound in the vast moving green was the hissing of the board over the water. A couple of times it almost dropped away under my feet, but I found it again and stood my ground.

"Shoot it, Gidget. Shoot the curl!!"

My own voice had broken away from me and I could only hear the echo coming from a great distance.

"Shoot it . . . shoot it . . . shoot it, Gidget!"

There was the shore, right there. I could almost reach out and touch it.

Well, this is it.

This was the summer I wanted to write about, the memory of which I wouldn't part with for anything.

Now I'm middle-aged, going on seventeen. I've learned so much in between. I've learned that virtue has its points. That you can grow up even if you don't grow. That men are wonderful.

As for Jeff—we're going steady now. He's shooting the curl at some boot-camp in Texas, being sponsored by the supreme commander himself. I got his fraternity pin before he left and—brother—do I make the most of it with those squares who think they're just *it,* because they have a few more inches upwards and sideways.

As for the great Kahoona: he had to fold up his stand at Malibu and now he's probably pushing some green water down in Peru, operating with a new set of sponsors.

My big love is still out Malibuways with some bitchen surf going.

When it struck me this summer with Jeff it could have just been the dream. With Cass curiosity. But with the board and the sun and the waves it was for real.

All things considered—maybe I was just a woman in love with a surfboard.

It's as simple as that.

# TWO

# KAHUNA:
# SURFING CHARACTERS

When Malibu legend and definitive surfer/outlaw Mickey Dora died at age 67 in 2002, the era of the Great Surfing Character died with him. Or that's the way a lot of older surfers view it, and they have a point. The sport still has its share of compelling figures. Tow-in pioneer Laird Hamilton, for one, seemingly belongs to a still-unclassified species of humanity that is at once primordial and futuristic, with giant muscles matched by giant reserves of courage and inventiveness. But today's surfing leaders are now all operating in waters that have already been charted and mapped. Maybe this explains why surfing celebrity is so much more expansive than in decades past, spilling over into nonsurfing regions as if wave-riding alone was a bit... not passé exactly, but not quite

interesting enough. Six-time world champion Kelly Slater is an *Interview* magazine cover boy and gets to record a CD with T-Bone Burnett. Surfer/attorney Mark Massara is a crusading environmentalist. Quiksilver CEO Bob McKnight is an action sportswear industry titan. Even Laird Hamilton has been grouped with skateboarders, BMX riders, and other extreme sports stars (maybe not such a great deal for Hamilton, as he finished ninth in a 2003 Extreme Sports Channel viewers poll, well behind winner Rodney Mullen, a Florida street skater).

Modern surfing is now more than 100 years old, and as it becomes more popular and familiar, the chance for a surfing personality to stand out as an original becomes correspondingly smaller. The sport already has a full pantheon of inventors, travelers, rogues, competitors, and stylists. While these archetypes are periodically refitted and redefined, never again can any of them be completely new. Meanwhile, in coastal zones worldwide the once-gaping chasm between surfers and nonsurfers has all but closed.

Surf culture has been appropriated by the culture at large since the late 1950s, but for years the sport was often vilified or mocked as a fad, like hula hooping or break dancing. Surf culture today does pretty much whatever it wants, on its own terms and often with fanfare, which reduces the opportunity for subversiveness, which in turn reduces the opportunity for true surfing greatness. Or that's the logic if you believe, as most surfers do, that cutting against the grain is a basic surfing character prerequisite. Mickey Dora is revered, as DAVID REASON notes in "The Legend Lives," mainly because he played off the tensions between the surfing and nonsurfing worlds—and then worked overtime by playing insurgent against the surf industry, his surfing peers, even his friends.

*Apocalypse Now* screenwriter and former Malibu regular JOHN MILIUS watched Dora closely through the early '60s, and brought some of the dark-haired surfer's grinning sedition to bear in writing the part of Colonel William Kilgore, who takes surfing fanaticism to wild new heights by firebombing a North Vietnamese village so that his men can slide a few waves at a nearby pointbreak. Surfer/novelist ALLAN WEISBECKER also returns to the '60s, with "Jock's Night Trip," recalling how Jock Sutherland rode twenty-five-foot Waimea Bay at night while dosed on a big hit of acid. Sutherland wipes out and loses his board, an emergency rescue squad arrives and announces that nobody could survive such conditions, then Sutherland quietly appears walking down the coast highway, having come ashore a mile to the east. The Surfer again gets one over on the Man. Two months later, with no advance notice, in a move that seemed to turn acquiescence itself into subversiveness, Sutherland enlisted in the military. It's a subjective call for sure, but Slater winning a sixth world title or Hamilton fading deep on a fifty-footer was child's play compared to Sutherland putting on a U.S. Army uniform.

## "THE LEGEND LIVES: FINDING MICKEY DORA"

Los Angeles–based journalist David Rensin began writing for *Rolling Stone* in 1972, and became a *Playboy* contributing editor in 1981. He's written or coauthored ten books, including 2003's *The Mailroom: Hollywood History from the Bottom Up.* "The Legend Lives," Rensin's feature on charismatic surfing icon Mickey Dora, was a cover story for a 1983 issue of *California* magazine.

> *"At the perfect surfing spot on the perfect day,*
> *Mickey Dora is probably the best surfer in the world."*
> —*Surf Guide* magazine, November 1964

Ten years later, Mickey Dora had disappeared. The onetime Malibu heavyweight—whose cool self-possession had, to many, epitomized the California surfing lifestyle—was missing from his favorite waves. Yet, unlike other aging surf stars, Dora hadn't retired to run a beachfront restaurant or surfboard shop. He had simply vanished.

Dora left in his wake only rumor and speculation. Though tales of his activities through the years washed him far beyond the ocean's pale, the surf magazines continued to muse about his fate. And Dora's name was always mentioned whenever conversations among old beach buddies turned to surfing nostalgia. Everyone, it seemed, had heard something different about "The King of Malibu," "Da Cat."

In the absence of facts, Dora's legend became embroidered with fiction.

Some said that Dora had gone Hollywood—that his innate charisma and work in early beach exploitation flicks had paid off—or that he had swapped his board and baggies for the Mercedes and tailored suits of a prestigious law career. Fantastic stories surfaced of his alleged hashish smuggling operation in the Middle East. Or was it gunrunning in Indonesia? Others claimed that Dora, who had once adorned his surfboard with swastikas, was living the *über*-life in Argentina. Or perhaps he was still searching for the perfect wave—Dora sightings were reported in Bali, New Zealand, Peru, France, Australia, Costa Rica, and New Guinea. Some even thought Dora was dead, but the faithful plastered their cars with DORA LIVES! bumper stickers.

I'd surfed in the sixties, and followed the entertaining, Dora-bylined accounts of his improbable international adventures in the genre magazines. But there were also the rare Dora interviews—all typically sardonic, aggressive, apocalyptic. First he would lambast the surf press's fascination with him. Then he'd castigate the "Valley cowboys and aircraft workers" who were overcrowding his beloved Malibu. He'd scorn the beach party movies he thought were responsible, insult well-known surfers by name, and predict the entire sellout subculture's imminent demise.

For these mouthfuls, Dora was tagged the "angry young man of surfing." His blasts seemed to some like theater. They often were. But Dora's outrage was more than simple self-conscious antiheroism. It revealed deep convictions about surfing's real nature, as far removed from the surf music / beach lingo/surf contest marketing of the California lifestyle as Dora's young James Garner looks were from the typically tanned and blond beach boy's. Dora never drove a woody. He didn't spend every moment at the beach. "When there's surf, I'm totally committed," he once said. "When there's none, it doesn't exist."

Dora's flip side was equally memorable. He was an avid partier and prankster. He was unpredictable, colorful, and attractive. "Mickey was the ultimate surfing celebrity," says an old Dora cohort. "He was flamboyant, charming, and a great storyteller with a go-for-it attitude. He spent his life searching for the ultimate wave, the best coq au vin, and an appreciative audience that he could hypnotize with his 'truth or illusion?' stories. But he was finally a loner. We all knew him as the Malibu Gypsy."

Through the anger and the antics, Dora kept the beach crowd entertained and his private life private. He regularly rebuffed questions about his image and his off-beach activities. Though Dora's growing legion of adherents could copy his graceful surfing style, the hand gestures and vocal inflections that were his trademark, and his rhetorical approach to conversation—always questioning the questioner—they could not decipher the enigma that was their idol. Nor could his many detractors. And his prolonged absence from the scene only intensified the mystique.

In late 1982 I decided to try to find the Malibu Gypsy. It wasn't Dora's style to leave many clues, so I sought out a cross section of people who had known him. Almost immediately, I realized that I had crossed the border into an intense, fraternal land peopled with characters who lived, in their hearts, on society's edge. They were territorial. Loyal. Fiercely protective. Some talked willingly, some didn't. But to all, Dora was a cherished anomaly—good or bad, he was one of their own.

Along the way I was given an old photograph of Dora, a Belmondo-esque head shot. He wore a week's stubby beard, and a cigarette dangled from parted lips. But where Belmondo's eyes would have been etched with possibility, Dora's were like one-way mirrors. I saw the unfolding challenge reflected. It was as if Dora and I were taking off on the same wave, but only one of us would finish the ride. And Dora was used to winning.

Picture Malibu without today's posh hamburger joints, exercise salons, or shopping centers. Send the sightseers home. Clean up the beach trash. Imagine a crystalline summer morning, cooled by an offshore breeze, and remember the waves—the long, sweeping south swells wrapping perpetually around the first and second points, many crashing virgin and unridden over the rocks and sand.

But not all of them. Out in the water a young surfer eyes the six-foot combers that have been rolling in since before daybreak. He is darkly tanned, and his curly hair is the color of wet mahogany. Now, breaking through a lip of mist, he drops to the bottom of a perfect wave, carving a white trail through the blue-green wall. He stalls for a moment and then, almost imperceptibly using his knees and ankles to position himself, rises into the curl. Once at the crest, he saunters casually to the nose of his board, bends his knees, and wraps his toes over the edge. Relaxed and yet arrogant, he taunts the wave—he moves like a matador, a ballet dancer, a cat. Suddenly, with feline reflexes, Mickey Dora abandons the wave and watches it crash before him.

"Mickey used to talk about the summer of '49 and how perfect Malibu was," says Jim Kempton, associate publisher of *Surfer* magazine. "Imagine the setup at that place without a crowd. You can understand, then, how the eventual commercialization of surfing, of California, made Mickey very resentful and bitter. Lifeguards, restrictions, people in the way . . ."

Introduced to the sport by his stepfather, Gard Chapin, a well-known surfer of his generation, Dora first surfed at San Onofre in the late 1940s. Though it was still a small scene then, centered on a few rugged individuals riding crude redwood boards, surfing great Phil Edwards remembers the teenage Dora as "a hot guy. . . . At San Onofre he made the rest of us look like idiots. Mickey had seen that there was more to surfing than riding straight in." By the early 1950s, Dora had gravitated to Malibu, where a few daring young surfers were perfecting their art on new streamlined boards and uncrowded waves. His star began to rise in the watery firmament of California surfing. Some say he was also beginning to earn a reputation as a rebel.

Dora's problems had started early. He was born Miklos Sandor Dora to Ramona, 17, and Miklos, 20, on August 11, 1934, and six years later the union ended. A friend says the divorce shook young Dora: "He wanted to live with his mother, but his father insisted that Mickey be raised as he was—in military schools. He hated them." Grant Roloff, a filmmaker who shot extensive surfing footage of Dora in the 1960s, recalls seeing an old photograph of Dora in a military school uniform. "He was probably in the seventh or eighth grade," Roloff says. "I can still remember how shocked I was by the anger and unhappiness in his face."

But Dora was a quick, intelligent child, and he found ways to survive while growing up among strangers. One was to withdraw. Another was to intellectualize situations and turn them into games. "Even today, games underlie everything," says a woman who met him in Malibu in the late 1950s and has remained close. "Next to surfing, games are his greatest passion." An extension of those games in later years was scamming—inventing ways to get something for next to nothing. In military school, Dora's scam was to smuggle candy in on weekends.

Ramona's second husband, Chapin, began taking Dora to the beach during his school vacations, and for a time Dora adopted his stepfather's surname. But if Chapin took Dora under his wing, he also took him to task for his behavior. "My stepfather had strange ideas about raising kids," Dora said in an issue of *Surf Guide*. "He devised some pretty stiff disciplinary programs for me...but he was also a unique frontiersman and a profound influence on my life." Chapin died in the mid-1950s, and Dora insisted that the circumstances were mysterious. "His untimely [death] in Mexico can only be linked with his individualistic personality," he told *Surfer* magazine in one typically cryptic interview.

Chapin's independence was characteristic of his surfing generation and an era when surfers were true bohemians. "The American dream then was a sedate, unhip little house in the Valley, two cars, a nice steady job, and a couple of bratty kids," says John Milius, director of the surf epic *Big*

*Wednesday.* "But this tight-knit brotherhood developed a lifestyle so they didn't have to get stuck in that rut. It was a matter of doing what you had to to get by, so you could go to the beach."

It is unlikely that Dora perceived his stepfather's legacy so philosophically back then. In a moment of rare candor, he told *Surf Guide* why he found surfing rewarding: "When I went to school, damn near everything was concocted around the buddy system. They never left you alone. But with surfing I could go to the beach and not have to depend on anybody. I could take a wave and forget about it."

In 1959 everything began to change. "Surfing U.S.A." was invented. Gremmies, kooks, hodads, and surfer girls swarmed the beaches. Peroxide futures skyrocketed. Woodies were resurrected. Surfing magazines were started and surf movies made. A whole California dream–oriented subculture exploded into the American consciousness, and Mickey Dora no longer had the waves at Malibu or anywhere else to himself. But he did have a front-row seat for the changing times as the youth revolution, with all its possibilities in tow, slammed headlong into the Malibu crowd.

Dora and his beach buddies were not quite prepared for the disorientation of meeting their idealized media images face-to-face, or for the aftershocks of celebrity. As the top dogs of surfing, they were hounded for interviews, photographed constantly, and used as stunt doubles, extras, and technical advisers in beach party movies. They were asked to compete in televised surf contests and hired to endorse rival manufacturers' products, and they were ultimately cast as role models for a new generation of surfers. All of a sudden Dora had a surfing "career"—a situation he constantly renounced. "I'm not a commodity to use in your cheap, quick-buck articles," he raged in *Surfer* magazine.

But Dora didn't so much reject the media as become adept at manipulating it. "Mickey understood how to get attention," says Jim Kempton. "He knew that saying less was far more interesting than saying too much. And he had a sure sense of self—he didn't need anyone to prick his finger and see if the blood ran blue. Mickey knew that much of his mystique would have been impossible without the media responding as they did. He just understood what people liked. And then he played with it."

Dora was always up to something, and he soon gained a reputation as a prankster. Classic, perhaps apocryphal tales include his shooting Army rocket flares off the Malibu pier, unleashing a jar of moths at a surf movie screening to watch them converge on the projector, and dropping his trunks for the crowd and TV cameras at a 1965 Malibu surfing contest. Another Dora pastime was party crashing. "We always had a party kit in the car so that we could dress to suit the occasion," says Dora's self-proclaimed Hollywood party connection. "We had everything from a Hawaiian shirt to a tuxedo. Even a glass with ice cubes." Mongoose, another Malibu regular, places Dora at a Bel-Air party given by the Beatles—"and not because he especially dug the Beatles."

"Mickey loved fraud," John Milius explains. "He was fascinated with the concept of deceit. He would come to the beach with a couple of young guys and the word would pass around that 'Mickey Dora is gay.' Three days later he'd show up with the most extraordinary girl on his arm. It was quite funny."

What wasn't funny, however, was the way Dora treated his beachside groupies. He relegated them to stooge status, using them as errand boys, chauffeurs, and the objects of his contempt. Other Dora victims were those surfers naive enough to try to share a wave with him—Dora adamantly defended his practice of sending the offending surfer and his surfboard in opposite directions. "These guys are thieves and they're stealing my waves," he railed in *Surfer* magazine. "If I get it first it belongs to me....I deserve it!"

Dora also deserved his reputation for rejecting the rewards of a steady job. When he did work, it was only temporary—he just did what he had to to get by. He bartended at La Scala restaurant in Beverly Hills for a few months in the mid-1960s, and there were his parts in the beach party films. (He once listed among his credits *Gidget, Gidget Goes to Rome, Ride the Wild Surf, Gidget Goes Hawaiian, Surfing Wild, Beach Party, Bikini Beach,* and *For Those Who Think Young.*) At one point he contracted with Greg Noll Surfboards to develop a signature model, da Cat, but it was only marginally successful, perhaps due to Dora's volatile ad copy: "I don't want some acne adolescent in Pratt Falls, Iowa, using da Cat as a car ornament or some show-biz creep in the Malibu Colony using da Cat as a coffee table, da Cat is too pure and sensitive for the clumsy touch of the occasional pseudosurfer." Other sources of Dora's income are largely un-known, though one friend remembers Dora as a credible silver speculator.

John Milius regards Dora's penchant for not working in a more ro-mantic light: "The heroic aspects of Mickey Dora are that he did resist the

work ethic, that he did live his own life, that he was his own man. Even if he was scamming to get by. Mickey understood that, especially in Los Angeles, appearance means everything. One just needs the proper trappings to play perfectly into whatever illusion one wants to create. If Mickey were being chased by the police, he'd probably pull over, figuring he could talk his way out of it. He scammed for the sheer joy of it. Like he surfed."

Mickey Dora turned 35 in 1969. Surfing hadn't lost its spiritual charm, but Dora found it increasingly difficult to exist in a California beach scene that fulfilled his every bitter prophecy. He became a frequent world traveler, riding the waves on a circuit followed by the international surfing clique, and his appearances in the surf press began to reflect the change— the angry interviews he once gave via written answers to written questions mellowed into capricious travel pieces laced with humor and cynicism.

In early 1970, Dora and three friends, including Mongoose, went to Rio de Janeiro for Carnival as guests of the Brazilian attaché in Los Angeles. The "four horsemen of the Apocalypse"—as Dora called the troupe in a Mongoose-ghosted *Surfer* article entitled "To Whom It May Underestimate"—had a fast time. They partied at Rio's best nightclubs, crashed the $10,000-per-ticket Governor's Ball, and claimed they were treated to a private performance by Brazil '66. The group's final destination was the Gran Hotel Dora in Buenos Aires. Ostensibly, the trip's initial purpose had been for Dora to meet his ailing "Uncle Kornel" and, as his only living heir, to discuss Dora's eventual interest in the hotel. A picture of Dora in front of the hotel accompanied the text. It was a classic of humor and bravado, and mostly fiction.

But underlying Dora's restless escapades was his quest for an ocean Eden. "Mickey was obsessed with the idea of apocalypse, of a world in ashes," says Mongoose. "The search was his favorite thing. He once wrote me a letter from New Zealand claiming he'd found an island with an economy and lifestyle based on coconuts. To me, this quest for the Holy Grail, a place where he could seek inner salvation, was simply metaphoric. I think he was just looking for some justification for his life. He had this cynical vision—he wanted to get away from the demons he thought were going to descend."

If so, he should have been more careful, because on April 3, 1973, the sky rained demons. Dora was arrested for buying skis and equipment in California's Mono County with a bad check, and was charged with felony fraud. The proceedings—motions, appeals, continuations—lasted nearly eighteen months. During that time Dora failed to appear and to post bail as ordered. He also changed his plea four times, finally pleading guilty on September 27, 1974. Dora was sentenced to three years' probation, the terms of which included a $1,500 fine, no credit cards, a job, an approved residence, and regular check-ins with his probation officer. All anathema to the now psychologically caged cat.

On April 11, 1975, the court issued an arrest warrant in Dora's name for probation violation. Bail was set at $10,000. What had happened? A friend insists that Dora had intended to stay in touch with his probation officer. But he didn't. Another suggests that he simply couldn't deal with the "restriction and the scrutiny [of probation]. He needed to be completely free." Yet Dora's craving for ultimate mobility actually locked him into the very narrow existence he sought to avoid. He was on the run.

Biarritz is a beautiful old town surrounded by the Basque country of France and Spain. Built for royalty in the 1800s, it was a seaside resort for the upper crust, and even today, despite its faded facades, it retains much of its former opulence. It is the La Jolla of the French Atlantic coastline, with a major franchise on natural beauty, and to some it is the European surfing mecca. "It's the September stopping spot," says Jim Kempton, who met Dora in Biarritz in 1971 and continued to see him there every year for nearly a decade. "The mountains begin to get cold, creating offshore winds, but the days are still sunny and warm. Indian summer. You get the big swells."

Though Dora would eventually make his way to Biarritz, drawn in part by the Indian summer surf and the variety of exotic paddle games played there (jai alai being the most familiar to Americans), his path was circuitous. He first set up housekeeping in New Zealand, on the Mahia Peninsula. A friend describes the stay as a brief spell of peace for the outlaw surfer—"the waves were great, and no one was around." But when the local authorities learned of Dora's fugitive status, he left for Australia. There, while horseback riding at a friend's ranch, he fell and shattered his arm. Dora traveled to Switzerland for a restorative operation, and finally settled in France.

In 1976, Dora and a girlfriend spent eight months in a Mercedes camper parked outside an ancient Biarritz farmhouse that Jim Kempton had rented. During the winter, a severe Atlantic storm kept Dora, Kempton, and his other guests locked inside for ten days. "I got to see different sides of Mickey," Kempton says. "There were times when he broke down and we became like normal people—an extremely rare circumstance with Mickey. He was in a fragile position. The French wouldn't extradite, but I think he was afraid of being kidnapped if word spread about him. We talked about how painful it was for him to be away, to not be free. It was a special thing, his opening up to me. Kind of a feather in the cap to have this living legend confide in me. But in other ways it was a pathetic picture—pathetic that a guy with so much charisma and intellect would degrade himself by doing stupid things that in the long term were minor in his gain and major in his downfall.

"Mickey could have been anything he wanted to be," Kempton continues. "An actor. A businessman. If only he'd played by the rules. But he was out to beat the system. The unfortunate part is that there was a moment, sociologically, when there was support for that attitude—all the sixties heroes were outlaws. What turned him bitter, I think, was that suddenly the whole thing went out of fashion, and Mickey was left holding the bag. He was on the outside, where he started."

As the seventies faded, Dora remained in France. Jim Kempton took a job in California. The Mongoose practiced landscape architecture. John Milius made his feature surf film, *Big Wednesday,* but the Dora character was only a minor role.

In 1981, Mickey Dora was arrested by French authorities. Friends say by coincidence. He'd been making transatlantic phone calls from a booth used by Basque revolutionaries—and under police surveillance. Once in custody, Dora's name probably made the computers sing, and his past deeds crashed before him like a closeout section at Waimea Bay. Though France didn't extradite him, three months in a French jail apparently convinced Dora to repatriate. He flew back to California in September 1981, first class. He told a friend that he laughed and joked with the passengers on the flight, sharing wine and stories, and that one traveler even offered him a lift home from the airport. But Dora already had a ride. FBI agents met him at Los Angeles International Airport and whisked him away to the L.A. County Jail.

I discovered the first public mention of Mickey Dora's whereabouts nearly a year later. Under the headlines EX-SURFER 'KING' SURFACES IN CHEYENNE JAIL and SURFER TO SERVE SIX MONTHS, two July 1982 stories in the *Rocky Mountain News* told of Dora's indictment by a Denver Federal Grand Jury. According to the indictment, Dora had forged a Diners Club credit card issued in his name in 1969 by altering the expiration date and one digit in the card number, and had used it on "a two-year-long spending spree through Europe and Asia." It was quite a scam. Dora faced ten years in prison if convicted, but he managed to plea bargain a misdemeanor charge of tampering with his own mail—that is, he threw away the Diners Club bills, thereby interfering with their prompt return to the Denver issuing offices. On July 22, 1982, he was sentenced to six months in federal prison.

Further research revealed that Dora had languished in a variety of correctional institutions since his return. From the L.A. County Jail he was sent to Terminal Island, and then to Bridgeport, in Mono County, to face probation violation charges. He pleaded guilty on October 6, 1981, and was given until January 2, 1982, to surrender. He did and was sent to the Vacaville medical facility for diagnostic study. Six months later, Dora was in the Bridgeport court again, facing the same judge who had tried him in 1973. He was once more put on three years' probation, with similar terms, except that he was now specifically required to reside in California for the duration. He would need written permission to leave. Dora was also ordered to serve another 161 days in the Bridgeport County Jail. But before his time was up, federal authorities took him to Denver on the credit card fraud charges. Upon conviction he was returned to California, and was sent to Lompoc federal prison. I learned of his whereabouts on December 19, 1982, and called the prison. He had been released two days earlier.

With Dora free and living somewhere in California, my original notion of finding him and filling in the mystery years took on an added urgency. Now I wanted to meet him, to get his version of the story that had unfolded. I asked whomever I interviewed for information but had little luck beyond Dora sightings: he'd been seen in a Santa Monica surfboard shop, and surfing at Rincon and Trestles. I was finally told to forget about meeting him. "Dora will never do it," said one former friend. "And if he does," said another, "you'll get taken for the ride of your life. Mickey is like a chimpanzee on a motorcycle, with a loaded shotgun. If he had coffee for breakfast, he'd tell you he had tea."

I called Dora's father in Montecito on the off chance that his son might be living there. He wasn't. Still, I asked the senior Dora if we could meet and talk. The old gentleman courteously declined. "It would complicate things," he said. "My son and I are on speaking terms, but we have a completely different outlook on life." He offered, however, to give my number to Dora when next they spoke. Weeks passed and Dora never called.

But a friend of his did. Cynthia Applewhite, a novelist, had met Dora at Malibu in 1959 and "was attracted to him immediately. He was just a beautiful man. We had a lovely chemistry." Cynthia heard about me from Dora, who had received my message from his father. Dora sent Cynthia to investigate.

We met at a Studio City coffee shop and sat at a table near the kitchen, amid the clatter of dishes. Cynthia was intrigued, though understandably cautious about my interest. "Mickey's tired and sick and wants to be left alone," she said. But she also felt that a story about a man she clearly admired might help him—that he needed to be remembered well, perhaps as the mysterious James Bond character she sometimes imagined him to be.

I asked Cynthia to fill in a few gray areas. How had Dora reacted to prison? "He's embarrassed at having been caught, but prison hasn't changed him," she said. "I'm amazed that he came through it so well. From his letters I could see that he really suffered. He knew he was going to prison, and I remember him doing as much surfing as he could just before he went in. He said the California surfer image was a detriment in jail, that people would slit his throat out of envy if they knew. When he got out he looked tired and beaten. Awful. But each time I see him he looks more and more healthy." I had seen pictures of Dora, but nothing recent. What did he look like today? "Mickey stands erect and still has that graceful walk," Cynthia answered. "He's also lost the fifteen pounds he gained on the prison diet. I think he's still very handsome—he still gives off those young Cary Grant vibes."

And then the essential question: could Cynthia arrange a meeting between Dora and me? Her answer was not surprising. "Mickey thinks this story is just another example of his being exploited," she said, and then she paused. "Actually, Mickey is afraid. He thinks the authorities are going to try and jail him again. He's working at a court-ordered job in Orange County to pay off his fines, and he feels... trapped."

I paid the check and we walked to our cars. Would Cynthia ask Dora for a meeting? She agreed, but suggested I prepare a list of questions to submit through her in case he refused. He had, after all these years, never met an interviewer face to face.

Cynthia called a few days later with mixed news. "Mickey is out of sorts and wants to leave the country," she said. "He's trying to get written permission, but it's not working." Then, a surprise—Mickey would talk, for a price. A one-way ticket to Europe, first class, in case he was granted permission to leave the country. It was pure Mickey. I had to refuse. But Cynthia wanted to explain. "Mickey wants to leave because he has this pet project. He's searching for this mysterious wave. A rogue wave. When he finds it, he's going to turn all his research over to scientists who can use it." She sighed. "It's funny, but Mickey has been talking a lot about the ocean lately. Just the ocean, not even surfing. It's as if he wants to become part of the ocean. He thinks he'll find his salvation there. Whenever he talks about the ocean or this wave, he glows—he seems young again." Her statement echoed what one Dora acolyte, who'd spent some time with him in France, had said. "Mickey carries a couple of pictures in his wallet. One is of his dad. The other is of a wave—an excellent, beautiful, hollow, giant tube...with no one on it. He treats waves like people."

During the following weeks, I began to receive some mysterious phone messages. One caller, who refused to identify himself, said he was a friend of Dora's who wanted to "shade the story with positive input." But he also sounded an ominous warning. "The story of Mickey Dora is the story of getting the story," he said. "The real story is unpublishable. It's more than a simple journalistic undertaking. There's more to it than words on a page." Amen. I felt as though any hope of my meeting Dora had finally evaporated.

Weeks passed. Then Cynthia called. "Mickey wants to meet you tomorrow at 7 P.M.," she said, "in the fourth-floor taping room of the Orange Coast College Library. He feels he may have handled this situation wrong. You can bring your tape recorder. Mickey is bringing his. I'm excited. Good luck."

I arrived early and waited in a reading area on the library's second floor. I kept one eye on the entrance and the other on the elevator—I wanted to see Dora before he saw me, before what I was sure would be our uneasy confrontation. I knew I would recognize him. But by 6:55 I was still waiting. Perhaps he wouldn't show. I quickly checked the first-floor entrance. Nothing. It was time. I called for the elevator and rode up.

Dora was waiting by the elevator, slumped against a floor-to-ceiling column, reading a magazine. He was darkly tanned, and his curly hair was flecked with silver and matted. Cynthia had mentioned a beard, but now only a thin wisp of moustache lined his upper lip. More wisps formed the outlines of a translucent goatee. Dora looked very tired, and his clothes were rumpled, almost as if he'd been sleeping on the beach. He was hardly the self-possessed legend I'd expected, the one who had told Cynthia "they'll never beat me." He stood up like a cautious animal. We shook hands.

"I'm, uh, I apologize that it's taken so long for us to meet," he said in a small, modulated voice, as if he had never avoided me. We settled into a glassed-in taping room with yellow walls, bean bag chairs, and a long, vinyl couch divided by a Formica table top. It was the kind of room you see used for group encounter sessions in the movies. Dora and I sat on opposite sides of the divider and turned on our tape recorders.

"I've been away from California for twelve years," Dora began. "I have nothing to do with surfing here. Why have you taken an interest in me?" His dark eyes watched me carefully.

"Well, I've wondered where you've been," I said.

"So has everyone else—so have the authorities."

"They found you."

"They didn't find me," Dora countered. "I came back voluntarily to settle this up—as an honorable gentleman. I thought they would reciprocate. But things like that don't occur anymore." Dora sounded tense but restrained, as if he were explaining right and wrong to a child with a discipline problem. We were both conscious of the whispering tape machines.

"I should never have come back to America," he said. "That was the great mistake of my life. But I did. And I have fulfilled my obligations to the state as far as I'm concerned. Even more so—a thousand percent of suffering. . . . My ambitions are to terminate this probation as soon as possible and continue my life abroad. I'm not happy in America. And I'm sure that many people here want to make me miserable and, if they can, put me back in prison."

"Why do people want to make you miserable?" I asked.

"Why are the prisons filled?" he answered. "Why are the psychiatric clinics filled? Why is the whole country neurotic? Because the system isn't working. I don't trust people, because I know the American mentality. It's competitive—it's a dog-eat-dog society."

I still wanted to know why Dora thought returning to America had been such a mistake.

"Because, since I've been back, I've been in more than twenty jails," he said. "I did four or five months in solitary in Bridgeport under horrible conditions. I went through hell up there. And if I told you about it, no one would possibly believe the abuse I took. I had a wonderful life in Europe. I thought I'd be here one or two months—my lawyer said, 'This is nothing. We'll settle the charges quickly and you'll be on your way.' And 99 percent was just gossip, just like your story is going to talk about. Hearsay. Unsubstantiated rumor."

Was he, in fact, saying that the Diners Club problem and breaking probation charges were all gossip?

Dora began to unleash some of his anger and resentment. "The state says the charges are true, and the state is right and I'm wrong and that's all there is to it. The prisons are full of innocent people who have been coerced into pleading guilty. But those are the facts of life, and now I'm a criminal. Now I have a record. My family is disenchanted with me." Dora paused, and then, as if it would drive home his frustration, said, "Look, it can happen to you. Maybe one day you'll be in there."

"And maybe you'll be a reporter who's doing a story on me," I said, "though I doubt it. I'm not yet a legend in my own time."

Dora responded instantly. "I have never considered myself a legend. I have never considered myself anything—as a way of survival, of living, in a very competitive sport. I'm an old man now. The sport is for young people. There are thousands of these kids, millions of them, all over the world, like polliwogs. It was a different sport in my day. It was a small community and everyone respected each other. Now that world and life are gone forever. Off the face of the earth. What's to discuss? . . . My only talent [today] is to try and live a free life. And that's been taken away from me."

Even if Dora didn't want to discuss the past, I still had questions about his philosophy. But he was more concerned with how this story might affect him in the present.

"I have to make a living in this country. I have to pay back certain fines. I must be very circumspect in my behavior. If I do one thing wrong I can go back to jail. And I feel I can't protect myself against the crackpots and the screwballs you've talked to."

I explained that many people had said good things about him. I also told him that most of his friends, sources who could have made positive contributions, had refused to help. Suddenly Dora shifted gears.

"I'm not afraid of this story, per se," he said. "I can stand on my own two feet. It's just that I'm afraid of the law in this country, this holy vendetta against the populace, this purification. I don't want to be a part of it. . . . But I'm walking a tightrope."

"Don't you think you're being a little paranoid?" I asked.

Dora's eyes widened. He laughed for the first time. The tension was broken. "I just don't want to be made crazy," he said. "I'm a healthy human being and I just want to find happiness and live a good life. The reaction to this story will make me crazy. Everyone will look at me as if I'm a freak of nature, some untrustworthy individual." Now it was my turn to laugh. Dora smiled. "I'm quite sure you've put in print my escapades—my supposed escapades—of the last 30 or 40 years. People interpret them as nefarious sometimes."

Then Dora suggested we end our talk. We turned off our tape

machines, and I asked if we could meet again. Dora said he would not be averse to working with me, but he wanted time to digest what we had already said. He was also unsure of what else I really needed from him. I ventured that he remained an enigma.

"I don't think of myself as an enigma," he said. "I don't think of things like that at all. But I guess I'm paying the price now for my charades with the surf magazines in the past. This is what I get for having lived here in the fifties and sixties."

The campus was empty. Dora declined my offer of dinner and a ride home. For a while we walked in silence. Though I knew more about Mickey Dora than I had thought possible, I realized I would never have his entire story. Too much of what I had heard could not be substantiated, and even a face-to-face meeting could be deceptive. Perhaps Dora can best be viewed in a sociological context. He said some important things about consumerism, the commercialization of the natural environment, hero worship—its dangers and transitory nature—and the joys of committing pure experience in and out of the water. In the end, the way Dora surfed reveals the most about the way he lived and would like to live again: aggressively, stylishly, milking the wave for all it's worth.

We lingered in the parking lot, making small talk. I still wanted to meet again. Dora promised to think it over. We shook hands.

On impulse, I took a quarter from my pocket and flipped it into the air. Mickey read this as his signal to leave, and he spun slowly and sauntered gracefully away. As I watched him, I remembered something Cynthia had said: "Mickey's always had this disappearing fantasy. He once told me that he wanted to paddle out beyond some second point and just disappear in the fog, leaving his surfboard to wash up on the shore." I caught the coin and cupped it on the back of my left hand. Heads, he would call me. Tails, he wouldn't.

It came up tails.

# JOHN MILIUS

## EXCERPT FROM
## *APOCALYPSE NOW* SCREENPLAY

Hollywood writer/producer John Milius put his bellicose stamp on a number of box-office hits, including *Magnum Force* (1973) and *Conan the Barbarian* (1982). His script for 1979's *Apocalypse Now* inspired a brilliant performance by Robert Duvall as Lieutenant Colonel William Kilgore, connoisseur of wartime violence and shapely point surf. *Apocalypse* follows Captain Benjamin Willard (Martin Sheen) as he goes deep into enemy territory to find and assassinate Colonel Kurtz, a renegade army colonel. Willard's upriver odyssey begins as he and Corporal Lance Johnson, a famous Malibu surfer, arrive on a beach in central Vietnam, just after Kilgore's airborne troops have destroyed a fishing village. Willard and Johnson watch as Kilgore puts his signature on the carnage by dealing Air Cavalry "death cards" on the North Vietnamese casualties.

KILGORE: (*bellowing*) Lieutenant! Bomb that tree line back about a hundred yards—give me some room to breathe.

*A lieutenant and radio man nod and rush off.*

*CLOSE VIEW ON WILLARD*

*He was not quite prepared for this.*

———————

(Note: Because the *Apocalypse Now* screenplay was revised, altered, and, in some cases, improvised throughout the shooting of the film, much of the dialogue in this excerpt is different from that which appears in the movie.)

*VIEW ON KILGORE*

*Turning to his guards*

KILGORE: Bring me some cards.

GUARD: Sir?

KILGORE: Body cards, you damn fool—cards!

*The soldier rushes over and hands him two brand-new packages of playing cards wrapped in plastic. Two other soldiers get out of the copter and walk over. They are well-tanned and carry no weapons. They seem more casual about the colonel than anyone else. The sergeant walks up, leading Willard and Lance.*

WILLARD: (*formally*) Captain B. L. Willard, sir—Fourth Record Group—I carry priority papers from Com-Sec Intelligence, 11 Corp—I believe you understand the nature of my mission.

KILGORE: (*not looking up*) Yeah—Na Trang told me to expect you—we'll see what we can do. Just stay out of my way till this is done, Captain.

*He cracks the plastic wrapping sharply—takes out the deck of new cards and fans them. The colonel strides right past Willard with no further acknowledgment. The others follow.*

*TRACKING VIEW*

*The colonel walks through the shell-pocked field of devastation. Soldiers gather around smiling; as Kilgore comes to each V.C. corpse, he drops a playing card on it—carefully picking out which card he uses.*

KILGORE: (*to himself*) Six a spades—eight a hearts. Isn't one worth a jack in this whole place.

*The colonel goes on about his business.*

*TRACKING ON KILGORE*

*Moving through the corpses, dropping the cards. One of the two tanned soldiers rushes up and whispers something to him. He stops.*

KILGORE: What? Here? You sure?

*The soldier points at Lance. Kilgore strides over to the young man, who almost instinctively moves closer to Willard.*

KILGORE: What's your name, sailor?

LANCE: Gunner's Mate, Third Class—L. Johnson, sir.

KILGORE: *Lance* Johnson? The surfer?

LANCE: That's right, sir.

*Kilgore smiles—sticks out his hand.*

KILGORE: It's an honor to meet you, Lance. I've admired your noseriding for years—I like your cutback, too. I think you have the best cutback there is.

LANCE: Thank you, sir.

KILGORE: You can cut out the "sir," Lance. I'm Bill Kilgore—I'm a goofy-foot.

*VIEW ON WILLARD*

*His entire top-priority mission has been put in the background.*

KILGORE (O.S.): This is Mike from San Diego and Johnny from Malibu—they're good solid surfers. None of us are anywhere near your class, though.

*Lance blushes, sort of mumbling "Thanks."*

WILLARD: My orders are from Com-Sec Intel—B. L. Willard, Fourth Recon...

KILGORE: Just hold up a second, Captain—I'll get to you soon enough. We've got things to do here.

*Willard eats it, for now. Kilgore puts his hand on Lance's shoulder, and continues flipping the cards indiscriminately on the bodies as they talk.*

KILGORE: (*continuing*) We do a lot of surfing around here. Like to finish up operations early and fly down to Vung Tau for the evening glass. Have you ever surfed the point at Vung Tau? I like the beachbreaks around Na Trang a lot—good lefts.

*He passes a twisted gun emplacement with about five bodies—sprinkles cards all over them.*

KILGORE: (*continuing*)...we keep three boards in my Command Huey at all times. You never can tell when you're gonna run into something good. I got a guy in Cam Ran Bay that can predict a swell two days in advance. We try to work it in.

*He stops at a particularly wild-looking Viet Cong who has died with his mouth agape—staring wild-eyed in horror at the sky. Kilgore pauses.*

KILGORE: (*continuing; to himself*) Hell, that's an ace if I ever saw one.

*He puts the card in the gaping mouth.*

CLOSE VIEW OVER THE VIET CONG

*We SEE the colonel; the others walk off—the dead Viet Cong and card are in the immediate foreground. The card has the shield of the Air Cavalry printed beautifully, and above it the motto: DEATH FROM ABOVE.*

ZONKER, DO YOU KNOW SOMEONE CALLED "OL' SURFER DUDE"?

9-9

OL' SURFER DUDE? SURE! HE WAS MY CHILDHOOD MENTOR!

WELL, HE CALLED. YOU CAN REACH HIM AT EDDIE'S BOARD SHACK.

I DON'T GET IT... OL' SURFER DUDE NEVER CALLS — HE HATES THE PHONE! IF HE CALLED ME, THEN HE MUST BE... BE...

WHAT?

DYING! MY GOD! HE MUST BE DYING!

"GETTING MARRIED. NEED SHIRT BACK."

EDDIE'S BOARD SHACK!

YEAH, I'M RETURNING A CALL FROM THE OL' SURFER DUDE.

9-10

ZONKER? IS THAT YOU, MAN?

MASTER! WHAT'S ALL THIS ABOUT MARRIAGE?

NO WORRIES, Z, I'M NOT GETTING MARRIED. I JUST LEFT THAT MESSAGE SO YOU'D CALL ME PRONTO!

WHAT A RELIEF! SO WHAT'S UP?

SOME MAD SPRAY OFF MALIBU! WANT TO GO OUT?

GOOD THOUGHT, MASTER. EXCEPT I'M IN CONNECTICUT AND YOU'RE 87.

THE RETURN OF THE PROTEGE.

AND SO AFTER THAT, I TOOK A FEW MORE YEARS OFF.

YOU HAVE LIVED WISELY, WATERBUG.

9-16

KILGORE: Where've you been riding, Lance?

LANCE: I haven't surfed since I got here.

KILGORE: That's terrible—we'll change that. I'd like to see you work—I've always liked your cutback; got a hell of a left turn, too.

*Later that day, Willard talks to Kilgore about getting started on his search for Colonel Kurtz.*

WILLARD: (*pointing to the map*) I got to get into the Nung River, here or here.

KILGORE: That village you're pointing to is kinda hairy.

WILLARD: Hairy?

KILGORE: I mean it's *hairy*—they got some pretty heavy ordnance, boy—I've lost a few recon ships in there.

WILLARD: So? I heard you had a good bunch of killers here.

KILGORE: And I don't intend to get some of them chewed up just to get your boat put in the mouth of the goddamn Nung River. You say you don't know Kurtz?

WILLARD: I met him.

KILGORE: You talk like him—I don't mind taking casualties, Captain, but I like to keep my ratio ten to one in this unit—ten Cong to one.

WILLARD: You'll find enough Cong up there.

KILGORE: What about this point here?

*He puts his finger on the map.*

KILGORE: (*continuing*) What's the name of that goddamn village—Vin Drin Dop or Lop; damn gook names all sound the same.

*He motions to one of the surfers.*

KILGORE: (*continuing*) Mike, you know anything about this point at Vin Drin Dop?

MIKE: Boss left.

KILGORE: What do you mean?

MIKE: It's a really long left slide, breaks on the short side of the point—catches a south swell.

LANCE: Nice.

*Willard looks at Lance—then at Kilgore.*

KILGORE: Why the hell didn't you tell me about that place—a good left. (*to Willard*) There aren't any good left slides in this whole shitty country. It's all goddamn beachbreak.

MIKE: It's hairy, though. That's where we lost McDonnel—they shot the hell out of us. It's Charlie's Point.

KILGORE: How big was it?

MIKE: Six to eight feet.

*Kilgore gazes out across the parked helicopters.*

KILGORE: (*to himself*) A six-foot left . . .

*Willard nudges Lance, who gets the idea.*

LANCE: Boss. What's the wind like?

MIKE: Light offshore—really hollow.

WILLARD: We could go in tomorrow at dawn—there's always offshore wind in the morning.

CHIEF: What are you talking about?

KILGORE: I'm talking about going surfing, son. Hunting up Cong, and going surfin'. I'm talking about a left slide six to eight feet. (*to Willard*) Hell, we'll pick your boat up and lay it down like a baby, right where you want it. This is the CAV, boy—airmobile. I can take that point and hold it as long as I like—and you can get anywhere you want up-river that suits you, Captain. Hell, a six-foot left.

(*he turns to an adviser*) You take a gunship back to division. Mike, take Lance with you—let him pick out a board, and bring me my Yater Spoon—the 8′6″.

TOM: I don't know, sir. It's—it's...

KILGORE: (*hard*) *What* is it?

TOM: Well, I mean it's hairy in there. It's Charlie's Point.

*Kilgore turns and looks to Willard, exasperated.*

WILLARD: Charlie doesn't surf.

*Kilgore's helicopter squadron moves on the fishing village at daybreak the following morning, Wagner's "Ride of the Valkyries" blaring from loudspeakers, and the area is blasted with machine-gun and mortar fire, grenades and napalm. As the village and nearby jungle burn, Kilgore, Willard, and Lance fly overhead in the command copter.*

KILGORE: We'll move in another company and then we'll own it. (*he laughs to himself*) Charlie's Point.

*He looks out toward the ocean.*

KILGORE: (*continuing*) Good swell.

LANCE: What, sir?

KILGORE: I said it's a good swell—hell of a good swell, about six feet. Let's get a look at it.

*Lance looks at Willard and then agrees.*

*FULL SHOT—COPTER, SURF*

*The pilots are used to this—they bank sharply and swoop in on the lineup of waves, coming in low over the point and streaking down a long, lined-up green wall as if surfing it. They tip over and up at the last minute as the wave breaks.*

*DISSOLVE TO:*

*FULL SHOT—BEACH HUTS, SOLDIERS*

*Americans line up blindfolded Viet Cong and North Vietnamese Army regular troops outside a burning hut. GUNFIRE is DISTANT and sporadic—an occasional MORTAR round SCREAMS in. The prisoners are marched away. Other soldiers are already setting up heavy weapons emplacements. Three helicopters ROAR in, fanning the smoke with their wind. The center one, the command ship, lands. Jets SCREAM over. The doors open, guards jump out and check the situation, and out steps Kilgore and Lance. From the other copters are more guards, Kilgore's surfers, and others. Willard follows.*

*FULL SHOT—THE POINT*

*They stride out across the debris-strewn beach. Kilgore stands majestically on the point watching the waves. A shell SCREAMS overhead.*

SOLDIER: Incoming!

*They all dive, except Kilgore. He is watching a big set—as the shell EXPLODES in the water about a hundred yards away, sending up a huge geyser of spray. Kilgore is unmoved.*

KILGORE: Look at that.

*They look.*

LANCE: It's still pretty hot, sir. Maybe we oughta stand somewhere else.

*Kilgore pays no attention.*

WILLARD: I'm waiting for the fucking boat, Colonel.

KILGORE: (*without looking*) It'll get here, soldier.

*He turns to Mike and Johnny who have their faces in the sand.*

KILGORE: Change.

MIKE: Wh—what?

KILGORE: Change. Get out there. I wanna see if it's ridable. Change.

MIKE: It's still pretty hairy, sir.

KILGORE: (*bellowing*) You wanna surf, soldier?

*Mike nods meekly.*

KILGORE: (*continuing*) That's good, boy, because it's either surf or fight.

*He cocks his M-16. Lance looks around uneasily. The colonel walks over.*

KILGORE: You think that section on the point is ridable, Lance?

LANCE: I think we ought to wait for the tide to come in.

*A shell SCREAMS over—they all hit the dirt except for Kilgore. It EXPLODES, throwing sand through the air. Kilgore leans down, yelling over the NOISE.*

KILGORE: Doesn't happen for six hours.

*Lance just looks up at him terrified, holding on to his helmet.*

KILGORE: (*continuing*) The tide—doesn't come in for six hours.

*DISSOLVE TO:*

*FULL SHOT—SURF—MIKE AND JOHNNY*

*They walk through the shallows carrying brightly colored boards. They look very scared. Jets SCREAM overhead, firing cannons. Helicopters wheel by carrying out wounded. They wear olive-drab surfing trunks with the Air Cavalry shield on the left leg. The same shield is emblazoned on the boards along with the word AIRMOBILE. They edge into the water and paddle through the mild shorebreak.*

*FULL SHOT—THE POINT—SURFERS*

*They paddle up the point in the calm channel—the beautiful waves breaking beyond them.*

*CLOSE SHOT ON JOHNNY, MIKE*

*They paddle on their stomachs, keeping low—constantly looking around, scared out of their minds.*

*MEDIUM SHOT—KILGORE AND LANCE*

*Kilgore looks at them with his field glasses. Lance kind of sits below taking cover in a shell hole.*

KILGORE: They far enough?

LANCE: Sure—fine...

*Kilgore turns and takes a giant electric megaphone from a waiting lackey.*

KILGORE: (*through the megaphone*) That's far enough—pick one up and come on in.

*FULL SHOT—THE POINT, SURFERS*

*They line themselves up on the point. A good set is building. Mike turns and strokes into it—takes off—drops to the bottom and turns—trims up into a tight section—everything right except he keeps looking around frantically.*

*CLOSE SHOT ON LANCE AND KILGORE*

*Another shell SCREAMS over and EXPLODES down the beach. Lance looks over at Willard.*

LANCE: (*to himself*) Maybe he'll get tubed.

WILLARD: What?

LANCE: Maybe he'll get inside the tube—where—where they can't see him.

*A series of shells ROAR in.*

WILLARD: Incoming!

*Lance ducks and puts his hands over his head. The shells SCREAM over Kilgore and out toward the point. Kilgore looks through his glasses—two EXPLOSIONS in the water are HEARD.*

KILGORE: Son of a bitch.

*Lance looks up and out toward the point in horror.*

*FULL SHOT—THE POINT*

*Two surfboards float in the channel bobbing up and down on the waves.*

*MEDIUM SHOT—LANCE AND KILGORE*

LANCE: (*to himself*) The tragedy of this war is a dead surfer.

*Willard looks over, beginning to think Lance is crazy, too.*

WILLARD: What's that?

LANCE: Just something I read in the *Free Press.*

KILGORE: They just missed a good set, the chickenshits!

*FULL SHOT—THE POINT, SURFERS*

*They come up near their boards and climb on—smoke hangs over the water.*

KILGORE (O.S.): (*through megaphone*) Try it again, you little bastards.

*BACK TO SCENE*

*Kilgore turns to Willard.*

KILGORE: I'm not afraid to surf this place. I'll surf this place.

*CLOSE SHOT ON KILGORE*

*He turns, glowering to his lackeys.*

KILGORE: Bring that R.T. [radio transmitter], soldier.

*He grabs it.*

KILGORE: (*speaks into R.T.*) Big Duke Six to Hell's Angels—Goddammit, I want that tree line bombed—yeah—napalm, gimme some napalm— son of a bitch—just bomb 'em into the Stone Age, boy.

*He throws the R.T. back to a soldier—another salvo WHISTLES over— everyone but Kilgore drops.*

KILGORE: (*to himself*) Son of a bitch.

*As the shells EXPLODE on the beach behind him, Kilgore raises his M-16 and EMPTIES it full automatic in the general direction of the trees. He mumbles a few unintelligible swearwords, jams a new clip into his rifle, and turns to Lance.*

KILGORE: We'll have this place cleaned up and ready for us in a jiffy, boy. Don't you worry.

*He FIRES another clip as the jets SCREAM overhead.*

*FULL SHOT—PHANTOM JETS—MONTAGE*

*Phantoms RAKE the trees with 20-mm CANNONS, FIRE five-inch rockets in salvo, "Bull Pop" missiles, DROP high explosive and cluster-bomb units, and finally SHOOT off an immense amount of napalm.*

*FULL SHOT—THE POINT—KILGORE, WILLARD, LANCE, OTHERS*

*Kilgore watches the waves with his field glasses—smoke drifts over.*

*Lance crouches below. Willard is looking off in another direction—the boat that will take him and his crew upriver has just been dropped into the river-mouth shallows. The jets are meanwhile making a hell of the tree line—a hell of fire and steam that nothing could live in.*

WILLARD: (*to Lance*) Look. There it is—the boat.

*Lance looks over, with tremendous relief on his face. But still there remains the threat of Kilgore, standing stark against the sky. Willard silently motions Lance toward the boat.*

LANCE: (*whispers*) He'll kill us.

WILLARD: He can't kill us. (*realizing as he says it*) We're on his side.

*Kilgore FIRES another clip into the tree line, then strides back without looking at them.*

KILGORE: (*almost to himself*) You smell that? (*louder*) You smell that?

LANCE: What?

KILGORE: Napalm, boy. Nothing else in the world smells like that.

*They reflect the glow from the burning trees.*

KILGORE: (*continuing; nostalgically*) I love the smell of napalm in the morning. One time we had a hill bombed for twelve hours. I walked up it when it was all over; we didn't find one of 'em ... not one stinking gook body. They slipped out in the night—but the smell—that gasoline smell—the whole hill. It smelled like ... (*pause*) victory.

*He looks off nostalgically.*

WILLARD: You know, some day this war's gonna end ...

KILGORE: (*sadly*) Yes, I know.

## "JOCK'S NIGHT TRIP"

New York–born writer Allan Weisbecker was a screenwriter for NBC's *Miami Vice,* and later wrote articles for *Men's Journal, Smithsonian,* and *Popular Photography. In Search of Captain Zero* (2001), Weisbecker's second book, details his life as a 1970s hardcore surfer and oceangoing pot smuggler. "Jock's Night Trip" was originally published in a 1992 issue of *Surfing* magazine.

1969 WAS, OF COURSE, the year Man first walked on the moon, and much was made of that fact when the Swell of the Century hit the Hawaiian Islands some six months later; the temptation to see cause and effect in these two unrelated though admittedly significant (and, let's face it, somewhat, uhhh . . . cosmic) events was very much in keeping with the long-haired psychedelicized pseudo-philosophies rattling around in our simple skulls in those days. (One guru of the heavily Karmaed-out Vegetarian Contingent theorized that it wasn't Man's walking on the moon that raised the ocean's destructive wrath—it was the fact that Man had left his excrement up there.)

In retrospect, it was a wild year, even not counting the Mets, Jets, Woodstock and assorted other Mainland follies. The same was true on the North Shore of Oahu. It was the year you'd buy a surfboard blank from a guy living in a treehouse, have it shaped by Dick Brewer down at his Waimea shack, then glassed by a maniac named Wolfman, within hooting distance up the road. Total outlay—eighty bucks in cash or smokeable trade. It was the year Lopez was doing fin releases at Pipeline and when that giant December surf had eased to comprehensible proportions, Greg Noll summarily retired after stroking into what was then the biggest wave ever ridden, admitting he'd finally scared himself.

Pundits of surfing history like to mark Noll's ride as a sort of symbolic end to the surfing decade—it sure sounds right—but I'll here put forth an alternative occurrence as fitting punctuation to the era.

Jock Sutherland was an unusual guy back then. Eschewing the shaggy badge-of-the-Sixties look, he wore his hair short, with a neat, middle class—I'd call it dweebish on anyone else—part. While his contemporaries sold dope and evaded the draft, Jock, in the ultimate maverick move, would soon enlist in the army, doing his duty as he saw it. In the midst of the aggro North Shore lineup chaos, Jock found no need to yell, whistle, grimace threateningly or pull pecking order rank, as the other name surfers often did. He'd slink around out there, simply out-positioning everyone, and thereby getting more than his share of waves and raising yodels from one and all with his deep barrel-riding style. Jock rode the North Shore well that winter—probably better than anyone—and was equally at home in four-foot Backyards or nutso Sunset Beach. He was a natural goofyfoot, although he was able to switch stance at will, even in big waves, and his skills as a regularfooter were just as impressive.

Jock was an unusual guy alright, but there was something more to him than astounding natural ability and quiet intensity. It was something in, or behind, Jock's eyes that got your attention. A surfer to respect, if not like.

One day at Waimea my respect for the guy exploded into fullblown, dumbstruck awe.

The Bay was breaking and getting bigger. I remember because I'd looked at it in the morning and thought seriously about going out; I'd never ridden the place but I'd survived twelve-foot-plus Sunset with only some minor puckering of the posterior. And I had that still-unwaxed nine-foot Brewer pintail and Dick kept *asking me if I liked it*. The sets at Waimea that day were maybe eighteen feet, a big drop then a flat shoulder. Minimal size for the place. But still Waimea.

Okay. I'll do it. Oh God.

I went home and tried to eat something, but you need spit to swallow food, even brown rice sogged down with milk.

My first emotion upon returning to the beach was immense relief. In an hour Waimea had gone from eighteen to a solid twenty (two feet at the Bay is not like two feet anywhere else) and had that Waimea look. BIG and getting BIGGER. I don't remember who was in the car with me but I turned to him and said, or yelled, something like, "I'm not going out, so fuck you anyway!"

I was a happy boy. I would survive the day.

About twenty surfers were in the lineup: Buffalo and the local boys; Hakman and the *haole* crew. They looked jittery, everyone seemed to be edging further outside; it was definitely getting bigger. The afternoon wore on and the boys worked out the peak and the pecking order. The Show got good, with hoots, whistles and almost continuous applause from shore. My stomach never quite settled down—a combination of fear and shame, I suspect. Fear because I'd almost paddled out, and shame because I hadn't.

Sometime that afternoon Jock appeared and stroked on out. He had trouble getting waves and even from shore it was obvious why—his board was about two feet shorter than anyone else's, forcing him to sit inside and try to pick up the dregs. It was fruitless and hairy and obviously frustrating, but Jock had been quietly asserting that the Bay could be ridden on an under-eight-foot board (I think his was 7'10") and he was out to prove it. Well, it wasn't working and I began to wonder why he didn't come in and switch sticks. The Bay doesn't break very often and here he was wasting a good day. The thing I didn't realize was that Jock had a plan.

The sun dipped below the hills south of Kaena Point, casting the Bay in slick gold shadow, and the lineup started to thin out. The twilights are short in the Islands and the light began to do a fast fade. Pretty soon there were maybe a dozen guys in the water, then a half dozen, then two or three. I don't remember who else was out at this point—it was impossible to tell one surfer from another in the failing light—except Jock. With the crowd gone he started getting waves, started doing his switchfoot dance on his undersize stick. Climbing and dropping like he was riding fun six-footers.

Okay, he'd made his point; you could ride the Bay on a shortboard.

The other couple of guys made it in and the spectators dispersed. Heading for my car I watched as Jock took what I assumed would be his last wave. I mean it was all but dark. The moon, pale and full, was rising down to the right, toward Sunset Beach...wait a minute. The sonofabitch was paddling back out. A few people noticed, pulled up short, and stayed.

I'd once surfed three-foot Chun's Reef by moonlight, with a couple of buddies, and it was very weird. I mean there are demons out there at night, reaching up out of the phosphorescence for dangling pink toes, creatures both finned and phantasmagorical with orb eyes glowing red and malevolent and...and...and the waves. I mean little knee knockers are tough to figure in the dark, as your depth perception goes bazooey, making it impossible to judge size and distance. Spooky.

But this thing Jock was doing was in a different realm. A foreign concept. It was insane. I mean wasn't it?...Hey, wait. What's that? A white streak there on that feathering wall, trailing off just ahead of the white explosion freight training across the Bay and shaking the earth under our blood-drained toes, curled tight as if trying to grasp the implications of what we were seeing.

A few small groups formed, the class strata of ability and race forgotten now, local boys and *haoles,* hot and not-so-hot, gathered together in the spectral half light of shore, watching as wave after wave was taken and mastered, deep snaking luminescent board-wakes, Jock himself invisible in the moon shadow under the lip.

And so it went. I don't really know how much time went by, or how many waves were taken that night—probably dozens—but it was late when a piece of Jock's board finally washed ashore, a forlorn shard chewed up and spit out by the angry Beast out on the reef.

So we waited, squinting uneasily into the hazy glow of the white-water, imagining the dark speck of a head, then Jock dragging himself to

land, wild-eyed and disoriented. But no one, nothing, not even the rest of Jock's little board, emerged from the shorebreak. Somebody must have made a phone call, because suddenly the fire trucks and ambulances were there, crackling radios and rotating lights adding an unnatural rhythm to the night. And then a rescue chopper was overhead, the beam of its gargantuan spotlight futilely searching the nearshore froth—a joke in those conditions. The road and beach were once again lined with people, and the night air was filled with half-whispered phrases and questions: "What's going on?" "Jock?" "He was what?" "But it's the middle of the night."

And the thought, left unspoken by Jock's surf-brethren, was finally voiced by a man in a firefighter's hat and boots, after examining the remains of Jock's board. "He's drowned, that's for sure. Nobody could survive out there."

Those who had witnessed Jock's moonlight romp were pulled aside and asked a few questions, with the authorities shaking their heads at the foolhardiness of it.

Later, much later it seemed—but I had no grasp of clock-time—as the crowd once again began to disperse, a figure was spotted walking down the road from the east. Lean, sandy hair, yellow trunks dry from what had apparently been a long walk—it was Jock alright.

"Anybody seen my board?"

"Broken, Jock."

"Bummer."

"Where'd you come in?"

"Down around Pipeline."

*Pipeline? That's over a mile.*

A few words were exchanged with the authorities and Jock hoofed it home. He was so calm, still so deep within himself, that nobody even thought to offer a ride, and I'm sure he would have refused it anyway.

The next day I ran into Jock's brother, Jim, and asked about Jock's state of mind that night. Jim laughed. "Who knows," he said, "he was dosed."

"What?"

"He'd dipped his finger in (Famous Name)'s baggie of Sunshine before he stroked out."

It was common knowledge that (Famous Name) was the keeper of the most potent Orange Sunshine LSD on the North Shore. It was in powder form and the dosage was measured by how deep you stuck your finger in the baggie.

"How much did he do?"

Jim shook his head. "Wet and deep."

Twenty-some-odd years later I've come to see LSD as a bad thing, but I did my share in the late Sixties and had surfed once or twice under the influence. I never believed you could perform well or even competently while whacked. Everything became too brilliant . . . too intense. Too many odd, distracting thoughts. You'd tend to either freeze up in paranoia or, deranged from synaptic misfire, attempt to spread imaginary wings. I mean people would jump off buildings, figuring they could fly.

And here Jock had ridden the Bay, at night, under a finger-lickin' big hit of it. (The size of his board—a major deal at first—quickly became a non-issue.)

It was as if Jock had jumped off a tall building and lo and behold . . . he *did fly*.

So hey, fellas, at least those of you aged enough to remember those days, those wacky incredible Sixties, what say you? If you are to believe my tale and have a bend towards the metaphorical view, as I do—shall we say the decade, if not ended, was at least somehow epitomized by this occurrence at Waimea Bay, in the winter of 1969?

# THREE

# OUT THERE: BIG WAVES, LONG JOURNEYS

Travelogues and big-wave stories together make up a pretty sizable chunk of all surf writing, but top-quality work in either genre is hard to come by. Surfing travel stories have become clichéd and formulaic to the point where magazine editors can serve them up to readers with a weary ironic smile: JUST ANOTHER INDO BOAT TRIP is the cover blurb for a recent *TransWorld Surf* article. With big-wave surfing comes the difficulty of rhythm and pacing; highlight rides often happen in clusters, and there rarely seems to be a narrative endpoint. Garret MacNamara's atom-blasting tuberide at Teahupoo in the summer of 2002, for example, was eclipsed a few months later by his fifty-footer at Jaws, which in turn was more or less matched an hour later by

Ross Clarke-Jones's barrel on a like-sized wave. Greg Noll's crash-and-burn thirty-five-footer at Makaha in 1969 remains the greatest big-wave story not just for its simplicity—one man, one giant wave—but its finality. Noll, a beefy thirty-two-year-old big-wave legend, crawled out of the water at Makaha, flew back to the mainland, bought a motor home, drove to Alaska, and began a new life as a fisherman.

As with just about any other kind of nontechnical writing, the problem with big-wave stories and travelogues is usually a failure to recognize that setting and situation alone aren't enough to carry the day, whether it's lunatic third-reef surf in Hawaii or unmapped tubes in the Andaman Islands. Interesting, funny, fallible characters are what really matter. Mark

Foo's impending death gives *Maverick's* its dramatic tension, but the story is animated by the prickly relationship between Foo and fellow Hawaiian big-wave rider Ken Bradshaw. Similarly, the roaring big-wave finale in JAMES HOUSTON's *A Native Son of the Golden West* holds interest only because Houston has slowly and carefully, over the course of a long period with no big surf whatsoever, developed the odd but credible rapport between soul-searching Hooper Dunlap and big-wave satyr Jonas Vandermeer. The story opens as Dunlap flies from California to Hawaii, and carefully sneaks into Jonas's funky Waikiki apartment in order to surprise his friend. When Jonas walks in and sees Dunlap lounging on the bed—the two haven't had contact for months—he blinks but otherwise doesn't react. No greeting, just a word of caution: "Dunlap, that bed is full of fleas, ya know."

Travel pieces are probably even more character dependent than big-wave stories. In "The Land Duke Forgot," DAVE PARMENTER is happy to report the discovery of an excellent snow-framed Alaskan pointbreak, but seems to have even more interest in his Haida Indian surf guide. Most of the natives, Charlie Skultka tells Parmenter, deal with Alaska's endless rain and snow and twenty-hour winter nights by drinking heavily. Skultka, a fisherman, then admits that he once dropped $3,000 on a payday bender that ended with him waking up in a sunlit Mazatlán hotel room with no memory of his arrival.

Surf can be chased, romanced, fetishized, even loved. As a narrative player, however, surf works best if placed in the background. You couldn't really call it a formula, but flea-ridden beds and alcoholic blackouts will put you a lot closer to a great story than a righteous eight-foot northwest swell.

# "THE LAND DUKE FORGOT"

California-born Dave Parmenter was a world pro tour surfer in the 1980s, and is now regarded as a top surfboard shaper/designer. His sharp, often-caustic articles and essays have been published semiregularly in the surf press since 1982. "The Land Duke Forgot" originally appeared in a 1993 issue of *Surfer,* and later that year was included in Houghton Mifflin's annual *Best American Sports Writing* collection.

O
N THE LEFT SIDE of the aircraft there's a great view of the Malaspina Glacier, which is bigger than the state of Rhode Island," came the Chuck Yeager–modulated voice of the pilot.

Halfway through our Naugahyde omelets, Brock Little and I looked at each other and chortled. We'd been in Alaska only a short while, and yet we'd run into this Rhode Island comparison a number of times. It had already become a private joke.

Thirty-eight thousand feet below, an impossible landscape scrolled past the portholes; brutal snow-caked mountain ranges hooked across the eastern Gulf of Alaska like a giant mandible of chipped teeth. Massive panes of crevassed ice creaked in glacial strain toward the ocean, some as big as . . . well, Rhode Island. The currency of measurement is as elephantine as the state itself. Features are constantly scaled to this Rhode Island standard: the glaciers, the forest tracts, the medicine-ball cabbages from the fertile Matanuska Valley, the manta ray–sized halibut. Rain is measured in feet, wholesale, rather than sissy California inches. Even the name itself is derived from the Aleut native word "Alashka," or "great land." If there is any "greater" or more bizarrely gorgeous land on the globe, George Lucas will have to build it at Industrial Light and Magic.

Surfing Alaska? Surely an oxymoron if ever there was one. A lot of things have drawn people to Alaska in the past: fur, fish, gold, oil, even elbow room. But never surfing. It's not exactly what Duke Kahanamoku had in mind.

People thought we were pulling their leg. Were we for real or just eccentrics on a cavalier whim, like mad flagpole-sitters intent on defining some new parameter in discomfort? We weren't sure ourselves, stepping off the plane into the mid-summer drizzle of Sitka. Wrangling bulging surfboard bags around like hog-tied steer, we drew quite a few quizzical stares.

"Whatcha' got there son, a canoe?" someone wearing a CPO jacket and hip-waders would invariably ask. Maybe we were potential canoe-borne invaders of his favorite trout lake.

"Naw, it's a surfboard."

Now in Alaska, it's a safe bet that if the rejoinder isn't a hearty, "Them's good eatin'!" you'll be of no further interest and can pass on your way without further scrutiny.

Brock Little, Josh Mulcoy, Bob Barbour and myself heaved and dragged our burdens into the terminal, and we felt a hell of a lot better when the entire surfing population of Sitka was there to greet us. Both of them.

Charlie Skultka and his brother-in-law Todd. We all shook hands, piled our gear into Charlie's truck, and within an hour or so were blasting out of Sitka Harbor in a 14-foot aluminum skiff, toward one of the innumerable swell-exposed islands that make up the Alexander Archipelago of Southeastern Alaska.

The no-wake rule in the harbor gave us plenty of time to take in the city's layout. It's a quaint yet utilitarian harbor town, set on the low terraces beneath snowcapped coastal mountains snaking around Sitka Sound.

Spruce trees carpet every square foot in verdant deep-pile, even on nearly vertical angles. Grimy, diesel-sooted fishing trawlers grappled with incoming cruise liners as immaculate and white as a first communion dress. Sea planes were hauled up on slanted docks, guzzling fuel with happy-hour zest.

Once clear of the fish and diesel smell of the inner harbor, we got our first lungfuls of pure Alaskan air. Glacier-chilled and imbued with the Christmas-tree scent of a billion spruce, the air was so rich and pure that it verged on being an intoxicant.

The outer harbor was dappled with dozens of small, craggy islands. Some were sizable enough to have cozy New England–style homes built on them. Others were mere tree-stubbied sea stacks.

Charlie had a dozen marine charts detailing more than 1,000 islands with something like 10,000 to 15,000 miles of potentially surfable coast-line. We'd point to a likely looking setup on a chart and yell over the drone of the outboard motor, "What about this point?" Every inquiry was an-swered with a shrug and, "No one's ever been down there."

Charlie and Todd had surfed a handful of spots that they knew well, bashing out into wild seas in small skiffs, sometimes camping on a deserted beach, trading rainy gray waves in the loneliest surfing real estate on earth.

Charlie was a Haida, a native Indian in the region. Solidly built and ruggedly handsome, he had a certain Hawaiian bearing, which showed up even more when he hit the water. A surfer of modest ability, he rode with a definite Hawaiian regalness—upright and proud—with none of the ex-aggerated Wilbur Kookmeyer flailings that plague most intermediates.

"A lot of folks say our people migrated here from Hawaii," Charlie told us. As if to support this claim, Charlie told us the story of his first board. A fellow fisherman had found it drifting far out to sea. It was a mossy, water-logged model called a "Tiki," a '60s longboard popout from Southern California. Most likely it drifted up from Hawaii in the northwesterly-flowing Japanese current. Charlie scraped off the moss, dried it out, and repaired the dings with bluish marine resin. He learned to surf at Sandy Beach in Sitka, the one sliver of swell window actually in town and accessible by car. If there's a 12-foot swell on the outer waters, Sandy Beach might be 3 feet and like a good day on Lake Superior.

I told Charlie about the hairball landing we had sweated out at Juneau. Fog kept us circling over aluminum-cleaving peaks for almost an hour until the pilot found a vein of clearness.

"Oh yeah. Happens all the time. Those glaciers above the city make their own weather," Charlie said. "You know, that ice field is bigger than Rhode Island."

We anchored off a low, spruce-shaggy point on the southern tip of a volcanic island. A black slab of pitted lava tilted into the ocean with that perfect inclination and sweep that sets surfers a'blubbering from Rincon to Raglan. There wasn't much swell, but a few glassy, head-high peelers wrapped around the point, rehearsing their lines for better days.

It resembled a small day at Third Point, Malibu, may it rest in peace. Except Gidget would have some pretty stiff nipples here, and the bears have even less patience with the Vals than Dora did. This was as far from the teeming SoCal mouse hole of surf culture as you could get in America. Well, almost. . . .

Let he who hath understanding reckon the number of the Beast, for he is a California refugee. We hadn't been in the water 10 minutes when a guy in an aluminum skiff like ours sidled up to the lineup during a lull. I instantly recognized the phylum and class. The beard, the dog as Man Friday, the vibe.

"I know what this guy ate for breakfast," I thought. "If we were on Highway One, that skiff would be an El Camino."

"You the *Surfer* magazine guys?" asked the guy, whom we called "Dick," for a number of reasons mutually agreed upon later.

"Yep," Charlie answered. He seemed to know Dick.

"Which one of you is the writer?" He had those oversize polarized glasses you see on fuddy-duddies timidly pulling out of Leisure World in Buick Le Sabres.

"That'd be me," I said, thinking, Laguna Beach? Santa Cruz? Palos Verdes? He's behind the times; nowadays you're supposed to hassle the photographer.

"You're not going to tell everyone about this place are you?" Dick asked. "I've been surfing here for 10 years." I looked for the bandanna on the dog. Nope, must have been in the wash.

"Uh . . . that's not the idea. We don't intend to . . ." I trailed off thinking, "This is unfuggingbelievable."

"Thank you," he said with finality and motored off into the channel, leaving us on a shriveling, ever-smaller planet. Even here, on a remote and uninhabited island, one of thousands in the Gulf of Alaska, where one wrong move or fey lash of weather means a mossy skeleton in six months, there is still the stereotypical Californian paranoiac looking over his shoulder to make sure Salt Creek isn't gaining on him, sweating out the fever of Invasion Fear, as if tomorrow we'd have introduced a leprosy of condos and 7-Elevens and parking meters at his personal retreat.

Charlie was pissed. He explained that Dick hadn't wanted us to come here. Dick was a bodyboarder, and, if that wasn't bad enough, he had also written a book about the self-same island, using personal or native endearments for place-names. Bob and I later read it, a deeply felt and poetic but overwrought Boy and His Dog love letter to the island. Reading between the lines, one could find that smug sanctimony so many refugee Californians assume, as if having the wisdom to turn their backs on Californication grants them the moral high-ground and the deed to their personal Walden Pond.

"Sorry, you guys," Charlie said, his eyes clouding over. "Not many people around here like that guy. No offense, but . . . they think he's a typical Californian."

The waves were fun, head-high on the sets, and for a half an hour the sun popped out and baked the shoulders of our wetsuits. I asked Charlie what this wave was like at 6 feet.

"Actually, this is the first time I've ever surfed this place," he replied.

"What?"

"I don't go backside very good," Charlie offered. "But this place is 'kill.' I'll have to come out here more."

The next day we decided to start fresh and begin exploring the outer coast of this Catalina-size island. There were a lot of places on the charts that looked suspiciously like a Klondike of Rincons, Burleighs and Mundacas. Venturing on such a quest into the open ocean here is not something to be taken lightly. If by definition "adventure" is adversity rightly viewed, then by all rights anytime you take a boat into Alaskan waters, it qualifies as adventure. Or certainly adversity.

Preparing for extended camping in this wilderness is a serious undertaking. Most camping in the lower 48 isn't real camping. You phone up Ticketron months in advance, and your credit card reserves you a sandbox-size cubical of "wilderness" that is really more Festival Seating Motel 6 than Communion with Nature.

But this was the real thing. Alaska has a total tidal shoreline of 47,300 miles. Virtually none of it can be reached by car. So it's boats or sea planes. The tidal range can be 12 to 18 feet. When the tide goes minus, it leaves a pre-tsunami scree of exposed sand and rock, often stranding your boat 100 yards from where you want it to be. When you're lost here, not even God can find you.

The region of Alaska we were in can get more than 200 inches of rain in a year—Cornwall on steroids. In medieval Cornwall, when the foul weather drove people batty, they invented witchcraft to cope. Here,

they just drink. After a week of constant rain, you can imagine the faintly audible gritty sound of whiskey bottles being unscrewed under rain-slashed roofs across town. After September, the tourist trade fizzles, leaving the local alone with four-hour days and 100 inches of rain.

"How do people cope?" I asked Charlie. Just one week of fog in Morro Bay and I look like Jack Nicholson just before he lost it in *The Shining*.

"Ninety-nine percent of the people drink," he said evenly. "The other 1 percent are court-ordered not to."

Charlie didn't drink, at least not anymore. Once, flush with $5,000 in cash after a long fishing job, he got so bombed he woke up in . . . Mazatlan. He couldn't remember how he got there; just woke up in a hotel in tropical Mexico with a hangover that would have toppled a Cape buffalo. He had $2,000 left.

As our strategy gelled, there remained one final obstacle—Mr. Bear. Alaska, first and foremost, is bear country. Bears, bear tracks, bear shit and bear lore all but cover the countryside. Every point in Alaska is Charlie Bear's Point. Charlie Bear don't surf, but he can run 35 mph, swim like Mark Spitz, and climb a tree faster than a scalded cat.

Even in the urban areas, according to a newspaper account, bears "ruined by their taste in garbage" hang out at dumps like ATM muggers.

In the coupon section of the local newspaper, sandwiched between the Renuzit Fragrance Jars and the Hostess Ho-Hos, is a device known as a Bear Bell. For 59 cents (with coupon) you get a cube-shaped bell that affixes to your clothing, the idea being that, when tromping over hill and dale, or taking an old mattress to the dump, you'll clang and peal like a Salvation Army Santa, thus signaling to any marauding bear, "Hey, comin' through."

Of course, the Bear Bell is the rock-bottom, low-end ticket in bear repellent. It's sensible and field-tested effective, and for about five bucks you can bell yourself, the family, the mailman, baby Herman, even Rover. But dammit, it's also un-American. It's what Gandhi would have done to ward off bears.

Which is why you should do what 99.999 percent of Alaskans do: purchase a big ol' mofo firearm and cart it everywhere like a fifth limb.

Not that you'll ever really need your "smokewagon." Chances are you'll never encounter a bear that will interrupt his berry-slurping or wood-shitting to charge you. But at least you can lend a hand in what seems to be a statewide industry of reducing wind resistance on road signs and mailboxes.

Being lower-48 greenhorns in Alaska, we were constantly teased. "Look out for them bears, boys," they'd warn us with a twinkle in their eyes. We'd explain that Bob, Josh and I were from the notorious Red Triangle in Central California, and that once a person reconciled the fear of a sudden, fatal attack by a white shark, well, "bearanoia" seemed almost laughable. One wildlife expert, stretching hard for a great sound-byte on a local news show, called the grizzly bear a "terrestrial version of the great white shark." We howled at that. Bears declare their major well in advance, unlike the stealth-torpedo tactics of a white. It's not like a grizzly suddenly rockets upward from some ursine gopher hole and takes your leg in a splintered second.

Still, something had to be done. We had our ultra-trick Patagonia rain gear, some Rubik's Cube North Face tents, and 14 cartons of Pop-Tarts, but it was time to step up and arm ourselves. Brock was elected sergeant-at-arms. He was the most macho and was used to dealing with big, grumpy locals. He was also the only one of us who had any money.

We went shopping for our peace-makin', lead-spittin' bear control at a little shanty perched over the harbor on stilts. It was called Ye Old Rod and Reel (no lie), and the scene inside was familiar to any veteran surf shop patron. Racks of guns, new and used, stood erect in an intentionally phallic way across the showroom. Two grizzled good ol' boys—one easily measuring on the Rhode Island Standard—sporting NRA sideburns and CPO jackets, tried to sell Brock the firearm equivalent of a 12-foot Brewer gun, when all he really needed was a Becker.

Brock was keen on a 30.30 Winchester. He cocked the lever and checked the "action," the gun version of kicking the tires on a used car. The elder gun nut scoffed.

"That won't stop no bear," he said, sucking his cigarette like a snorkel, partially obscured in that pall of acrid smoke that most Alaskans live and work in. "What you need is sumthin' like this here 7mm." He brandished a huge rifle, a dreadnought with a bore like a garden hose. "This'll stop 'im right in his tracks." Yeah, and uproot the tree behind him. It would also come in handy if you wanted to bore a new cylinder into an engine block.

But Brock was set on the 30.30. Ten minutes later, he left the shop cradling his rifle, beaming proudly. The day's provisioning was over.

"I've got a rifle, some wool socks, rain paints and a sleeping bag," Brock exclaimed with satisfaction. "I'm ready to go surfing."


No sooner had we packed the boats when the unthinkable happened... the weather cleared. A rogue slab of glacial high pressure nosed into the soupy overcast, and soon we were smack dab in the middle of the best weather of the year.

Alaska has a feminine, brooding beauty—gorgeous and enchanting even when cloaked in a chador of rain and gloom. But when the sun comes out and the mountains glow green, you feel singled out and special. Your heart lifts. It's as if you've just passed Greta Garbo in a crowd, and she smiled directly at you.

Of course, as soon as the weather turned glorious, the swell hissed flat like a punctured tire. We motored around the far side of the island for half a day, finally making camp near a rivermouth deep in a wide bay, with a melding of forest and foreshore that made Big Sur look like a wilted Disneyland diorama. Three conical Puerto Escondido–style sandbars were scattered about near the rivermouth, teasing us with 1-foot replicas of perfect surfing waves.

The weather stayed great while the surf remained flat, so we put on our camping heads. Our setup was idyllic. Salmon were endlessly spinning and pirouetting above the surface of the river. Bob, the photographer, would stand in the icy river for hours, jacking huge dog salmon onto the bank, his voice fairly cracking with emotion: "This is the J-Bay of fishing. . . . It's like some beautiful dream."

The biggest fish caught was one Bob spotted trapped in a large longshore pool, cut off from river and sea by the extreme low tide. Josh, Brock and I chased it through the pool like a greased pig in a rodeo event. Brock finally cornered it, quickly rolled it up the bank, and drilled its head with three lightning-quick North Shore haymakers. Within two hours eight pounds of salmon steaks were grilling over our campfire.

Walking through the forest you could snack on raspberries and blueberries, which grew everywhere, and wash them down with ice-cold, snow-fed river water. On sand banks deeper in the interior, we found fresh bear tracks and the leftover viscera of salmon lunch. One set of prints were big as dinner plates. Charlie extended his rifle overhead to show us the approximate size of that bear. Great. No surf, but at least the bears were double-overhead.

A couple more no-swell days followed, and we started to wonder if perhaps we weren't camped out at Rincon waiting for a big north swell in July.

The weather began to sour one afternoon, with the portent of an approaching winter in a Stephen King story. By nightfall, a gale was upon us. We moved camp into the protection of the forest, and huddled around the fire, grilling the last of the salmon as all hell broke loose out at sea.

Brock and I lay in our tent listening to the creaks and groans of the gale-torn forest, waiting for a bear in the Double-Overhead Club to take us like a nylon Bon-Bon. There'd be a horrid ripping of fabric and he'd come and he'd...

The tent flap flew open and a dark head poked through. It was Charlie. "I need some help with the skiff." Charlie had that understated, taciturn manner that most Alaskans have, as if constant exposure to the grandeur of their surroundings had stripped them of all futile adjectives. We geared up, abandoned our warm cocoon, and followed Charlie's swinging, fluttering lantern out onto the beach.

The skiff was sunk. Luckily it was sunk right near shore, but regardless, it was well on its way to a more traditional burial. The millpond anchorage of the previous day was now a heaving, wind-nagged 4-foot shoredump. The skiff was broadside to the waves, which were breaking directly into the sorry craft. Half a ton of sand had gathered along the floor, pinning the skiff in the ceaseless shorebreak. And the incoming tide was still two hours from peaking.

The three of us wrestled the motor off the mount and set about reclaiming our vessel, scooping water and sand in gut-busting desperation, trying to stay a beat ahead of the incoming flushes. Rain slashed through the lantern's wavering sphere of light at a 45-degree angle. The wind screamed and moaned. Waves broke completely over us as we grappled with the boat. A few times the lantern blew out, and one of us had to relight it as the other two bailed furiously.

By 2 A.M., we were able to monkey the skiff up out of reach of the tide. The last of the dry driftwood was thrown onto the fire back at camp. I put a pot of coffee on, and we squatted near the flames, steam beginning to waft from our sodden clothes. For some perverse reason, this moment was the highlight of the trip, and we all sensed it. "Welcome," Charlie deadpanned, "to the real Alaska."

One of us said in the morning, and I don't recall who, "Enough of this boat shit!" We broke camp and limped back to Sitka in the remnants of the storm. Confused spikes of windswell hammered our 14-foot skiff, and it took most of the day to gain the calmer waters of Sitka Sound.

The next morning we were on the dawn flight to a place I'll call Cape Tanis, leaving Charlie and Todd to their lonely sentinel in Sitka. We'd heard tell of a better swell window a few hundred miles up the coast. Best of all, the area had dirt roads leading out to most of the surrounding coastline. The prospect of not having an outboard hangover every day pleased us, as did eliminating the expense of hiring two boats.

Cape Tanis was a small, remote fishing and hunting Mecca, sort of a salmon Tavarua. In August and September the silver salmon head upstream and the few local lodges fill up. The population swells to 900, three times the winter size of 300. People in Sitka warned us that people in Cape Tanis weren't too friendly, that they didn't like outsiders, but we found it to be one of the friendliest places any of us had ever been. Every single person waved when passed on the road. It was a habit that came remarkably easy to we veterans of the 405 Freeway. All you had to do was extend the remaining four fingers normally folded over in the customary L.A. freeway greeting.

We stayed at the Happy Bear Lodge. The bar and restaurant were wallpapered with the skins of bear and lynx. Stuffed salmon gaped vacantly from mahogany plaques, and over the kitchen door was what had to be the world's largest taxidermied king crab. Over by the jukebox stood a posthumous member of the Double-Overhead Club, stuffed and mounted in a snarling rictus. A placard at the base read: "Old Rover, shot by Bad Bob Fraker in May 1979. R.I.P."

The hunters and fishermen regarded us with curiosity, but most were so ensnared in the fishing *plak tow* that they didn't even notice us. We

were as out of place as a luge team in Bali. But we all had the same spirit, more or less. At the bar I read a magazine called *Alaskan Hunter,* and a passage in the "Taxidermy Tips" column caught my eye:

> Each year as we get out the hunting gear for the first time, there's a feeling of excitement and anticipation as we think of the hunt. Maybe this will be the year we finally get that big one we've been looking for all these years. As we gaze at our living room wall, or think of how we'd feel if our bear or sheep was standing proudly in a public place for all to see, we dream of that moment, when we finally realize our big dream!

It's obvious we were of a breed. We were brothers.

Force 7 winds had whipped up a solid 8-foot swell. We'd heard quite a few fish stories about a left point at Cape Tanis; on the charts it looked too good to be true. We set out in our rented van and drove as far as we could in the general direction of the point. When we could go no farther we got out and hiked through the foliage, Brock on point with the 30.30.

We found ourselves at the terminus of a large bay. A mile seaward was the graceful sweep of a sand-shoal left point, so we hiked along the beach to get a better look. The wind was offshore here, and at the top of the point, thick, lumpy swells staggered around the cape, punch-drunk and slobbering from a beating out to sea. They refracted into the stiff offshore wind, sifting and smoothing into progressively cleaner lines. Halfway down the quarter-mile point certain waves would bend so severely that they actually became thick Trestles-like rights that wound to the beach like spokes around a hub. It was possible to ride a hundred yards or so from the top of the point on a left, and then bank off a swelling hump on the shoulder that in turn swung its energy right for another 50 yards, ultimately depositing you on the sand with burning quads. From there, it was a short jog back to the top of the cape for another circuit.

To the north was a staggering backdrop, as alien and transfixing as a Martian landscape. The Saint Elias Mountains, at 18,000 feet the highest coastal range in the world, soared into the chilled Alaskan sky, crusted with snow and flanked by the ivory shards of some of those Rhode Island glaciers.

Having access to roads set us free. After a day or so of scouting, we were able to make surgical strikes at the point and various beachbreaks. On smaller days we hit the beachbreaks at high tide for some thick, wedgy bowls that strongly resembeled Hossegor. In one week we got two 8-foot swells. We spent these at the point, surfing five or six hours a day, stopping only for peanut butter sandwiches shared around a roaring bonfire, which we kept stoked between quarter-mile rides down the sand point.

So what was it like to surf Alaska? How different was it than, say, Oregon or Northern California? All I can say is that it wasn't a matter of how the water felt or what wax to bring, or even how your lungs burned running up the point, sucking in volcanic ash from a nearby eruption. I felt something so much bigger than mere... surfing.

They call Alaska the "Last Frontier," but it's more than that. It's the last place where America, its true atavistic spirit, exists. It's the America of John Ford, where accountability and self-reliance still mean something. It's not the litigation-snarled America we have today, full of blame-shirkers and moral cowards. If you break down, you don't call Auto Club. If a bear looms up on the trail ahead, you don't slap an injunction on him or sue the state because you weren't notified by warning signs every 10 yards. And if you get into trouble surfing, you don't flag down the rescue helicopter to save your lily-white helpless ass.

Elephants, rhinos, even spotted owls all have their sanctuaries now. But what of that breed of Americans also so endangerred? The wild-eyed misfits who webbed prairie and desert with the ruts of countless wagon wheels, beating the wildest continent on earth into docility, staying always one step ahead of the preachers and lawyers and bureaucrats. What of them? Maybe they just took a dogleg turn north when they ran out of "West" generations ago. Alaska is their reserve.

Studying my creased and fish-stained Alaskan chart one night, I happened upon a discovery that made my heart swell. A 50-mile chunk of coast, some accident of desolation, was inscribed with that rarest and loveliest of all words: "Unsurveyed."

EXCERPT FROM
# A NATIVE SON OF THE GOLDEN WEST

U.C. Santa Cruz professor James Houston coauthored *Surfing: A History of the Ancient Hawaiian Sport,* originally published in 1966 as the first in-depth study of surfing's origins. *A Native Son of the Golden West,* Houston's first novel, was released in 1971; he went on to write several other well-received fiction and nonfiction books, including *Continental Drift* (1978) and *Snow Mountain Passage* (2001), and his essays have appeared in the *New Yorker* and the *New York Times. Native Son* is set in the mid-1950s, and opens with California surfer Hooper Dunlap flying into Honolulu, where he tracks down his friend Jonas Vandermeer in a dingy Waikiki hotel room.

JOE IS TWENTY-ONE, has lived in the sun for eight years on California beaches wearing no more than he wears this morning, an old pair of striped golf knickers trimmed above the knee. And Joe has never tanned. Nor has he burned, or even reddened. The sun can do nothing to Joe's skin but assault each layer till it flakes away and hope the one below is thinner or newer or somehow subject to change. But Joe's skin has never changed, always dusty white, sprinkled with blond hairs and stretched over knots and clumps and welts of muscles hardened in his daily wrestle with the sea.

He says to Hooper, "You want to go in the water?"

"Can you get me a board?"

"Where's yours?"

"I sold it."

Jonas jumps up and stands over him, grimacing and blinking. "Jesus Christ, Hooper, why'd ya do that?"

"I needed the money."

Joe shouts, "That was a great board! A fan*tas*tic board!"

"I said I needed the money."

"What're you gonna do without a board?"

"Rent one, or borrow one, I guess."

"Shit, you can't rent a board. Soldiers rent boards. Summer coeds rent boards."

Joe paces for a few moments, then slaps a fist into his palm and observes the action of his triceps in the long mirror on the closet door across the room.

"I really feel good this morning. I feel like getting wet. You know how it feels after you take a good, quick, heavy dump?"

"Sure."

"Well, let's get going then. You can use my extra board."

"Wait'll I change."

"I have to move my truck. The meters start at nine. I'll meet you at the corner." Joe is reaching for the blind.

And in a single silent stride and lift and ducking slide Joe is out the window, dropping into a net of vines, an albino Tarzan squeaking shut the rusty screen.


Jonas won't surf at Waikiki. It's against his principles. Not only soldiers and summer coeds rent boards and ride there, but also bank clerks on vacation, paunchy middle-aged men, canoes full of smirking tourists. Joe doesn't consider himself a tourist. Nor does Hooper. They put themselves in a different, unnamed category of island visitor. And Joe does his surfing at Sunset Beach, forty miles through cane and pineapple fields to the north shore. They drive out there in his Reo, a one-time baker's delivery van, a high metal box fitted inside with bunks slung from chains, decorated outside with movie posters and cartoons and random inked and painted slogans, and roofed with two surfboards that jut over the windshield like cannons on a gunboat.

See them shirtless side by side. Next to Joe's white bulging wedge, Hooper is a bundle of sticks, his limbs coated, as Joe often jokes, with "Indian muscles," hardly seen on the surface, but there, and waiting, somewhere next to the bone. Joe is weaving from side to side, ducking and stretching, as the traffic shifts in front of him, to find the best view among all the cracks in his windshield. And Hooper, with one lanky arm on the hot sill, is doing two things at once.

He watches this land they're driving through, brownwood shacks of country towns, and road walls of sugarcane, meanwhile remembering earlier trips after waves in all the old cars they once owned, clanking from Los Angeles north to Santa Barbara, or south to Baja California and Mazatlan, clanking and sputtering and flat-tire cursing as far south as they could get without leaving the land, cars lashed with balsa boards, stuffed with bedrolls and diving gear—rusty station wagons, rickety Model A's, abandoned laundry trucks, and taxicabs, and hearses. They had to be old and battered and barely running. The closer to dead the better. Some had belonged to Jonas, some to Hooper. The most treasured was the car that could travel the farthest on five cylinders, or four; three tires; or no lights. And the same measure applied to houses. And to clothing. And to food. Everything had to be old, or discarded, or cheap, or free.

Hooper's father could never understand this, having been himself, at Hooper's age, starving in Oklahoma, scratching hopeless soil for stillborn potatoes, and how lucky he was, coming west in the pit of the Great Depression, to find any work at all, and then when the war came along to land a job at Boeing. He's a supervisor there, with a fine home in Glendale, and a congregation elder to boot, Brother Andrew Dunlap, a man much respected among those two hundred worshippers, most of whom traveled out with him from the South. World War Two made their dreams come true, the Korean just multiplied their blessings, and Andrew's still feeling lucky about the way things worked out, which is why he has told Hooper so many times how tough it was in those early days, eating cornbread and red beans all winter, hiking barefoot through deep mud to a country school that wasn't always open when you got there. He tells such tales, of course, with considerable pride, having endured it all, and having prospered. And this is what Hooper remembers, the pride, the virtue of such denial. Sidestepping his father's hardwon prosperity—the Chrysler, the deep-freeze—he covets the ragged, the barefoot, and the cheap. But not the suffering. No. Sidestep the suffering too. Be ragged, but the farther south the better: Chickasha, Glendale, San Diego, Mazatlan, Oahu. Always someplace warmer. Someplace where it's always warm, and the fields are filled with available fruit, and the sea with fish.

Now Joe is starting to talk about the waves they'll ride today. But Hooper only half listens. He's envying Joe this truck, wondering how he can top, or even match it. The upholstery is bursting, one running board drags, the tires are bald, the horn seldom works, it reeks of oil and unwashed clothes and the pungent resin Joe uses to patch his boards. In Hooper's eyes it is the ultimate vehicle. And he has to admit it'll be hard to beat. He'll just have to wait and see what comes his way. Meanwhile—and this comes to him just as they clear a final rise before the island slopes down to its northern rim—he figures he can at least stay even, since minimum investment and painless self-denial are the first terms of their bond and private legend, by having no car at all. Which Hooper instantly decides to do. And he is so relieved at one-upping Joe by bumming a ride in the very car he covets, and so taken with the look of this new ocean spreading out and up—the appeal water always has for him when the land falls away to reveal it—he yells out the window.

It interrupts but does not stop Joe's loud explanation that this now calmly tropical stretch of sea curves north to Alaska, where earthquakes and winter storms make waves as high as houses, with nothing to stop them once they start until they hit this shoreline. Joe says he's ready for them whenever they get here. They're way overdue, as it is. And Hooper understands the loudness, the urgency in his description. It's the way Joe used to describe Hawaii when they were both back home. These islands have the one natural resource that interests him. Not the coco palms, or the trade winds, or the spirit of Aloha. No. Oahu sits in the path of those northern swells, and it has the reefs that lift them to twenty-five, thirty, sometimes forty feet, shaped right for riding if you can get to where they break, and Joe's one ambition is to catch a bigger wave than any other man has ridden.

Waves have never been this important to Hooper. Before he left, he sold his guitars and his surfboard, not only because he (1) needed the cash and (2) wanted no possession he couldn't carry on his back, but also because he (3) wasn't flying out here particularly to play music or ride waves. Yet now, listening to Joe describe waves he has already caught these past few months, the speed and steeper wall and seething tunnels you can shoot through, Hooper feels old juices reviving. And when they finally leave the sea road and break through a line of hibiscus flame and wind-tattered palms, and reach the spot, the nose of land that flares out onto lava reefs, and see swells humping blue, molting green across the sandy bottom to peak and break with hoofbeats, curling and clattering and rushing white over inshore placid green, Hooper, and Jonas too, are unstrapping boards and waxing the surfaces frenzied, as if the last wave for all future time is scheduled to break in the next five minutes. They slide down a short sandy cliff, leave the beach, and race for the breaking place, boards aglitter in the near-noon overhead sun, their arms digging in like four adzes chipping at the water.

They swing wide to the left, paddle in behind the break, Jonas leading now, and suddenly stop, drop legs over the sides. Like that oldtime statue of the hunching brave on his sagging horse, they sit hump-shouldered in a lull of surf, and wait, as if this in itself is enough, frantic paddle to end up perched offshore where sunlight ripples from the bottom, and a mile stripe of beach to edge volcanic ridges.

Waiting, silent, and after a while Joe explains the lineup.

"They peak fast, Hooper. It's a fast takeoff, and you better only go right. Until you see how they feel. You go left and it's pretty shallow over there. A lot of coral."

A new set is humping. They watch it. Slyly Jonas adds, not to scare, but just to hone the edge of their sport a little sharper, since for him it isn't sport at all, "Guy cut his legs pretty bad last week on the coral. Water was sucking up into his wave, and the tide was so low the heads were popping out in front of him. He got spooked and fell right into one."

With underwater kicks Joe swings his board around, telling Hooper to try for the first one, take a short ride, and paddle back in time to get the last wave of the set. He isn't that hungry. Hooper watches Joe take the first alone, to see how he handles it. He has never seen Joe make a mistake in the water. Joe always knows where the surf is best, where to wait, when to take off, how the reefs look, and why the currents change.

Joe flattens, waits a moment for the green slope to backtilt his board, then one white plunge of arms and his board is sliding. He jumps to his feet, crouched, cuts right just as the wave center snaps up and over, an exploding tube, and from behind, all Hooper can see is shaggy blond hair shooting along the rim just ahead of each erupting section.

Ten seconds and his board slices back through the wave. Joe is nearly aloft with forward motion channeled into his pullout, white arms spread like wings for balance, feet lightly holding the deck. Then he's flat again, paddling back like a water machine, as if pacing himself by a metronome, each stroke striving to move maximum water, just as each wave ridden is not simply a ride, but another, more perfect step toward what he came to Hawaii to do.

A week goes by.

Daily Jonas scans each view of the horizon for any sign of change in the ocean's face. On the sixth day, when he finally sees something, a flicker in the dawn light that seems to roll shoreward, but becomes, as Joe sprints to the water's edge to watch it, nothing more than that distant flicker, on that day Joe climbs back in and gives himself up to the whimsy and appetite of his Reo. And the Reo, satisfied at last, makes one more lap around the island and out to Sunset Beach, where it comes to rest.

Witness the community Joe and Hooper just joined. This parking space—a stubbled clearing on the low cliff between two battered palms—which a week ago was empty, is now occupied by three other vehicles that function much like Joe's: an old Ford station wagon, the kind with real wood paneling; a La Salle sedan, with a mattress where the backseat used to be, extending into the trunk; and a prewar Dodge pickup, with a plywood shed over its backend. They're all nosed up close to the sandy precipice.

The owners are well known to Jonas. All come from California, all flew over about the same time he did, all are sitting out this unaccountable flat spell with the same apathy of outraged impatience, waiting through January for waves they expected in November. One or two are usually out here, or parked over at Makaha when Joe surfs there. This is the second time in history all four have arrived at Sunset on the same day. The first time it happened they named their mobile community *Sunset Automotive,* and in the breezeless heat of this Tuesday afternoon these are its citizens.

STANLEY MOREHEAD, called Sheepdog, baby-faced and trying to conceal it, not by growing a beard, but by letting stringy blond hair grow down to cover his ears and eyes, with no other part of him covered between the bridge of his nose and the line where his red pubic hairs start. A rotten pair of green satin basketball shorts hang from that line, and

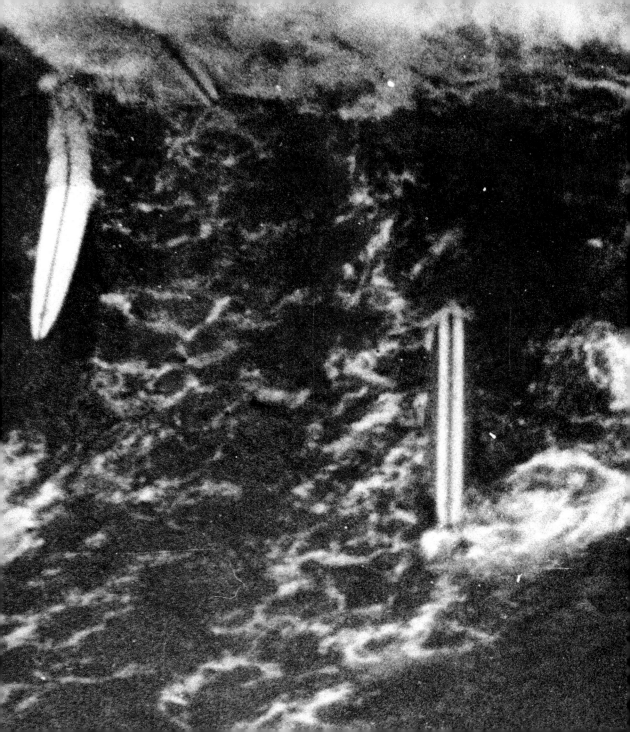

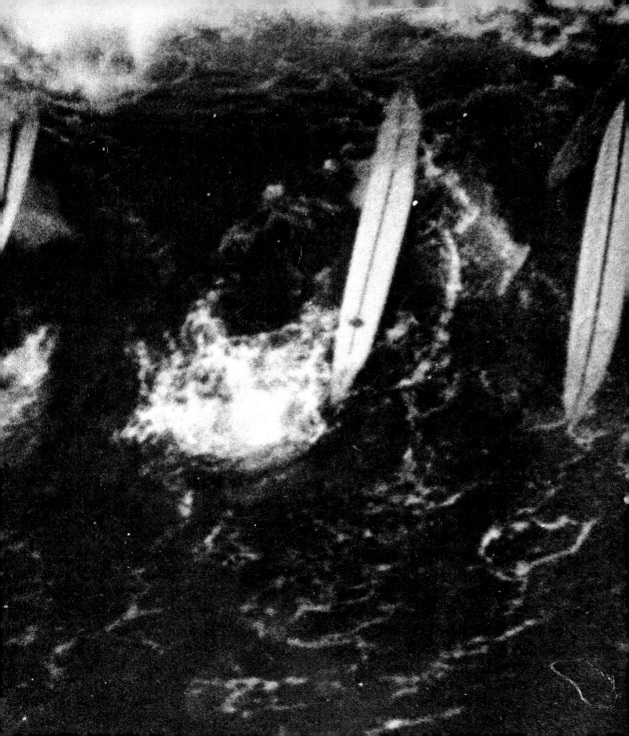

these reveal, as he hunkers at the cliff edge next to his station wagon's front bumper, half his buttock cleavage.

BYRON BASSIAN, called Black Bass, a weightlifter in the off-season, has been known to shave everything and oil his body, although this isn't necessary, since his body's always chocolate brown and shining with sweat like a Turkish wrestler's. He combs his black hair back, so it hugs his neck and scoops down and out Johnny Weissmuller style. He's now lying on a blanket on the metal roof of his black La Salle, a beer can balanced on his chest.

WALTER CONQUEST is the only married man among them, and his truck, the pickup with the plywood shed, which was once a community showpiece—mats on the floor, shelves for food—is now going to hell. Walter's wife flew back to the mainland last week to have a baby, at home, where her mother could help. Walter would have gone with her, but the surf was due at about the same time, and she understood, and he is still waiting for both events. Short, balding, husky, a miniature Black Bass bending over a surfboard set on two sawhorses behind his pickup, sanding fiberglass away to patch a tiny hole in the balsa. Sweat keeps falling from his forehead onto the sanded surface, and Walter keeps wiping it off with a red bandana.

Joe's engine coughs and dies. No one moves. Stanley hunkers hypnotized by the sea's absolute blue flatness. Black Bass is a chocolate corpse about to slide into it. The only sound is the ssshhh ssshhh ssshhh of Walter's sandpaper. Fronds hang limp. Joe and Hooper sit surprised by the sudden stopping after all this endless jolt and steady rumble, bodies dazed, eyes glazed, staring at hundreds of miles of nothing.


This morning on Walter's radio the newsman reported earthquakes in the Aleutians. Small-craft warnings are out. A new rip is running along the beach, and another runs straight out from shore toward the break, as if pumped from a great pipe under there. Signs. Portents. Shock waves pushing into the north Pacific are already giving southbound shape to ice water moving past the bergs, not the water moving, but the shape itself, fanning out, picking up speed. Some of them will hit Wake Island, some New Guinea, some Antarctica, some hit nothing, but swing around the Horn or south Australia and roll on till they dissipate, shape giving out, settling down weeks later, limp, finished, flat. But one band of these oceanwides will hit Oahu, pile up on reefs out there, piling till there's more water than the shape can hold, and Jonas knows no man yet has ridden a wave as large as the one he'll ride when the quake shocks and high tide and storm that's due all hit at once.

Joe knows the story of Shorty Baker, in fact heard it from Shorty's lips, and stored it away in his catalogue of wave lore, cross-filed under B for Baker, S for Sunset, C for close-out. It was late in '54, the first year in modern times anyone tried the winter surf out here. Shorty was the pioneer, the same way he pioneered Makaha a few years earlier, and is said to have pioneered the Tijuana Sloughs right after the Second World War, riding an oldtime redwood plank. According to Shorty, in December of '54 it just came up all of a sudden, overnight, bam, the biggest waves he'd ever seen. Shorty and two others got caught in a close-out set, and the rips started carrying them north, a mile or so in the direction of Kauai. Shorty knew the reefs and currents well enough to get everyone back to the beach, but it took two hours of hard paddling to make it, all of them vomiting their guts out, curled up on the sand and too sick to walk. And Shorty later admitted that none of them took off on the biggest waves that broke that day. Being out there among them was enough in itself.

Joe also knows the story of Holoua, a man of Kauai, whose house was washed out to sea in the great tidal wave of 1868. Tearing a plank from the wall of his living room, Holoua is said to have ridden the next wave, a fifty-footer, back to shore. This is, of course, only a legend. Even if it were true, Joe figures Holoua most likely rode the wave lying down. Which in any case wouldn't count.

Jonas knows all the stories, likes to tell them, and hear them told, and to know that soon he too will be remembered in the backends of station wagons, all along the running boards of old limousines around the coastlines of the world.

The sun's up, but still behind the mountain, three trucks at Sunset Automotive and six boards scattered, waiting, like rifles in a gun room before the alarm goes out. Oyster light of post-dawn tints them, two boards up against Sheepdog's wagon, one on the ground, two on sawhorses next to Walter's pickup, one at the cliff edge, resting on its skeg, uptilted. In this lot of dented cars and charred scoops of campfire and tin-can litter and rotten clothes hung from limbs in the breezeless morning air, these boards gleam like armor, like firetrucks, like shipboard cannon. Every deck is waxed for surefootedness, every onetime hole now patched and waterproof, everything else can go to hell but the boards stay sleek, slabs of balsa finely rounded, sheathed with fiberglass.

Now Joe and Sheepdog and Walter come tumbling from the trucks to stand among these boards, rub eyes, stare at the waves that have made sleep impossible. The ocean's sigh and murmur that become a moan and growl is now a howl and grinding roar, and this isn't surf any more. It's a hissing stampede avalanche of water walls erupting. The waves breaking a second time, fifty yards offshore, are the size of those they rode yesterday—now the first barrier to push through. The outside break is something none of them has ever seen before, except in pictures, and the pictures lied because they don't make the sound, or show the heave of a whole ocean in front, behind, on all sides of the great waves that seem to be the purpose of all the rest.

There isn't much to say. It's what they've been waiting for. They stand in a row along the cliff for thirty minutes, watching it, timing the sets, stony-faced. Then Sheepdog and Walter, like deputy sheriffs called to duty, grab two boards from the armory, and kneel in the dry grass fiercely waxing their decks.

Jonas tries to fry some eggs, but can hardly squat over the tiny fire. He's shivering with morning overcast, leaves the eggs to blacken in the skillet, and reaches for his board, waxes it, leads the others down the cliff path. They wait ten minutes for a short lull to let them past the inside break, Jonas all this time squeezing at his sphincter to keep his bowels from falling out. Finally three boards hit the water, splat splat splat.

The current along shore is a river now, as wide as the beach. Beyond it the surface chop is almost breaking, and the white water after each big wave breaks is as high as the cliff they park on—speedup of a continental glacier burying territories in its push.

Three is always the magic number, Sheepdog tells himself, paddling out. All good things come three. Bad things too. Trinity is nonpartisan, and three any way you look at it is the one to watch. Three blind mice. Three bears. Three strikes you're out. Three little words. Rubadubdub three men in a tub. Three times this month the surf comes up. Today's the third day of the third pulse. I'm third man paddling behind Joe and Walter, and every third stroke I push a little harder. One—two—THREE. One—two—THREE. I will wait for the third set after we get out there, and I will take off on the third wave of that set.

Three cars pull into the clearing just about the time the surfers reach the takeoff zone. Joe and Walt join Sheepdog in letting the first two sets roll through untouched, looking them over, every wave a twenty-footer and no one anxious to try till they see how these look up close. This gives the new arrivals time to hop out and set up cameras. Tripods on the cliff edge, telephoto lenses. One man, in a hooded sweatshirt, is making a movie. Another is looking for a sports feature to sell the Honolulu paper. More equipment is on its way. Shutterbugs and spectators.

The third car, a Model A sedan, carries three surfboards strapped to its roof and three more Californians who've been mainly riding at Waikiki and who would remain for a long time today sitting in this car, contemplating these outlandish waves, were it not that the third set is humping out there and someone has paddled over right in under the peak and has barely missed getting swamped by two waves the size of department stores and now seems ready to actually try for the third, from a position that would only be taken by a blind man who couldn't possibly perceive what he's getting into. He's starting too late, it's going to break on top of him. They leap from the car and run to the cliff edge waving, shouting, "No! No! No!" One runs back to blare the horn waaaaaaah, waaaaaaah.

None of this reaches Sheepdog. He only hears the rumble all around of waves broken and threatening to break, he only knows that the third one is ready now, so it's three hard strokes, and three strokes more. It's one—two—three, and one—two—three, and one—two—THREE, and the wave of his choice scoops Sheepdog to its high crest.

Below him there's no slope. A sheer wall. The wave lets go. The blond board plummets. White water's roaring above him before he hits the trough.

On shore the new arrivals are cringing with the hurt. Their faces contort, watching him hit the bottom. He seems suspended there, floating, and the whiteness itself is suspended above, giving him one saintly moment of terrible grace, tiny brown body upright and waiting, with palms out from his waist, not Christ-like, but as if to say, "You see? You see?" before the tumbling wave falls all over him like ten thousand sacks of wet cement.

Overcast today, oyster sky turning pewter, the first lick of water at his instep and Joe's scrotum draws, he has to hold his face together. Flesh feels old and loose and useless. Water colder than he's ever known it in the islands, starts him paddling fast to keep warm, warm the chest. Pecs tight with little spasms as he hits the current that sweeps him toward the break. Easy to get out there now. Too easy. Double hard getting back, if you have to swim. Slow down then. Don't paddle too fast. Save the calories. Save the arms for getting into waves fast. Get out fast too, on the first few rides. Less chance of losing it. Won't have to swim so much. That's what wears you down. Shorty said four out of seven is a good average in surf this size. Make four, swim for three, you're not doing too bad. I can beat that. One thing at a time. First, get the takeoff wired. Then the long wall.

He watches Sheepdog's Kamikaze drop, later sees him bobbing far inshore, boardless and hacking at the foam, trying to swim for it. On the fourth set, Joe tries a wave, like looking down a canyon, cuts a half-moon as he slides under, up, over the top and out the back. Test flight. He paddles toward the takeoff zone again, still shivering, still cold and rubbing palms as he waits out there for Walter, who took the wave behind him, and made it. Sheepdog is far down the beach, evidently dogpaddling against the rip, two hundred yards below the clearing, and still no board in sight.

By midmorning five more riders have paddled out. Two paddled back in after a few halfhearted tries. Two took wipe-outs—neither as spectacular as Sheepdog's since no one dares get that far into the curl— and decided to swim for shore. One man remains out there with Joe and Walter, a Hawaiian named Horse who works at Waikiki Beach.

The clearing has filled with spectators, lenses, more boards and battered cars. Down the coast road a quarter of a mile, where the trees open up, there's another patch of cars, people perched on hoods with binoculars, a touring bus parked, a score of cameras, narrow-brim straw hats.

Joe's shivering has stopped. He's finding the rhythm now. And it's easier to try the big ones when you know shutters are clicking, reels are whirring to record it all. No more legends. These rides will be preserved. Still shots to blow up later and measure with calipers.

Horns are honking too, all the time. It's a way for spectators to get into the act. Cliff-watchers can see farther than someone in the water, so when a set starts to build, you send signals. One honk means take the wave right in front of you. Two means wait for the next one. Three honks means wait for the third, it's the biggest, looks the best.

The swells are five feet higher than when Joe first paddled out. And they're growing. Each set seems bigger than the last, seems to peak a little farther out each time. Now a new set rises, and Joe and Walter and Horse paddle toward it, paddle hard, not to get caught when it breaks. On shore everyone is honking in unison ONE, ONE, ONE, which means the wave following is either too big or will break too far out to reach. Horse and Walter swing into position. But Joe thinks to himself, "Fuck all those assholes," and he paddles up the face of it, pushes through the slapping crest, drops to the valley, with a glump of his vital organs, arms driving into water marbled scummy white from back foam. He hears the horns again, blaring ONE, ONE, ONE, pleading Take *this* one, for Christ sake. Again Joe paddles toward it, climbs the front, and blinks salt water out, craning. From its spuming crest he sees the third bulging toward him, and beyond that the fringes of a fourth so big it's already frothing, and beyond those stand others, like endless Himalayan ridges, clouding the horizon.

He sinks into this valley, thinking "Close-out set," figuring three will have to be the one, and doesn't notice that all the horns along the cliff are silent. He sees the spot he wants, ten yards away, digs for it till the wave is bulked above him, jade green, foam-veined, cupped with silver from the graying sky. He swings his board, curved palms stroking for speed, looking back to judge the time, up and up and up to see the top. Stroking. Hard. Hard. Harder. A breath-grabbing lift, an instant glance down the deep well of it, then a thirty-foot fall, plowing to the bottom where his board catches, spurts out across the curving wall, and Joe knows he has it, hears the sharp clean hissing as it steepens and knows he can't make a mistake. Thunder of the first peak behind him. Loud tunnel thundering shut, while in front of him it opens still wider, endless, expanding before it contracts, green-walling, tingles all the flex, and poise, and stinging him with salt spray.

And so intent is Joe upon the speed and balance, he doesn't hear the horns that now begin to bellow, choral triumph of squawks and beeps and waa-waa-waas. From the clearing sweatshirted girls are yelling. Sheepdog is leaning on his horn and yelling, "Go Jonas! Go go go!" Grown men are shouting at the ocean. Engines roar. A Minnesota husband at the tour bus turns to sun-hatted wife, "That fella's having himself quite a time out there."

Quite a time, yes, and going all the way, flawless ride, milking it be-cause he knows it'll be the day's last. He rides a hundred yards, and as it dwindles from thirty-plus to fifteen or so, just before the great swell grades out too flat to ride, jumps to another moving from the west, renegade heap of backwash about to break, and takes that ten-footer the other way, toward the crowd, now frenzied with delight, and makes it almost to the beach before he drops to his knees, board still moving, and starts to paddle for a five-foot lick of shorebreak that carries Jonas right up onto the drain-ing sand, where well-wishers have already run down to meet him, camera-men pushing in close with expensive lenses to get every moment of this fantastic ride, from takeoff to beach-walk. And Joe, as if he's all alone somewhere in the South Pacific, bends and gathers up his board, and starts his slow stroll back along hard sand to the cliff path, dragging feet in the tide rush, glancing seaward from time to time, checking it out, ignoring all the hands extended, smiling once as he climbs the path. Without dry-ing off, while the cameras whirr and snap, he breaks out a long can of Danish sardines, keys it open, sitting on his caked running board and be-gins to eat them one at a time, his long-awaited breakfast, dark grease dripping off his wrist, running to his elbow, dropping to the hairy thigh.

# MATT WARSHAW

## EXCERPT FROM
## *MAVERICK'S*

THE BIG-WAVE REVIVAL began in 1983, and it was at least in part a collective act of surf-world self-purification. Pro surfing events were fighting for attention (and usually losing) with adjunct bikini contests and sponsor-product giveaways. Beach fashion had turned to muscle shirts and tightfitting shorts in cornea-burning neon colors. Zinc oxide, the original sun block, once chalk-white, was now available in green, yellow, blue, and hot pink. When the 1982–83 winter season produced the biggest North Pacific surf since 1969, with one prodigious swell following another, it was almost as if a terrestrial statement were being made against the new commercial vulgarity. Surfers once again got a long draught of what Greg Noll had called "the big, damn terrorizing wave," and many of them realized that this was something worthy of more attention. Indeed, it all looked so dramatic and exciting that it was hard to figure out why big waves had gone out of vogue in the first place.

*Surfer* magazine helped things along with a mildly bellicose article titled, "Whatever Happened to Big-Wave Riding?" As author Leonard Brady noted in the introduction, just a dozen or so surfers in the early eighties were interested in riding waves twenty-five feet and bigger. And these "gladiators of the sea," these "fighter jocks who went surfing," were, in Brady's estimation, the sport's only true heroes. Pretty much everyone else was suspect. "What happened?" Brady asked. "Will lavender be the board color of the '80s? Have surfers turned into candyasses?"

Hawaii's Mark Foo rode Waimea Bay for the first time in 1983, almost simultaneous to the publication of "Whatever Happened to Big-Wave Riding?" and it's easy to imagine the twenty-five-year-old Foo staring at the *Surfer* article pages the way a teenager from the early forties might have stared at an "Uncle Sam Wants You" recruiting poster. Foo was in a rut. He was surfing well, but not well enough to put his name anywhere near the top of the year-end pro circuit rankings—in four seasons he hadn't finished higher than sixty-sixth. He was a big believer in the power of positive thinking, but self-doubt was creeping in, he was nearly broke, and his mother and father were both unhappy (and vocally so) with Mark's occupational choice. "Good Chinese boys don't surf for a living," as Mark's sister SharLyn would say, in a gently mocking tone to convey their parents' disappointment. Foo's mother had flat-out called him a "surf bum."

Big waves hadn't been much of a consideration for Foo up to that point. In early 1982, he'd talked eagerly about another go-round on the pro circuit, but at season's end he finished sixty-seventh. Now, looking ahead to 1983, he was warming to the idea that real opportunities might be found in big surf. Money and fame, yes, but more importantly a prolonged career in the sport he loved.

Foo had been surfing since 1969, when, as an eleven-year-old, he bought a secondhand surfboard with money saved from his paper route. One year later his father, a midlevel employee with the U.S. Foreign Service, was reassigned to Washington, D.C., and the family moved from Honolulu to Rockville, Maryland. SharLyn Foo says her surf-touched brother was miserable. "He'd have tantrums and fits," she remembers. "He'd lay on the floor and kick and scream. Everyone knows how intense he was about surfing as an adult. Well, he was intense about it as a kid, too." At age fourteen, Foo left for Pensacola, a Florida beach town, to live with the family of a friend. Two years later the Foo family, Mark included, moved back to Honolulu. Nobody was surprised when Mark graduated from Roosevelt High School in 1975, one year ahead of his class; he was ambitious and smart. Nobody was surprised, either, when he blew off the commencement ceremony to jump on an early season south swell.

Foo moved to the North Shore that fall. He wanted to compete with the pros in the contests, and to fully immerse himself in the top-level sessions endlessly taking place at Haleiwa, Pipeline, and Sunset. And he hoped to get his picture in the magazines.

Foo surfed well, but not as well as the prime-time pros, and he invariably lost early in the competitions. But if the contest judges didn't love him, the camera did, and before the end of the decade Foo was on the cover of *Surfer* and *Surfing* as often as the world champions. He drafted across the beautiful pellucid-blue North Shore waves in a compact, aerodynamic stance, and accoutered himself in the brightest colors possible—in a famous 1978 Pipeline photo, he's riding a pink-and-yellow surfboard and wearing scarlet-red trunks. Leveraging as best he could, Foo made small-money sponsorship deals with three or four surf companies. The goal all along, for Foo and the rest of the pros, was to make a living in surfing. Not by making or selling surfboards, or other surf-related items, or working surf-retail, but from riding waves. Prize-money contests were a means to that end. So were sponsorship deals, whereby surfers, in exchange for placing a company logo on their board, were paid in some combination of merchandise, salary, travel expenses, and "photo incentives" (a quarter-page black-and-white photo in *Surfer,* logo showing, might be worth fifty dollars; a cover shot could bring five hundred dollars). The pro surfing formula was simple. More magazine photos meant a higher surf-world "profile" (one of Foo's favorite words), which meant a higher personal market value. Sponsorship money plus contest winnings added up to an annual salary, and if it didn't add up to much for Foo, it didn't add up to much for anybody else, either. Peter Townend earned just over twenty-five thousand dollars when he won the world title in 1976. Three years later, Mark Richards, the new champion, made about forty thousand dollars. Surf company CEOs, a few of them, were making millions. Pro surfers were eating at Denny's and car-pooling from contest to contest.

Townend and Richards and the other top-rated pros, though, were at least respected by their peers. Mark Foo wasn't. The spectacular amount of media exposure he received was in fact out of proportion with his good-but-not-spectacular talent, and it didn't help matters when, after signing a contract with Anheuser-Busch brewery, he marched down the beach in the winter of 1981 with a lens-catching metalflake-gold surfboard bearing a gigantic red-and-white Michelob logo across the deck. Foo became known as a "photo slut," implying that he wouldn't bother paddling out until lighting conditions were of studio quality and the photographers were setting up their tripods along the beach.

The charge wasn't entirely fair. Surfing was Foo's rapture and joy, and he rode constantly in gray, windblown, nonphotogenic conditions. Never for a moment, though, did he feel that it was anything but honorable to reap income and status from the sport, and to that end he was indeed tireless. He would eventually host his own surfing radio show (and later a cable TV show), write articles for the surf magazines, do voice-overs for surf movies and color commentary for surf contests, and open a surfer's bed-and-breakfast. He darted back and forth across the North Shore in a business-fueled blur, making appointments, showing up on time, and working the phones with great entrepreneurial flair. Local schools invited him to speak on professional surfing during Career Day assemblies. The money wasn't great, he would tell the kids, but the hours were flexible, and daily surf sessions were part of the business plan.

Foo was social, garrulous, and funny, always eager to connect with people emotionally and openly. But behind the steady line of business talk and social chatter, he kept a fundamental part of himself in watchful reserve. Detachment, in fact, proved to be Foo's greatest big-wave asset.

When he rode Waimea Bay for the first time in 1983, he was alert and thrilled, but suffered none of the shrieking emotional feedback common to Waimea rookies. "Mark had this thing where he'd just get calmer and calmer as the conditions got gnarlier," says Bobby Owens, a former pro surfer and one of Foo's best friends. "He told me his breathing and heart rate actually slowed down on those giant days."

It was strange how Foo reacted in big surf, and Foo himself realized it. "I always drive really slow," he said in 1988. "I don't like heights. I'm afraid of roller-coasters. I pretty much don't like doing anything where I might get hurt." Yet riding big waves, as he pointed out, combined all of these things. Not long after his first Waimea experience, Foo seemed to arrange the disparate aspects of his character into a kind of big-wave Calvinism, where the prudent 55-mph driver, the diligent capitalist, and the swashbuckling surfer all merged in the name of a higher power.

"There has to be a bigger purpose to what I'm doing," Foo said. "It's a plan God has. It's destiny."


Foo had a sensational big-wave coming-of-age moment on January 18, 1985, after a cloud-splitting fifty-foot closeout wave roared through Waimea, steamrolling Foo and three more surfers. The others lost their boards and began the long, rough swim toward shore. Foo's board popped up nearby, still attached to its leash, and he swung up onto the deck, realizing that he was now alone in some truly giant surf. From a relatively safe position just past the lineup, he watched the fire department helicopter move in, a rescue basket dangling thirty feet below the cockpit, to pluck one of the surfers out of the water and deposit him on the sand. Beach spectators stood and applauded, and cars parked along either side of the bay honked their horns excitedly. The other two swimming surfers were also lifted to the beach, then the helicopter banked around to pick up Foo.

Thirty-footers were rolling through at a fairly steady rate, breaking in no discernible pattern twenty or thirty yards out past the normal Waimea lineup. A few of the waves, though, in Foo's estimation, looked ridable. The helicopter was now floating overhead, waiting. Foo ignored it.

After letting a few waves pass, Foo just missed catching a twenty-footer. He then wheeled his board around and saw that the following wave was bigger, maybe thirty feet, and that it was backed by a set of bigger-still waves. No choice: He'd have to catch the first one or get walloped by the next few. For ten seconds he paddled farther out, looking to intercept the wave at the exact right place, then he turned suddenly, pointed for shore, and dug in. There was a rush along his board's keel, the tail section lifted up, and Foo snapped to his feet.

The ride came apart in stages. Foo and his board disconnected as a unit from the crest of the vertically pitched wave, then Foo disconnected from his board and fell like a statue thirty feet to the trough. The wave hit, and he actually heard his board splinter and snap in the underwater concussion. His watch was stripped from his wrist. Pinpoint specks of light were flickering across his eyelids by the time the turbulence began to ease, then Foo broke the surface and drew a shuddering breath. The rescue basket was dangling just to his right, and he climbed inside, sat on the nylon mesh floor, steadied his breathing, and watched the tail section of his board twirl and spin at the end of its leash as he rode to the sand.

Ten minutes later, as Foo walked back to his Kam Highway home, he started blocking the event into prose. "I awoke early on January 18," his soon-to-be-published *Surfing* magazine article began, "unaware that I had a date with destiny."

Big-wave surfing lent ballast to Foo's life, personally and professionally. He was now respected and admired by the surfing world at large. His annual income was on the rise. His mother now saw him as a businessman, rather than a surf bum.

Foo also developed a free-ranging interest in death. "It's not tragic to die doing something you love," he said in a 1986 interview. "It's like the *[Challenger]* astronauts. When they died, they were doing something they'd geared their whole lives to do. They were at the climax of that, and it's not a bad way to go." Foo's big-wave peers thought his death musings were a bit theatrical. Foo didn't mind. It *was* theater, in part. There was craftsmanship in quotes like "If you want the ultimate thrill, you have to be willing to pay the ultimate price." But that didn't mean that he was putting anyone on—himself included. Good surfers weren't dying in big waves. Foo knew this. Yet he accepted it as an article of faith that big-wave surfing was dangerous to the point of being deadly.

While most of Foo's peers rolled their eyes and smiled at his dramatically rendered versions of big-wave surfing, fellow big-wave surfer Ken Bradshaw grew to see in Foo everything that was wrong with the sport. The two began feuding, and in 1988, the Foo-Bradshaw conflict was presented in an *Outside* magazine feature article titled "The Divided Rulers of Waimea Bay." The article pointed out a huge, congenital difference between the two. Foo was an impatient big-wave surfer, a late-starter not overly concerned with big-wave legacy and hierarchy. Bradshaw was a traditionalist—and in a sense had been since his 1967 surfing baptismal, in the placid mud-colored breakers of Galveston, where as a ninth-grader he rode his first wave on a rented Greg Noll surfboard. Bradshaw, a high school runaway, arrived on the North Shore at age nineteen, an artless but gutsy surfer, and brick-by-brick constructed a life and career for himself in big-wave surfing. He began to shape his own boards—the way old-timers Pat Curren and Greg Noll had. He scrupulously took care of his six-foot, 185-pound body; vegetarian diet, no drugs or drinking, plenty of nonsurfing exercise. He put the time in, made steady gains, and in 1982 he won the Duke Kahanamoku contest at Sunset Beach.

Bradshaw was deferential at all times to his big-wave elders. To most others, he was a brute. He'd paddle up to a surfer who had interfered with one of his waves, knock the surfer off his board, flip the board over, and with frowning Gestapo efficiency whack off a fin with the base of his hand. In a more emotional state—and to the horror of onlooking surfers—he would sometimes bite into the edge of the board and spit out a mouthful of foam and fiberglass.

Mark Foo, as far as Bradshaw was concerned, had been crossing the line as early as 1977, by grabbing too many waves at Sunset, and it was nearly a *pro forma* act when Bradshaw paddled up to Foo later that season and folded the smaller surfer down into an underwater headlock.

But the Foo-Bradshaw rivalry didn't really solidify until 1985, after Foo's first-person "date with destiny" Waimea account hit the newsstands. Bradshaw had aced a dozen huge waves on January 18 before Foo had even gotten to the beach, but that didn't get into print. Foo, on the other hand—and this was what really burned Bradshaw—had taken off on just *one* wave and hadn't even come close to making it. Then he'd gone home, written the article, and gotten famous! Bradshaw understood at some level that Foo had quickly and impressively made himself over into a big-wave rider. But that wasn't the point. He was acting like a punk. He was *pushing* it. Big-wave riding had tradition and custom, and Foo, as Bradshaw saw it, was just lifting a leg on the whole thing. It was a *business* hustle. Christ, he had *nine* sponsors' stickers on the deck of his board!

It got to the point where Bradshaw found fault with nearly everything Foo did. "Just the way he warms up before he surfs," Bradshaw told *Outside* in 1988. "He's down there at the edge of the water, this big public display, like 'Here I go, everyone! I'm getting warmed up now!'"

Foo responded with a smile and shrug. He was impatient. He admitted it. But he didn't consider himself a disrespectful person, and he got along pretty well with most other big-wave surfers. Bradshaw's animosity, he told *Outside,* had less to do with tradition and etiquette and more to do with jealousy. "Right when he's getting some real attention for what he's doing at Waimea, all of a sudden I'm out in the lineup with him. And making more money at it, too. I know what his sponsors pay."

But the gap between Bradshaw and Foo wasn't quite as chasm-like as they believed. Foo's impolite boasting aside, the sport was affording both surfers the exact same middle-class wages—about thirty thousand dollars in 1987. Bradshaw could be pushed into a grudging admission that he, too, like Foo, was a brightly accessorized (his trademark colors were orange and yellow) and attention-seeking big-wave rider. And Foo said that if he had to choose one person to surf with on a really huge day, he'd probably pick Bradshaw.

Animosity, though, was the rule. Bradshaw was incredulous when Foo told *Surfer* magazine that "good surfing is about making it look easy; Kenny's always had a make-it-look-hard approach." And Foo was embarrassed when, as reported in the *Outside* article, Bradshaw lumbered up one afternoon along Kam Highway and reached out with thumb and forefinger to tweeze one of Foo's sparsely grown chest hairs. "Hey, what's this?" Bradshaw boomed, squinting as he held up the lone black hair for inspection. "Foo-Foo! Check it out! You *are* becoming a man!"


Ken Bradshaw and Mark Foo were puffy-eyed and a bit faded as they walked through the United Airlines terminal at San Francisco International Airport. It was 5:20 A.M., which meant 2:20 Hawaiian time. Bradshaw led the way to the baggage area. He told Foo he'd deal with the car, then rolled off toward the Alamo booth. Foo located the "odd size" luggage depot, wrestled his enormous two-surfboard travel bag from the metal chute, set it against the wall, then stretched out alongside and closed his eyes. Bradshaw hadn't brought any boards, as he had one stashed in local big-wave rider Mark Renneker's garage. A half dozen times over the past two seasons he'd flown from Honolulu to San Francisco to ride Maverick's. Just six days earlier, in fact, he'd made the same trip. The big-wave chase was kind of exciting, Bradshaw thought. Then again, it was a lot simpler and less expensive when the whole thing pretty much began and ended on the North Shore.

Just after 7 A.M., Renneker handed Bradshaw a cup of green tea, and both men stood in front of Renneker's third-story dining room window and looked out to the twelve-foot Ocean Beach surf. Maverick's would be bigger; how much bigger was hard to say. Bradshaw lowered his gaze to the rental car, where Foo was curled up in the back seat. "Foo-Foo," he said, with a dismissive shake of the head. "Look how excited he is."

The tone was sarcastic, but not cutting. The Foo-Bradshaw hostilities had been over for two or three years. Neither surfer had officially stepped down, resolution hadn't been sought or acknowledged, but the nastier accusations and insults—not to mention the chest-hair tweezing and underwater headlocks—were a thing of the past. Foo had toned down his act, which helped. In fact, at age thirty-six, he was now a tenured member of the same big-wave establishment he'd once ignored or railed against. He could even be magnanimous, neatly and honorably defining his peers in a *Surfer* magazine interview as "artists, athletes, and professionals."

Foo, Bradshaw knew, could still be breathtakingly crass. His "photogenic looks and athletic prowess," as noted in Foo's two-page, four-color 1994 résumé, were key to his "spiraling media career as a print, radio, and TV personality." Elsewhere in his c.v., Foo declared himself "surfing's preeminent big-wave rider" as well as "surfing's consummate living legend." Bradshaw would sigh and wearily rub his eyes at this kind of florid PR

work. Then again, Bradshaw, like Foo, always kept his appointments with the surf magazine photographers, and Bradshaw's brightly colored boards, like Foo's, were dappled with surf company logos. The sport had long ago become a pleasure/business fusion for both men.

And so, on December 22, when Bradshaw heard that the surf at Maverick's was due to come back up, he called Foo and suggested an overnight strike. Ninety minutes later Foo was able to book a pair of airline tickets, but the plane left in three hours, so they had to move fast. Bradshaw packed a bag and drove to Foo's house near Waimea Bay, then stood in the driveway talking with Foo's fiancée Lisa Nakano—twenty-eight-year-old former model and a marketing department employee for Levi Strauss in Honolulu—while Foo shouldered his boards into the car. Nakano watched with a tight little smile. *This is what Mark does,* she told herself, accepting his odd vocation with its fire-drill departures but not liking it much at the moment. Christmas Eve he'd be back. Surfed out and worthless, probably. But happy.

Foo tossed a duffel bag onto the back seat and was ready to go. Nakano looked at Bradshaw as she gestured toward Foo. "Take care of him," she ordered. "Make sure he gets back okay." Nakano told Foo to take care of Bradshaw, too, and after a fast round of good-bye hugs and kisses, it was full-speed for the airport.


Foo revived as Bradshaw steered into the dirt parking lot at Maverick's, just behind Renneker's van. It was almost 9 A.M. The weather, again, was lovely—sharp blue skies and a gentle offshore wind. Foo, suddenly energized, bounded outside and unloaded a gaudy yellow-and-purple airbrushed surfboard from the top of the car. He crouched, rested the board perpendicularly across his thighs, and vigorously rubbed a bar of traction-enhancing wax back and forth across the deck, perfuming the air with a sweet chemical-coconut scent. Not too cold, he said to Renneker. How about the water, though? Should he wear a wetsuit hood? Hold on—maybe he was waxing the wrong board. Switch to the nine-six, or stay with the ten-footer? Which way was the tide going? Leave the clothes here, or bring everything to the beach? Hey, is that Jeff Clark's van? Foo often got this way before riding big waves, especially at a place he'd never before surfed. Not nervous, exactly, but restless and chattering, the staccato-voiced questions following one after the other. He'd never fit the low-key, slow-grinning big-wave archetype. Or he didn't on land. In the surf he always leveled out.

Thirty minutes later, as they paddled through Maverick's north channel, Renneker began doing most of the talking, explaining to Foo in a lively, helpful, somewhat pedantic voice about the Boneyard, the rocks, the Second Bowl section. Both surfers watched an empty twelve-footer lift up into the familiar pyramidal shape. Sunlight was absorbed into the blue face, then blindingly reflected off the frosted-white crest. The curl hit the trough with a low tearing sound that seemed to emanate from behind the surfers as well as in front of them—a strange aural deception that sometimes happens in big surf. "Some juice there, huh?" Foo noted.

Foo, Bradshaw, and Renneker paddled toward the Maverick's take-off area, where a dozen local surfers were loosely clustered. The waves were well-formed, but no bigger than fifteen feet. Maybe an eighteen-footer every hour or so, Foo hoped. Renneker didn't quite apologize for the smaller-than-expected surf, but did preface a comment or two by saying, "On Monday and Wednesday, when it was big . . ."

Foo wasn't the only famous big-wave surfer making his debut at Maverick's; Mike Parsons and Brock Little were as well. Parsons, from San Clemente, had been an amiable pro tour journeyman during the eighties and early nineties, but over the past few years had changed his focus to Todos Santos, and was now southern California's premier big-wave rider. He'd arrived in Half Moon Bay the night before, late, after a droning, seven-hour, coffee-fueled drive up Highway 101. Hawaii's Brock Little had also arrived the night before, flying in from Los Angeles. He wiped out on his first two Maverick's waves, breaking his leash on the second, which forced a long board-retrieving swim to the harbor jetty about a half mile from the lineup. Little would nonetheless describe the surf as relatively mild. "Pretty easy for the most part," he said. "A beautiful day. A nice size to check the place out."

All attending surfers, in fact, were content to settle into what looked to be a bright and airy morning of moderately big waves. The locals were wrung out after a fortnight of oversize surf. The newcomers, as Little said, were happy that their Maverick's introduction was being conducted under such pleasant conditions.

Visiting members of the surf press, meanwhile, were a little disappointed. Twenty-four hours earlier this had been shaping up as a real big-wave summit. The surf was going to rise, the weather would hold. Surf magazine editors moved photographers and writers to Half Moon Bay like chess pieces, and big-wave captains Foo, Little, Parsons, and Bradshaw were expected to gather for the laying-on of hands. Now everyone was in place, the color was perfect, but the surf was five or ten feet smaller than it needed to be to produce any atmosphere-crackling big-wave drama.

Or so it seemed. At about 9 A.M., as Foo, Bradshaw, and Renneker were walking down the trail toward the beach, local surfer Shaun Rhodes fell on a twelve-footer and was jostled downward until his wetsuit-covered feet brushed the reef. Rhodes was startled; in three years of riding Maverick's, he'd never touched the bottom. He swam up and ducked three more waves, the last of which again pushed him to the reef—except this time his left leg, just above the knee, suddenly wedged tight into a narrow crevasse. Rhodes twisted his hips and lower torso, but the leg held fast. Reaching down to brace his hands on the rocky ledge, he pushed, kicked, kicked again, and came free. Back to the surface a moment later, freaked out and short of breath, Rhodes reeled in his surfboard and paddled for shore. Nobody on the beach asked him about it. Nobody had noticed.

Mark Foo promptly caught three waves, none spectacular, but invigorating just the same. "It's good," he told Ken Bradshaw. "I'm stoked. Glad we came." Then the nearly requisite add-on, one gnarly big-wave vet to another: "Wish it had a little more size, though." Over the next hour, Foo rode one wave with Bradshaw, another with Little, and got two or three more to himself.

A lull settled in about 11, and the lineup became almost pool-like. The surfers' black neoprene wetsuits absorbed and distributed the sun's midmorning warmth, and everyone went deeper into an assortment of relaxed positions, sitting or lying on their boards. Conversations were easily picked up and just as easily dropped. Mostly it was quiet.

The hundred-or-so cliffside spectators were also relaxed. Some were standing, others were sitting in the dry scrub grass, arms back for support, eyes closed, faces tilted up to the sun. Nearly everybody had shed at least one layer of clothes, and a few men were shirtless. Fifteen minutes passed without a single breaking wave, at which point surf videographer Eric Nelson, standing behind his camera, squinted out across the level blue ocean and said to a friend, "Guess that's about it." Sometimes the surf just shuts off like that. Nelson hunkered down, picked at the grass, and began thinking about lunch.

At 11:20, he straightened up and murmured, "Here comes something," as the distant water stirred and changed color slightly. A minute passed. An underdeveloped first wave went unridden, but the second wave was bigger—about fifteen feet—and Nelson pressed "record" as Bradshaw and Foo both turned and paddled. Bradshaw was about five yards north of Foo, deeper in the peak, and holding priority. But he was too deep and pulled back at the last moment. Foo stood on his purple-and-yellow board, rode halfway down the steepening face, then dropped off the right side of his board. Still filming, Nelson aimed again for the takeoff area, where Mike Parsons and Brock Little were paddling hard for the third wave, another fifteen-footer. Both surfers got to their feet at the same time—so few waves had come in over the past hour that riders were doubling up—and Nelson muttered "Go, go, go," under his breath. Parsons then caught an edge and fell on his back, arms and legs in the air and scrambling uselessly as the falling curl drove scythelike through his torso. Little continued for another ten yards before being erased by whitewater. Three more waves passed, all too small to catch, then Bradshaw got a long ride on the final and best wave of the set.

Just after Bradshaw's wave, people on the cliff noticed that Little and Parsons were being swept toward a stand of rocks separating the surf break from a lagoon. Five or six waves rushed over and around the ridges and crags, spume bouncing up, then settling into a mist, and there was no telling from this distance just what was happening with Little and Parsons. Surfers usually were flushed directly through the rocks into the lagoon, but not always; most of the Maverick's locals remembered two years ago when Jeff Clark had been pinned atop a room-sized rock for nearly an hour. Now it looked as if Parsons and Little were both trapped somewhere on the west side of the rocks—but no, here came Little's surfboard bouncing into the lagoon, with Little just a few yards behind. Then another wave and Parsons washed through as well. Both surfers got to their feet and began walking through the lagoon's tidal zone, moving slowly, but apparently unhurt. Little went back out and continued surfing. Parsons, done for the day, paddled into the channel and headed for *The Deeper Blue,* a hired fishing boat he'd rode out with that morning.

Surf filmmaker Steve Spaulding extended a hand and helped Parsons into the boat, then listened with surprise as Parsons described his tour through the rocks—which had in fact nearly killed him. Parsons's leash had snagged on an outcropping. For two consecutive waves he'd been pinned underwater, then a quick breath, then back down for another two waves, this time thrashing wildly for the surface. Little, fifty feet over, was strung up in near-identical fashion. Then Little's urethane cord sawed through as it rubbed against the rocks, and Parsons's Velcro-lined ankle strap, through no doing of his, somehow pulled open—an amazing bit of good luck. "I thought for sure I was dead," Parsons told Spaulding, who had turned on his camera. "Brock, too. Both of us." Spaulding commented that the wipe-out looked pretty heavy as well. Yeah, it was, Parsons answered, but more so for Little "because I was coming up, and I could feel Brock underneath me, banging up underneath me—he was still down there, really deep."

Parsons was a reliable and plain-spoken big-wave surfer, and Spaulding was impressed. "Words of advice for anyone thinking about surfing Maverick's?" he asked. "Avoid the rocks," Parsons answered with a wan smile, trying to keep it light.

Spaulding kept the tape rolling as he tried to think of another question. Nothing came to mind. Just an afterthought: "So where's Foo?"


Mark Foo was floating face-down and drifting idly to the southeast, his water-filled lungs keeping him low on the surface. Wavelets rippled over the back of his head. His arms and legs were slightly open, like a paper-doll cutout, and the tail section of his broken surfboard was still tied to his ankle. Nobody had looked for Foo after what seemed to be an unremarkable wipeout on an unremarkable wave, and now his dead body moved slowly out of the Maverick's lineup without notice or comment.

"You have to fight to hold on to consciousness," Foo said in 1986, after he nearly drowned during a two-wave hold-down at Waimea Bay. "That's a fallacy, you know—when people say to relax and go with it. That's a crock of shit. First you relax, but after a while you have to fight. You gotta have your eyes open. You have to find out which way's up, where it's bright and green, not black. You actually look at death in those situations, and if you just relax and go with it, the wave's going to hold you down forever."

Brock Little, one year later, had his own close call at Waimea. "I think I know what it would be like to drown," Little said afterward. "A desperate fight—then peacefulness as you black out."

An hour after Spaulding asked about Foo, Evan Slater spotted the purple-and-yellow surfboard fragment floating near the Pillar Point harbor entrance. Slater, Parsons, and Spaulding were gathered near the cabin of *The Deeper Blue,* motoring back to the harbor after an onshore wind had roughed the ocean surface and cleared the lineup. They watched Foo's board for a moment or two as it rocked gently in the current. Everyone knew Foo had broken his board after his late-morning wipeout—the nose section had turned up right away. Foo had no doubt swam to the beach and gone back to the parking lot for his reserve board; it was a process that could easily keep him out of the water for an hour or more.

Slater blinked at a shadow next to Foo's board. Adrenaline bombed through him, and he yelled for the boat driver to turn back. Thirty seconds later he and Parsons jumped into the water and with an awkward tandem effort got beneath Foo and lifted him up to the others, all of them now swearing and shouting high-pitched instructions. Foo was laid on his back across the engine housing, his half-open eyes staring up blankly. Somebody pressed his sternum and water flowed from both sides of his mouth, splashing onto the deck. The boat captain radioed the harbormaster, sped past the breakwater, then throttled back as two harbor paramedics intercepted *The Deeper Blue,* jumped aboard, and began a half-hour's worth of diligent but pointless resuscitation efforts.

Brock Little didn't see Mark Foo's blanket-covered body as it was lifted onto a stretcher and placed in an ambulance bound for the San

Mateo County morgue, but it looked as if somebody had posed Foo in such a way as to illustrate Little's notion of life-ending struggle and peace. His hands were clenched fists, the knuckles and tendons pushing out against the skin. His face, though, was composed and untroubled. When Ken Bradshaw arrived at the harbor, just before Foo was taken away, he pulled the blanket down from Foo's head and shoulders. It was a surreal, heartbreaking sight, but not grotesque. Foo had a small cut over his right eye and a light abrasion across his forehead, but neither injury was serious, and he was otherwise unmarked.

Bradshaw kept looking. He rested a hand on Foo's shoulder. "Then I kneeled," he remembers, "and held him, and prayed, and just kept saying, 'Why, why, why?'" Bradshaw at that point noticed that the corners of Foo's mouth were slightly turned up in what looked like a wry smile.

During a 1994 BBC interview, Mark Foo said that dying in big surf "would be a glamorous way to go; a great way to go." He told *Surfer* that "it's not tragic to die doing something you love." But nobody who knew Foo believed he had a genuine death wish. He left for Maverick's engaged to be married. He talked about having children. He was excited about upcoming work projects. Furthermore, as defined by big-wave standards, Foo was a courageous but not reckless surfer. Jose Angel, a North Shore notable from the sixties, would paddle into a twenty-five-foot wave and purposely back-flip off the tail of his board, straight into the vortex, just to see what would happen. Foo wouldn't dream of such a thing. He rode huge waves with deliberation and calculation. Dying in big waves was something he talked about the way other people talk about dying in their sleep—as a preferred choice against other types of death, not as something to be wished for, or planned for, or acted upon.

But it probably wasn't something he was scared of, either. And of course he was right—death by big-wave misadventure was indeed a glamorous way to go. "Dennis Pang and I sat under a tree at Waimea the other day," Bradshaw said just after Foo's memorial service, "and Dennis looked at me and said, 'Mark's just *laughing*. He couldn't have done it any better.' And he's right. Mark rode a ton of big waves, he surfed all over the world, he got to be famous, and he went out in a big way. He wanted to be a legend. And, boy, is he ever going to be a legend now."

# FOUR

# SURF CITY, HERE WE COME: SURF CULTURE

An Internet search in early 2004 for "surf culture" produces more than 9,000 listings, including "Surf Culture: The Art History of Surfing," "Surf Culture: The Surfer's Directory," "Stoked! A History of Surf Culture," "Sexism in Surf Culture," and "Surf Culture Canada." It's a tricky phrase. "Surf culture" might be defined as everything having to do with surfing except the actual wave-riding part—in other words, all surf-associated music, art, movies, fashion, and language. Except sometimes "surf culture" *does* include wave-riding—it depends on who's doing the defining—at which point the phrase may become broader than "surfing," which in turn might be read as synonymous with wave-riding only, and not all the accompanying movie/art/fashion stuff. Yes, well. Bring on the semantics and look what happens.

And there's more. Maybe a few dozen surfers can say "surf culture" conversationally, in a natural voice, but most have no use for the phrase, or speak it only with a light-to-moderate tone of scorn. The logic is: We *surf.* That's it. "Culture" is a fussy little highbrow suffix, attached to the sport thirty or forty years ago by a journalist or, worse, an academic. "They don't know what any of it means," TOM WOLFE wrote in "The Pump House Gang," when he described the marketers and product developers beetling across popular Southern California surf beaches in the early and mid-1960s. "It's like archaeologists discovering hieroglyphics of something, and they say, god, that's neat—Egypt!—but they don't know what the hell it is."

Given how surfing has been put to use by Hollywood, department stores, museums, automakers, toothpaste companies, fashion houses, brokerage firms, and anybody else hoping to draft a bit on the sport's dressed-down, sexed-up, sun-bleached cool, it's worth remembering that surf culture in its original form was insubordinate. California surfboard-manufacturer and big-wave crusher Greg Noll helped set the tone in the early 1950s by showing up for eighth-grade homeroom in a battered black trench coat with a rotting anchovy tucked in the side pocket. What Noll later described, somewhat uncomfortably, as "the surfing lifestyle"—the word "culture" won't likely pass his lips in this lifetime—was launched as a way to put distance between surfers and the rest of society. Non-surfers have over the past four decades learned to reproduce the language and markings of the surfer. But a difference between the two remains; because surfers are still living a life less ordinary, surf culture remains of interest.

Surf culture, by any definition, has evolved to the point where it can be held up and presented one facet at a time. SUSAN ORLEAN's "Surf Girls of Maui" wryly uncovers the genial mindlessness of teenage surfer-girl existence, but the author is also charmed by the ease and beauty of life in the wave-rich tropics. CHARLIE RUBIN's "Surf Dudes of Beach 89," set on the opposite end of the American surf spectrum, describes Rockaway Beach regulars as they arrive from Manhattan by subway and hit the waves after racing past boardwalk hookers, drug dealers, punks, and thugs.

The world pro tour is the subject of CINTRA WILSON's "Jesus Christ, Personal Friend of Surfing." Wilson, more cutting than Orlean, has a good long laugh at surf culture's expense. But she also acknowledges the attraction. "All the petty parts of surfers' brains seem blasted away by the overpowering waters," Wilson notes in an exquisite backhanded compliment, "and they have the weird, gentle majesty of giraffes or monks."

And that's the thing about surf culture. It's hard to say if it really adds up to anything. Or anything significant. But once it catches your eye, it's often hard to look away.

# "JESUS CHRIST, PERSONAL FRIEND OF SURFING"

San Francisco–born journalist/humorist Cintra Wilson began writing essays for *Salon* in 1995. Her first book of essays, *A Massive Swelling: Celebrity Re-Examined as a Grotesque, Crippling Disease and Other Cultural Revelations,* was published in 2000; *Colors Insulting to Nature,* her debut novel, was released in 2004. Wilson has also written columns for the *San Francisco Examiner* and *The Wave.* "Jesus Christ, Personal Friend of Surfing" first appeared in *Salon* in 1999. Wilson lives in New York.

CHEESE, three or four times a day! Enlarged duck organs and marinated ox problems! Fat guys with cigarettes leaning out of their mouths, wearing nothing but Speedo swimsuits and espadrilles. Ooh la la, La France!

I went to write about the 1999 Lacanau Pro, a professional surfing event wherein the Top 44 surfers in the world compete against each other on a French stretch of the Atlantic, down southwest with the Bordeaux grapes. I don't know that much about surfing, but I have a deep (if dilettantish) affection for it, and I read *Surfer* magazine every month, because for me it's sort of a semi-extreme sports version of *Tiger Beat.*

The most famous pro surfer is naturally the six-time world champ, the emerald-eyed and demure Kelly Slater, a sleek wave yogi light years beyond the rest, Neptune's Beautiful Son who rose fully formed from the seas of Florida and joined mankind to dance with the veiled and giggling ocean mysteries, and who also had a minor role on "Baywatch" for a few seasons. The international press got out of hand for Slater earlier this year when he was schtupping Pamela Anderson; Tommy Lee was released from jail or rehab or wherever he was and there was an unceremonious breakup and all the lager-dribbling press yobs in Australia and the world hounded the shit out of Kelly, because Pam Anderson is way more incredible to them than unprecedented quantum leaps in surfing artistry.

There wasn't much driving need on Slater's part to be the official Best in the World for the seventh time in a row since everyone knows he is anyway, so Slater took a break from the limelight this year, which left professional surfing without its biggest mainstream face, but it also gave everyone else in the Association of Surfing Professionals' Top 44 a fighting chance for the G-Shock ASP World Championship title.

I was dying to see the ASP in Lacanau because of my slavering personal interest in the careers of several pro surfers (I disclaim in advance the accuracy of these assessments):

**1. Cory Lopez.** I have a Cory Lopez screen saver. He's not the greatest surfer, but he's a fabulous, scowling young malcontent with diamond-hard, grapefruit-sized balls, who will take off on anything—anything, even the glass cliffs of death in Tahiti. And he can really spice up a mushy little wave session with all manner of whippy skate park aeronautics. He's a rudely talented, visceral show-stealer with unpredictable bolts of infernal genius; a monosyllabic, antisocial strange boy from an essentially momless upbringing. As a former juvenile delinquent, my bosom heaves and aches for him; I wish I was his favorite aunt or waitress or something. My main ambition for the whole trip was to see Cory walking around Lacanau with some preposterous-looking slag girlfriend, so I could ogle.

**2. Shea Lopez.** Cory's long-suffering Good Older Brother, kind, handsome and helpful, who seems blessed with a totally serene brain chemistry and an amazingly triangular waistline, which is pleasantly obvious due to the fact that he wears his pants slightly below his pubic hairline. Shea, though a connoisseur of greasy kid tricks, seems more elegant than flashy, and appears to have a diligent and mature aesthetic approach. He's also done a remarkably graceful and ego-less job of being Cory's Brother (second in line for the Lopez limelight). I read an article once that said that when they were kids, Cory used to hit Shea for breathing too loud.

**3. Mark Occhilupo.** Aka "Occy," a big koala bear of a boy, the most charming, affable, regular Australian human ever, with a big, square, blond head and an underbite. He was headed for a serious shot at the World Championship in the late '80s when he decided to stop surfing, lie on his couch, watch TV and get really fat for a few years. Now he's 33, he's trim, he's back, and he wants the title, and it's kind of weepily inspirational how great he's doing.

There was also a gaggle of surfers that I was crazy to see because I so love to hate them:

**1. Ken Bradshaw & Layne Beachley.** Ken Bradshaw is not a surfing professional but an older, veteran hard-ass—a surfboard shaper and Sunset Beach local, with an ancient reputation for ultra-hardcore big wave surfing and a general tone of ass-holically judgmental macho outdoorsmanship. Bradshaw seems to have built Layne Beachley, his much younger girlfriend, out of the refuse of his own frustrated ambitions. He coaches the living shit out of her. She is his creature; they walk around the beach smug and tan like the Tom & Nicole of the watersports set, and he shapes her surfboards with obnoxiously classified measurements and she publicly gushes over him whenever she wins anything and it's all kind of grimy. Beachley, last year's women's world champion, is fearfully unstoppable and most likely going to be world champ again this year.

**2. Damien "Iceman" Hardman.** A two-time former world champion and Occy's biggest threat to this year's championship, he is monstrously capable but strangely cursed to be the Richard Nixon of the surfing world. He's rigid with media unlovability, broody, uncute and super ambitious. He also colors inside the lines and racks up the points by being a ruthless and precise techno-surgeon. The Iceman is coldly serious and basically impossible for teenage girls to get a crush on. The utterly heart-melting bonhomie of Occy makes Hardman come off like everyone's Evil Stepdad.

**3. Andy Irons.** Andy has a knack for showing up on videos half drunk and talking in an especially depraved-sounding Hawaiian patois—a nearly unintelligible mélange of surfer dude-isms and mangled English—and coming off like a real parking lot alky with a big foam head. But on the positive side, he's a really exciting surfer with the kind of brute animal energy that makes your blood pay attention. You can find Andy on the last page of the latest issue of *Surfer,* charging the tube holding a can of Bintang Pilsner, with his eyes rolling half up into his head, looking red, bloated and poisoned like fat Elvis.

Andy's little brother Bruce is another legendary surfer; I keep having this horrible "Afterschool Special" plot premonition about the Irons brothers, wherein Andy gets dropped from the ASP Top 44 as soon as Bruce qualifies, then Andy gets thrown in jail and Bruce's career drags down after him in some hopeless brother-loyalty drama, filled with lots of painful sunset shots and loud young manly agony.

We showed up in Lacanau on the second day of the competition. The Mister and I ended up in the eye of the hurricane when I flashed my press credentials and we lucked into being spontaneously mentored by Sarge, a famous old Australian hippie photojournalist who began his career by taking the first published shots of Occy, way back in Cronulla, Australia, in the Day-Glo '80s. "We lo-o-o-ve Occy," I confessed, which is true enough—the Mister and I admittedly own and watch a lot of surf-porn videos, "The Occumentary" being one of our top faves—lots of hardcore, cum-shot surf action, unimpeded by bogus plots or excessive living-room lo-jinks.

"Oh, I assure you," twinkled Sarge Santa-Clausishly in a thick Aussie brogue, "you cain't love him helf as much as Oy do." Aww, sweet.

It was like walking in the Green Room at the Oscars, or in the locker room of the Chicago Bulls. Seventy percent of the people around us were centerfolds from *Surfer*. As if on cue to make me scream, in walked Dark Prince Cory Lopez, with a girlfriend who surpassed all of my most fiendish voyeuristic hopes: a cobra of an unsmiling hula princess with eyebrows plucked into fierce black commas. I was beside myself with visual gratification; it was one of those transcendental vacation moments.

A vast majority of surfers are built like sea turtles—short as hell. Most of the women are barely over 5 feet; many of the men are barely over 5-5—with wide torsos and really short legs and arms with wide hands like flippers, and long, rubbery spines that seem to have too many vertebrae, like the Ingres Odalisque. Extremely low center of gravity. The Brazilian pros are practically Oompa Loompas—they weigh little more than the chicks, and it does nothing but magical things for their wave ability.

Shea Lopez, who is uncharacteristically tall, was standing right next to me, so I throttled my nerve and went up to him, wild with too much saliva and agitated fan-girl fear, to ask what I figured was a Good Question: "Uh—Mr. Lopez? Is there anything you'd like to complain about in the world of professional surfing?" "Uhhh...well, not really..." "Nothing? What about the judging criteria? Anyone you'd like to personally assassinate?" He shook his head and shrugged. "It all looks pretty good... we're pretty fortunate..." "Nothing? You wouldn't change *anything*? Not if you were king of the world?!" "Well," he said patiently, "if you want to change things, then you're not happy where you are. I'm a lot happier here than I would be on Wall Street. We're in the sun, at the beach..."

I mumbled something conclusive and shriveled away, feeling like a corrupt, scab-picking New York vampire. It was a moment like the one in that Bob Marley documentary, when the idiot journalist asks Bob how he justified using the "fruits of Babylon" (i.e., the technology of the recording

industry) in order to further his message of Jah Love, and Bob, not meaning to hurt the guy or humiliate him but inadvertently doing it anyway, looked at the guy quizzically and said, "Babylon don't got no fruits!"

Anyone who has fallen in love with a group of uniformed firemen at the supermarket—noticing their polite, jokey teamwork and easy, 100-proof manliness while they shop together for the station—would probably like being around surfers. Like firemen, they've seen it all. They've plunged over the blue edge of eternity and been held underwater until their lungs turned to cannonballs; they've been scraped on sharp animals and poisonous invisible landscapes until all that remained of them was the basics of throbbing humanity: good sense, casual good feeling, good sportsmanship, respect for life.

There are the odd bullheaded tantrum-throwers like Hawaiian tiki monster Sunny Garcia, who had a couple of colorful shit-fits and poked some guy in the chest while we were there, but for the most part, all the petty parts of surfers' brains seem blasted away by the overpowering waters and they have the weird, gentle majesty of giraffes or monks. Something about living enslaved to an element like fire or water, I suppose, gives them that 1940s Royal Air Force, movie-hero kind of self-possession. Anyway, I felt dirty and mean after talking to Shea Lopez, and kind of sick with admiration for him.

I tried to think of a different Good Question, but all I could think of was "Would you rather have flippers or an extra dick?" so I abandoned the role of interviewer and decided to soak up the *atmosphere.*

Cory Lopez, to my dismay, was quickly out, beaten down into 17th place by one of the tiny Brazilians. Surf contests whittle down quickly and dramatically after the initial elimination heats.

The high point of the quarterfinals was when Luke Egan, Aussie good guy, friend of Occy, beat ruthless point-eater Damien Hardman, Occy's biggest threat to the world title, which was the surf-war equivalent to sitting on the land mine and saving the batch of little children. "Puissance!" the French announcer yelled. "Très radical, et très fort!"

Besides the surfing, the best show was the enormous windfall of bronzed tube-top blond, preening surf-groupies with 12-pack abs who looked like L.A. strippers: professionally huge tits and Japanimation-quality round asses, high shoes and short shorts. A real TV-quality hooter show, which stood out starkly in comparison to the top female surfers like Megan Abubo, who had a quietly bratty manner and big Walkman earmuffs on her head, and dressed way down in shapeless casuals like a sullen teenage raver, looking like she needed to be grounded or spanked or something.

Bradshaw was hulking around for the women's surf-offs, overzealously rubbing so much wax on Layne Beachley's surfboard we thought it might sink from the weight.

Surfers are a spiritual bunch; a great many of them are big Jesus freaks, in a real Old Testament, Book of Jeremiah, the-Apocalypse-cometh kind of way. Christian surfers like Glyndyn Ringrose and Tim Curran are always doling out quotes about how "He's coming soon!" and attributing all their victories to personal favors from Christ. He was the first shredder to walk on water, I suppose.

Apropos of Jesus, Sarge handed me a couple of articles he'd recently written for various surf magazines about the Top 44 at the midpoint of the '99 tour. We were a little stunned by what he had to say about Occy:

> After a comeback that nearly rivaled that of Jesus Christ, Occy came from obese proportions and a non-surfing recluse four years ago to show the world that anything is possible... The highlight of the life of Jesus Christ was his rising from the dead, after dying nailed to a cross. He was 33; so is Occy. He has already come back from the "dead" and he is currently doing the nailing. Should he be uplifted to world champ this year, the blinding glare and reverence

from the surfing world will be every bit as stunning as that which befitted the ascension into heaven of Jesus Christ! God Bless Him!

Wow, we thought. We really don't love Occy half as much as Sarge does. I read on; Sarge had a quote about Shea Lopez: "He remains outspoken and indignant at the current judging criteria, and refuses to change from surfing 'his way.'"

Shea *himself* is quoted in the document as saying, "The judging is stuck in the '80s contest pack-'em-in routine." OK, Shea. I'm just... (sniff)...I'm hurt, OK? Why would you complain to Sarge and not *me*? Is it my *body*? (sniff, sob). Don't touch me.

The final contest came down to Occy vs. Tim Curran, the Jesus-loving bantamweight from Ventura, who happens to be an ankle-high wave virtuoso. We thought it was a real dilemma; if Jesus is on Tim Curran's side and Occy is Jesus, who gets to win?

After a tense if uneventfully flat-watered heat, Curran was smiled upon by Occy and won, but it didn't matter—Occy, securing second place, ended up surfing way ahead of Damien Hardman in the points toward World Championtude, which is what mattered most. Shea Lopez came in third, launching him impressively past his rock-star brother in the ASP ratings to a solid 18th, which was surely some kind of karmic victory. Megan Abubo beat Ken Bradshaw's "Champion Beachley" prototype, and all was right with the world. Even Andy Irons looked healthy and relatively sober, despite the fact that he was wearing a wool stocking cap over his ears to cover a terrifying self-imposed 3 A.M. beer-binge haircut.

We left Lacanau feeling grateful, knowing that Occy has a sacred plan for us all. Praise him!

## EXCERPT FROM
# *THE PUMP HOUSE GANG*

Virginia-born Tom Wolfe invented the smart and exclamatory New Journalism with a 1963 *Esquire* feature titled "There Goes (Varoom! Varoom!) That Kandy-Kolored Tangerine-Flake Streamline Baby." He's one of America's most popular and acclaimed authors in both fiction and nonfiction, and his bestselling books include *The Right Stuff* (1979), *The Bonfire of the Vanities* (1987), and *A Man in Full* (1998). "The Pump House Gang," Wolfe's look at Southern California surf culture, first appeared as a feature in a 1966 issue of the *New York World Journal Tribune;* two years later it was the lead essay in a book of the same title.

OUR BOYS NEVER HAIR OUT. The black panther has black feet. Black feet on the crumbling black panther. Pan-thuh. Mee-dah. Pam Stacy, 16 years old, a cute girl here in La Jolla, California, with a pair of orange bell-bottom hip-huggers on, sits on a step about four steps down the stairway to the beach and she can see a pair of revolting black feet without lifting her head. So she says it out loud, "The black panther."

Somebody farther down the stairs, one of the boys with the *major* hair and khaki shorts, says, "The black feet of the black panther."

"Mee-dah," says another kid. This happens to be the cry of a, well, *underground* society known as the Mac Meda Destruction Company.

"The pan-thuh."

"The poon-thuh."

All these kids, seventeen of them, members of the Pump House crowd, are lollygagging around the stairs down to Windansea Beach, La Jolla, California, about 11 A.M., and they all look at the black feet, which are a woman's pair of black street shoes, out of which stick a pair of old veiny white ankles, which lead up like a senile cone to a fudge of tallowy, edematous flesh, her thighs, squeezing out of her bathing suit, with old faded yellow bruises on them, which she probably got from running eight feet to catch a bus or something. She is standing with her old work-a-hubby, who has on *san*dals: you know, a pair of navy-blue anklet socks and these sandals with big, wide, new-smelling tan straps going this way and that, *for keeps.* Man, they look like orthopedic sandals, if one can imagine that. Obviously, these people come from Tucson or Albuquerque or one of those hincty adobe towns. All these hincty, crumbling black feet come to La Jolla-by-the-sea from the adobe towns for the weekend. They even drive in cars all full of thermos bottles and mayonnaisey sandwiches and some kind of latticework wooden-back support for the old crock who drives and Venetian blinds on the back window.

"The black panther."

"Pan-thuh."

"Poon-thuh."

"Mee-dah."

Nobody says it to the two old crocks directly. God, they must be practically 50 years old. Naturally, they're carrying every piece of garbage imaginable: the folding aluminum chairs, the newspapers, the lending-library book with the clear plastic wrapper on it, the sunglasses, the sun ointment, about a vat of goo—

It is a Mexican standoff. In a Mexican standoff, both parties narrow their eyes and glare but nobody throws a punch. Of course, nobody in the Pump House crowd would ever even jostle these people or say anything right to them; they are too cool for that.

Everybody in the Pump House crowd looks over, even Tom Coman, who is a cool person. Tom Coman, 16 years old, got thrown out of his garage last night. He is sitting up on top of the railing, near the stairs, up over the beach, with his legs apart. Some nice long willowy girl in yellow slacks is standing on the sidewalk but leaning into him with her arms around his body, just resting. Neale Jones, 16, a boy with great lank perfect surfer's hair, is standing nearby with a Band-Aid on his upper lip, where the sun has burnt it raw. Little Vicki Ballard is up on the sidewalk. Her older sister, Liz, is down the stairs by the Pump House itself, a concrete block, 15 feet high, full of machinery for the La Jolla water system. Liz is wearing her great "Liz" styles, a hulking rabbit-fur vest and black-leather boots over her Levis, even though it is about 85 out here and the sun is plugged in up there like God's own dentist lamp and the Pacific is heaving in with some fair-to-middling surf. Kit Tilden is lollygagging around, and Tom Jones, Connie Carter, Roger Johnson, Sharon Sandquist, Mary Beth White, Rupert Fellows, Glenn Jackson, Dan Watson from San Diego, they are all out here, and everybody takes a look at the panthers.

The old guy, one means, you know, he must be practically 50 years old, he says to his wife, "Come on, let's go farther up," and he takes her by her fat upper arm as if to wheel her around and aim her away from here.

But she says, "No! We have just as much right to be here as they do."

"That's *not the point*—"

"Are you going to—"

"*Mrs. Roberts,*" the work-a-hubby says, calling his own wife by her official married name, as if to say she took a vow once and his word is law, even if he is not testing it with the blond kids here—"farther up, *Mrs. Roberts.*"

They start to walk up the sidewalk, but one kid won't move his feet, and, oh, god, her work-a-hubby breaks into a terrible shaking Jell-O smile as she steps over them, as if to say, Excuse me, sir, I don't mean to make trouble, please, and don't you and your colleagues rise up and jump me, screaming *Gotcha*—

Mee-dah!

But exactly! This beach *is* verboten for people practically 50 years old. This is a segregated beach. They can look down on Windansea Beach and see nothing but lean tan kids. It is posted "no swimming" (for safety reasons), meaning surfing only. In effect, it is segregated by age. From Los Angeles on down the California coast, this is an era of age segregation. People have always tended to segregate themselves by age, teenagers hanging around with teenagers, old people with old people, like the old men who sit on the benches up near the Bronx Zoo and smoke black cigars. But before, age segregation has gone on within a larger community. Sooner or later during the day everybody has melted back into the old community network that embraces practically everyone, all ages.

But in California today surfers, not to mention rock 'n' roll kids and the hot-rodders or Hair Boys, named for their fanciful pompadours—all sorts of sets of kids—they don't merely hang around together. They establish whole little societies for themselves. In some cases they live with one another for months at a time. The "Sunset Strip" on Sunset Boulevard used to be a kind of Times Square for Hollywood hot dogs of all ages, anyone who wanted to promenade in his version of the high life. Today "The Strip" is almost completely the preserve of kids from about 16 to 25. It is lined with go-go clubs. One of them, a place called It's Boss, is set up for people 16 to 25 and won't let in anybody over 25, and there are some terrible I'm-dying-a-thousand-deaths scenes when a girl comes up with her boyfriend and the guy at the door at It's Boss doesn't think she looks under 25 and tells her she will have to produce some identification proving she is young enough to come in here and live The Strip kind of life and—she's *had* it, because she can't get up the I.D. and nothing in the world is going to make a woman look stupider than to stand around trying to argue *I'm younger than I look, I'm younger than I look.* So she practically shrivels up like a Peruvian shrunken head in front of her boyfriend and he trundles her off, looking for some place you can get an old doll like this into. One of the few remaining clubs for "older people," curiously, is the Playboy Club. There are apartment houses for people 20 to 30 only, such as the Sheri Plaza in Hollywood and the E'Questre Inn in Burbank. There are whole suburban housing developments, mostly private developments, where only people over 45 or 50 can buy a house. Whole towns, meantime, have become identified as "young": Venice, Newport Beach, Balboa—or "old": Pasadena, Riverside, Coronado Island.

Behind much of it—especially something like a whole nightclub district of a major city, "The Strip," going teenage—is, simply, money. World War II and the prosperity that followed pumped incredible amounts of money into the population, the white population at least, at every class level. All of a sudden here is an area with thousands of people from 16 to 25 who can get their hands on enough money to support a whole nightclub belt and to have the cars to get there and to set up autonomous worlds of their own in a fairly posh resort community like La Jolla—

—Tom Coman's garage. Some old bastard took Tom Coman's garage away from him, and that means eight or nine surfers are out of a place to stay.

"I went by there this morning, you ought to see the guy," Tom Coman says. Yellow Stretch Pants doesn't move. She has him around the waist. "He was out there painting and he had this brush and about a thousand gallons of ammonia. He was really going to scrub me out of there."

"What did he do with the furniture?"

"I don't know. He threw it out."

"What are you going to do?"

"I don't know."

"Where are you going to stay?"

"I don't know. I'll stay on the beach. It wouldn't be the first time. I haven't had a place to stay for three years, so I'm not going to start worrying now."

Everybody thinks that over awhile. Yellow Stretch just hangs on and smiles. Tom Coman, 16 years old, piping fate again. One of the girls says, "You can stay at my place, Tom."

"Um. Who's got a cigarette?"

Pam Stacy says, "You can have these."

Tom Coman lights a cigarette and says, "Let's have a destructo." A destructo is what can happen in a garage after eight or 10 surfers are kicked out of it.

"Mee-dah!"

"Wouldn't that be bitchen?" says Tom Coman. Bitchen is a surfer's term that means "great," usually.

"Bitchen!"

"Mee-dah!"

It's incredible—that old guy out there trying to scour the whole surfing life out of that garage. He's a pathetic figure. His shoulders are hunched over and he's dousing and scrubbing away and the sun doesn't give him a tan, it gives him these... *mottles* on the back of his neck. But never mind! The hell with destructo. One only has a destructo spontaneously, a Dionysian... *bursting out,* like those holes through the wall during the Mac Meda Destruction Company Convention at Manhattan Beach—Mee-dah!

Something will pan out. It's a magic economy—yes!—all up and down the coast from Los Angeles to Baja California kids can go to one of these beach towns and live the complete surfing life. They take off from home and get to the beach, and if they need a place to stay, well, somebody rents a garage for twenty bucks a month and everybody moves in, girls and boys. Furniture—it's like, one means, you know, one *appropriates* furniture from here and there. It's like the Volkswagen buses a lot of kids now use as beach wagons instead of woodies. Woodies are old station wagons, usually Fords, with wooden bodies, from back before 1953. One of the great things about a Volkswagen bus is that one can . . . *exchange* motors in about three minutes. A good VW motor exchanger can go up to a parked Volkswagen, and a few ratchets of the old wrench here and it's up and out and he has a new motor. There must be a few nice old black panthers around wondering why their nice hubby-mommy VWs don't run so good anymore—but—then—they—are—probably—puzzled—about—a—lot of things. Yes.

Cash—it's practically in the air. Around the beach in La Jolla a guy can walk right out in the street and stand there, stop cars and make the candid move. Mister, I've got a quarter, how about 50 cents so I can get a *large* draft. Or, I need some after-ski boots. And the panthers give one a Jell-O smile and hand it over. Or a guy who knows how to do it can get $40 from a single night digging clams, and it's nice out there. Or he can go around and take up a collection for a keg party, a keg of beer. Man, anybody who won't kick in a quarter for a keg is a jerk. A couple of good keg collections—that's a trip to Hawaii, which is the surfer's version of a trip to Europe: there is a great surf and great everything there. Neale spent three weeks in Hawaii last year. He got $30 from a girl friend, he scrounged a little here and there and got $70 more and he headed off for Hawaii with $100.02, that being the exact plane fare, and borrowed 25 cents when he got there to . . . blast the place up. He spent the 25 cents in a photo booth, showed the photos to the people on the set of *Hawaii* and got a job in the movie. What's the big orgy about money? It's warm, nobody even wears shoes, nobody is starving.

All right, Mother gets worried about all this, but it is limited worry, as John Shine says. Mainly, Mother says, *Sayonara,* you all, and you head off for the beach.

The thing is, everybody, practically everybody, comes from a good family. Everyone has been... *reared well,* as they say. Everybody is very upper-middle, if you want to bring it down to that. It's just that this is a new order. Why hang around in the hubby-mommy household with everybody getting neurotic hang-ups with each other and slamming doors and saying, Why can't they have some privacy? Or, it doesn't mean anything that I have to work for a living, does it? It doesn't mean a thing to you. All of you just lie around here sitting in the big orange easy chair smoking cigarettes. I'd hate for you to have to smoke standing up, you'd probably get phlebitis from it—Listen to me, Sarah—

—why go through all that? Its a good life out here. Nobody is mugging everybody for money and affection. There are a lot of bright people out here, and there are a lot of interesting things. One night there was a toga party in a garage, and everybody dressed in sheets, like togas, boys and girls and they put on the appropriated television set to an old Deanna Durbin movie and turned off the sound and put on Rolling Stones records, and you should have seen Deanna Durbin opening her puckered kumquat mouth with Mick Jagger's voice bawling out, *I ain't got no satisfaction.* Of course, finally everybody started pulling the togas off each other, but that is another thing. And one time they had a keg party down on the beach in Mission Bay and the lights from the amusement park were reflected all over the water and that, the whole design of the thing, those nutty lights, that was part of the party. Liz put out the fire throwing a "sand potion" or something on it. One can laugh at Liz and her potions, her necromancy and everything, but there is a lot of thought going into it, a lot of, well, mysticism.

You can even laugh at mysticism if you want to, but there is a kid like Larry Alderson, who spent two years with a monk, and he learned a lot of stuff, and Artie Nelander is going to spend next summer with some Outer Mongolian tribe; he really means to do that. Maybe the "mysterioso" stuff is a lot of garbage, but still, it is interesting. The surfers around the Pump House use that word, mysterioso, quite a lot. It refers to the mystery of the Oh Mighty Hulking Pacific Ocean and everything. Sometimes a guy will stare at the surf and say, "Mysterioso." They keep telling the story of Bob Simmons' wipeout, and somebody will say "mysterioso."

Simmons was a fantastic surfer. He was fantastic even though he had

a bad leg. He rode the really big waves. One day he got wiped out at Windansea. When a big wave overtakes a surfer, it drives him right to the bottom. The board came in but he never came up and they never found his body. Very mysterioso. The black panthers all talked about what happened to "the Simmons boy." But the mysterioso thing was how he could have died at all. If he had been one of the old pan-thuhs, hell, sure he could have got killed. But Simmons was, well, one's own age, he was the kind of guy who could have been in the Pump House gang, he was . . . *immune,* he was plugged into the whole pattern, he could feel the whole Oh Mighty Hulking Sea, he didn't have to think it out step by step. But he got wiped out and killed. Very mysterioso.


Immune! If one is in the Pump House gang and really keyed in to this whole thing, it's—well, one is . . . *immune,* one is not full of black pan-thuh panic. Two kids, a 14-year-old girl and a 16-year-old boy, go out to Windansea at dawn, in the middle of winter, cold as hell, and take on 12-foot waves all by themselves. The girl, Jackie Haddad, daughter of a certified public accountant, wrote a composition about it, just for herself, called "My Ultimate Journey":

"It was six o'clock in the morning, damp, foggy and cold. We could feel the bitter air biting at our cheeks. The night before, my friend Tommy and I had seen one of the greatest surf films, *Surf Classics.* The film had excited us so much we made up our minds to go surfing the following morning. That is what brought us down on the cold, wet, soggy sand of Windansea early on a December morning.

"We were the first surfers on the beach. The sets were rolling in at eight to 10, filled with occasional 12-footers. We waxed up and waited for a break in the waves. The break came, neither of us said a word, but instantly grabbed our boards and ran into the water. The paddle out was difficult, not being used to the freezing water.

"We barely made it over the first wave of the set, a large set. Suddenly Tommy put on a burst of speed and shot past me. He cleared the biggest wave of the set. It didn't hit me hard as I rolled under it. It dragged me almost 20 yards before exhausting its strength. I climbed on my board gasping for air. I paddled out to where Tommy was resting. He laughed at me for being wet already. I almost hit him but I began laughing, too. We rested a few minutes and then lined up our position with a well known spot on the shore.

"I took off first. I bottom-turned hard and started climbing up the wave. A radical cut-back caught me off balance and I fell, barely hanging onto my board. I recovered in time to see Tommy go straight over the falls on a 10-footer. His board shot nearly 30 feet in the air. Luckily, I could get it before the next set came in, so Tommy didn't have to make the long swim in. I pushed it to him and then laughed. All of a sudden Tommy yelled, 'Outside!'

"Both of us paddled furiously. We barely made it up to the last wave, it was a monster. In precision timing we wheeled around and I took off. I cut left in reverse stance, then cut back, driving hard toward the famous Windansea bowl. As I crouched, a huge wall of energy came down over me, covering me up. I moved toward the nose to gain more speed and shot out of the fast-flowing suction just in time to kick out as the wave closed out.

"As I turned around I saw Tommy make a beautiful drop-in, then the wave peaked and fell all at once. Miraculously he beat the suction. He cut back and did a spinner, which followed with a reverse kick-up.

"Our last wave was the biggest. When we got to shore, we rested, neither of us saying a word, but each lost in his own private world of thoughts. After we had rested, we began to walk home. We were about half way and the rain came pouring down. That night we both had bad colds, but we agreed it was worth having them after the thrill and satisfaction of an extra good day of surfing."

John Shine and Artie Nelander are out there right now. They are just "outside," about one fifth of a mile out from the shore, beyond where the waves start breaking. They are straddling their surfboards with their backs to the shore, looking out toward the horizon, waiting for a good set. Their backs look like some kind of salmon-colored porcelain shells, a couple of tiny shells bobbing up and down as the swells roll under them, staring out to sea like Phrygian sacristans looking for a sign.

John and Artie! They are—they are what one means when one talks about the surfing life. It's like, you know, one means, they have this life all of their own; it's like a glass-bottom boat, and it floats over the "real" world, or the square world or whatever one wants to call it. They are not exactly off in a world of their own, they are and they aren't. What it is, they float right through the real world, but it can't touch them. They do these things, like the time they went to Malibu, and there was this party in some guy's apartment, and there wasn't enough *legal* parking space for everybody, and so somebody went out and painted the red curbs white and everybody parked. Then the cops came. Everybody ran out. Artie and John took an airport bus to the Los Angeles Airport, just like they were going to take a plane, in khaki shorts and T-shirts with Mac Meda Destruction Company stenciled on them. Then they took a helicopter to Disneyland. At Disneyland crazy Ditch had his big raincoat on and a lot of flasks strapped onto his body underneath, Scotch, bourbon, all kinds of stuff. He had plastic tubes from the flasks sticking out of the flyfront of his raincoat and everybody was sipping whiskey through the tubes—

—Ooooo-eeee—Mee-dah! They chant this chant, Mee-dah, a real

fakey deep voice, and it *really bugs people.* They don't know what the hell it is. It is the cry of the Mac Meda Destruction Company. The Mac Meda Destruction Company is . . . an *underground* society that started in La Jolla about three years ago. Nobody can remember exactly how; they have arguments about it. Anyhow, it is mainly something to *bug* people with and organize huge beer orgies with. They have their own complete, bogus phone number in La Jolla. They have Mac Meda Destruction Company decals. They stick them on phone booths, on cars, any place. Some mommy-hubby will come out of the shopping plaza and walk up to his Mustang, which is supposed to make him a hell of a tiger now, and he'll see a sticker on the side of it saying, "Mac Meda Destruction Company," and for about two days or something he'll think the sky is going to fall in.

But the big thing is the parties, the "conventions." Anybody can join, any kid, anybody can come, as long as they've heard about it, and they can only hear about it by word of mouth. One was in the Sorrento Valley, in the gulches and arroyos, and the fuzz came, and so the older guys put the young ones and the basket cases, the ones just too stoned out of their gourds, into the tule grass, and the cops shined their searchlights and all they saw was tule grass, while the basket cases moaned scarlet and oozed on their bellies like reptiles and everybody else ran down the arroyos, yelling Mee-dah.

The last one was at Manhattan Beach, inside somebody's poor hulking house. The party got *very Dionysian* that night and somebody put a hole through one wall, and everybody else decided to see if they could make it bigger. Everybody was stoned out of their hulking gourds, and it got to be about 3:30 A.M. and everybody decided to go see the riots. These were the riots in Watts. The *Los Angeles Times* and the *San Diego Union* were all saying, WATTS NO-MAN'S LAND and STAY WAY FROM WATTS YOU GET YO' SE'F KILLED, but naturally nobody believed that. Watts was a blast, and the Pump House gang was immune to the trembling gourd panic rattles of the L. A. *Times* black pan-thuhs. Immune!

So John Shine, Artie Nelander and Jerry Sterncorb got in John's VW bus, known as the Hog of Steel, and they went to Watts. Gary Wickham and some other guys ran into an old man at a bar who said he owned a house in Watts and had been driven out by the drunk niggers. So they drove in a car to save the old guy's house from the drunk niggers. Artie John had a tape recorder and decided they were going to make a record called "Random Sounds from the Watts Riots." They drove right into Watts in the Hog of Steel and there was blood on the streets and roofs blowing off the stores and all these apricot flames and drunk Negroes falling through the busted plate glass of the liquor stores. Artie got a nice recording of a lot of Negroes chanting "Burn, baby, burn." They all got out and talked to some Negro kids in a gang going into a furniture store, and the Negro kids didn't say Kill Whitey or Geed'um or any of that. They just said, Come on, man, it's a party and it's free. After they had been in there for about three hours talking to Negroes and watching drunks collapse in the liquor stores, some cop with a helmet on came roaring up and said, "Get the hell out of here, you kids, we cannot and will not provide protection."

Meantime, Gary Wickham and his friends drove in in a car with the old guy, and a car full of Negroes *did* stop them and say, Whitey, Geed'um, and all that stuff, but one of the guys in Gary's car just draped a pistol he had out the window and the colored guys drove off. Gary and everybody drove the old guy to his house and they all walked in and had a great raunchy time drinking beer and raising hell. A couple of Negroes, the old guy's neighbors, came over and told the old guy to cut out the racket. There were flames in the sky and ashes coming down with little rims of fire on them, like apricot crescents. The old guy got very cocky about all his "protection" and went out on the front porch about dawn and started yelling at some Negroes across the street, telling them "No more drunk niggers in Watts" and a lot of other unwise slogans. So Gary Wickham got up and everybody left. They were there about four hours altogether and when they drove out, they had to go through a National Guard checkpoint, and a lieutenant from the San Fernando Valley told them he could not and would not provide protection.

But exactly! Watts just happened to be what was going on at the time, as far as the netherworld of La Jolla surfing was concerned, and so one goes there and sees what is happening and comes back and tells everybody about it and laughs at the L.A. *Times*. That is what makes it so weird when all these black pan-thuhs come around to pick up "surfing styles," like the clothing manufacturers. They don't know what any of it means. It's like archaeologists discovering hieroglyphics of something, and they say, god, that's neat—Egypt!—but they don't know what the hell it is. They don't know anything about ... *The Life.* It's great to think of a lot of old emphysematous pan-thuhs in the Garment District in New York City struggling in off the street against a gummy 15-mile-an-hour wind full of soot and coffee-brown snow and gasping in the elevator to clear their old nicotine-phlegm tubes on the way upstairs to make out the invoices on a lot of surfer stuff for 1966, the big nylon windbreakers with the wide, white horizontal competition stripes, nylon swimming trunks with competition stripes, bell-bottom slacks for girls, the big hairy sleeveless jackets, vests, the blue "tennies," meaning tennis shoes, and the ... *look,* the Major Hair, all this long lank blond hair, the plain face kind of tanned and bleached out at the same time, but with big eyes. It all starts in a few places, a few strategic groups, the Pump House gang being one of them, and then it moves up the beach, to places like Newport Beach and as far up as Malibu.

Well, actually there is a kind of back-and-forth thing with some of the older guys, the old heroes of surfing, like Bruce Brown, John Severson,

Hobie Alter and Phil Edwards. Bruce Brown will do one of those incredible surfing movies and he is out in the surf himself filming Phil Edwards coming down a 20-footer in Hawaii, and Phil has on a pair of nylon swimming trunks, which he has had made in Hawaii, because they dry out fast—and it is like a grapevine. Everybody's got to have a pair of nylon swimming trunks, and then the manufacturers move in, and everybody's making nylon swimming trunks, boxer trunk style, and pretty soon every kid in Utica, N.Y., is buying a pair of them, with the competition stripe and the whole thing, and they never heard of Phil Edwards. So it works back and forth—but so what? Phil Edwards is part of it. He may be an old guy, he is 28 years old, but he and Bruce Brown, who is even older, 30, and John Severson, 32, and Hobie Alter, 29, never haired out to the square world even though they make thousands. Hair refers to courage. A guy who "has a lot of hair" is courageous; a guy who "hairs out" is yellow.

Bruce Brown and Severson and Alter are known as the "surfing millionaires." They are not millionaires, actually, but they must be among the top businessmen south of Los Angeles. Brown grossed something around $500,000 in 1965 even before his movie *Endless Summer* became a hit nationally; and he has only about three people working for him. He goes out on a surfboard with a camera encased in a plastic shell and takes his own movies and edits them himself and goes around showing them himself and narrating them at places like the Santa Monica Civic Auditorium, where 24,000 came in eight days once, at $1.50 a person, and all he has to pay is for developing the film and hiring the hall. John Severson has the big surfing magazine, *Surfer.* Hobie Alter is the biggest surfboard manufacturer, all hand-made boards. He made 5,000 boards in 1965 at $140 a board. He also designed the "Hobie" skate boards and gets 25 cents for every one sold. He grossed between $900,000 and $1 million in 1964.

God, if only everybody could grow up like these guys and know that crossing the horror dividing line, 25 years old, won't be the end of everything. One means, keep on living *The Life* and not get sucked into the ticky-tacky life with some insurance salesman sitting forward in your stuffed chair on your wall-to-wall telling you that life is like a football game and you sit there and take that stuff. The hell with that! Bruce Brown has the money and *The Life*. He has a great house on a cliff about 60 feet above the beach at Dana Point. He is married and has two children, but it is not that hubby-mommy you're-breaking-my-gourd scene. His office is only two blocks from his house and he doesn't even have to go on the streets to get there. He gets on his Triumph scrambling motorcycle and cuts straight across a couple of vacant lots and one can see him . . . *bounding* to work over the vacant lots. The Triumph hits ruts and hummocks and things and Bruce Brown bounces into the air with the motor—*thragggggh*—moaning away, and when he gets to the curbing in front of his office, he just leans back and pulls up the front wheel and hops it and gets off and walks into the office barefooted. *Barefooted;* why not? He wears the same things now that he did when he was doing nothing but surfing. He has on a faded gray sweatshirt with the sleeves cut off just above the elbows and a pair of faded corduroys. His hair is the lightest corn yellow imaginable, towheaded, practically white, from the sun. Even his eyes seem to be bleached. He has a rain-barrel old-apple-tree Tom-Sawyer little-boy roughneck look about him, like Bobby Kennedy.

Sometimes he carries on his business right there at the house. He has a dugout room built into the side of the cliff, about 15 feet down from the level of the house. It is like a big pale green box set into the side of the cliff, and inside is a kind of upholstered bench or settee you can lie down on if you want to and look out at the Pacific. The surf is crashing like a maniac on the rocks down below. He has a telephone in there. Sometimes it will ring, and Bruce Brown says hello, and the surf is crashing away down below, roaring like mad, and the guy on the other end, maybe one of the TV networks calling from New York or some movie hair-out from Los Angeles, says:

"What is all that noise? It sounds like you're sitting out in the surf."

"That's right," says Bruce Brown, "I have my desk out on the beach now. It's nice out here."

The guy on the other end doesn't know what to think. He is another Mr. Efficiency who just got back from bloating his colon up at a three-hour executive lunch somewhere and now he is Mr.-Big-Time-Let's-Get-This-Show-on-the-Road.

"On the beach?"

"Yeah. It's cooler down here. And it's good for you, but it's not so great for the desk. You know what I have now? A warped leg."

"A warped leg?"

"Yeah, and this is an $800 desk."


Those nutball California kids—and he will still be muttering that five days after Bruce Brown delivers his film, on time, and Mr. Efficiency is still going through memo thickets or heaving his way into the bar car to Darien—in the very moment that Bruce Brown and Hobie Alter are both on their motorcycles out on the vacant lot in Dana Point. Hobie Alter left his surfboard plant about two in the afternoon because the wind was up and it would be good catamaranning and he wanted to go out and see how far he could tip his new catamaran without going over, and he did tip it over, about half a mile out in high swells and it was hell getting the thing right side up again. But he did, and he got back in time to go scrambling on the lot with Bruce Brown. They are out there, roaring over the ruts, bouncing up in the air, and every now and then they roar up the embankment so they can...fly, going up in the air about six feet off the ground as they come up off the embankment—*thraaagggggh*—all these people in the houses around there come to the door and look out. These two . . . nuts are at it again. Well, they can only fool around there for 20 minutes, because that is about how long it takes the cops to get there if anybody gets burned up enough and calls, and what efficient business magnate wants to get hauled off by the Dana Point cops for scrambling on his motorcycle in a vacant lot.

Bruce Brown has it figured out so no one in the whole rubber-bloated black pan-thuh world can trap him, though. He bought a forest in the Sierras. There is nothing on it but trees. His own wilds: no house, no nothing, just Bruce Brown's forest. Beautiful things happen up there. One day, right after he bought it, he was on the edge of his forest, where the road comes into it, and one of these big rancher king motheroos with the broad belly and the $70 lisle Safari shirt comes tooling up in a Pontiac convertible with a funnel of dust pouring out behind. He gravels it to a great flashy stop and yells:

"Hey! You!"

Of course, what he sees is some towheaded barefooted kid in a torn-off sweatshirt fooling around the edge of the road.

"Hey! You!"

"Yeah?" says Bruce Brown.

"Don't you know this is private property?"

"Yeah," says Bruce Brown.

"Well, then, why don't you get your ass off it?"

"Because it's mine, it's my private property," says Bruce Brown. "Now you get *yours* off it."

And Safari gets a few rays from that old apple-tree rain-barrel don't-cross-that-line look and doesn't say anything and roars off, slipping gravel, the dumb crumbling pan-thuh.

But . . . perfect! It is like, one means, you know, poetic justice for all the nights Bruce Brown slept out on the beach at San Onofre and such places in the old surfing days and would wake up with some old crock's black feet standing beside his head and some phlegmy black rubber voice saying:

"All right, kid, don't you know this is private property?"

And he would prop his head up and out there would be the Pacific Ocean, a kind of shadowy magenta-mauve, and one thing, *that* was nobody's private property—

But how many Bruce Browns can there be? There is a built-in trouble with age segregation. Eventually one *does* reach the horror age of 25, the horror dividing line. Surfing and the surfing life have been going big since 1958, and already there are kids who—well, who aren't kids anymore, they are pushing 30, and they are stagnating on the beach. Pretty soon the California littoral will be littered with these guys, stroked out on the beach like beached white whales, and girls, too, who can't give up the mystique, the mysterioso mystique, Oh Mighty Hulking Sea, who can't *conceive* of living any other life. It is pathetic when they are edged out of groups like the Pump House gang. Already there are some guys who hang around with the older crowd around the Shack who are stagnating on the beach. Some of the older guys, like Gary Wickham, who is 24, are still in *The Life,* they still have it, but even Gary Wickham will be 25 one day and then 26 and then...and then even pan-thuh age. Is one really going to be pan-thuh age one day? Watch those black feet go. And Tom Coman still snuggles with Yellow Slacks, and Liz still roosts moodily in her rabbit fur at the bottom of the Pump House and Pam still sits on the steps contemplating the mysterioso mysteries of Pump House ascension and John and Artie still bob, tiny pink porcelain shells, way out there waiting for godsown bitchen *set,* and godsown sun still turned on like a dentist's lamp and so far—

—the panthers scrape on up the sidewalk. They are at just about the point Leonard Anderson and Donna Blanchard got that day, December 6,

1964, when Leonard said, Pipe it, and fired two shots, one at her and one at himself. Leonard was 18 and Donna was 21—21!—god, for a girl in the Pump House gang that is almost the horror line right there. But it was all so mysterioso. Leonard was just lying down on the beach at the foot of the Pump House, near the stairs, just talking to John K. Weldon down there, and then Donna appeared at the top of the stairs and Leonard got up and went up the stairs to meet her, and they didn't say anything, they weren't *angry* over anything, they never had been, although the police said they had, they just turned and went a few feet down the sidewalk, away from the Pump House and—blam blam!—these two shots. Leonard fell dead on the sidewalk and Donna died that afternoon in Scripps Memorial Hospital. Nobody knew what to think. But one thing it seemed like— well, it seemed like Donna and Leonard thought they had lived *The Life* as far as it would go and now it was running out. All that was left to do was—but that is an *insane* idea. It can't be like that, *The Life* can't run out, people can't change all that much just because godsown chronometer runs on and the body packing starts deteriorating and the fudgy tallow shows up at the thighs where they squeeze out of the bathing suit—

Tom, boy! John, boy! Gary, boy! Neale, boy! Artie, boy! Pam, Liz, Vicki, Jackie Haddad! After all this—just a pair of bitchen black panther bunions inching down the sidewalk away from the old Pump House stairs?

## "SURF GIRLS OF MAUI"

Susan Orlean's "Surf Girls of Maui" originally appeared in a 1998 issue of *Outside,* and was the inspiration for Universal's 2002 movie *Blue Crush.* The New York–based Orlean has published two collections of essays, *The Bullfighter Checks Her Makeup: My Encounters With Extraordinary People* (2001) which includes "Surf Girls," and *Saturday Night* (1990). The award-winning movie *Adaptation* was based on her 1999 nonfiction bestseller *The Orchid Thief.* Orlean is a staff writer for the *New Yorker.*

THE MAUI SURFER GIRLS love each other's hair. It is awesome hair, long and bleached by the sun, and it falls over their shoulders straight, like water, or in squiggles, like seaweed, or in waves. They are forever playing with it—yanking it up into ponytails, or twisting handfuls and securing them with chopsticks or pencils, or dividing it as carefully as you would divide a pile of coins and then weaving it into tight yellow plaits. Not long ago I was on the beach in Maui watching the surfer girls surf, and when they came out of the water they sat in a row facing the ocean, and each girl took the hair of the girl in front of her and combed it with her fingers and crisscrossed it into braids. The Maui surfer girls even love the kind of hair that I dreaded when I was their age, 14 or so—they love that wild, knotty, bright hair, as big and stiff as carpet, the most un-straight, un-sleek, un-ordinary hair you could imagine, and they can love it, I suppose, because when you are young and on top of the world you can love anything you want, and just the fact that you love it makes it cool and fabulous. A Maui surfer girl named Gloria Madden has that kind of hair—thick red corkscrews striped orange and silver from the sun, hair that if you weren't beautiful and fearless you'd consider an affliction that you would try to iron flat or stuff under a hat. One afternoon I was driving two of the girls to Blockbuster Video in Kahului. It was the day before a surfing competition, and the girls were going to spend the night at their coach's house up the coast so they'd be ready for the contest at dawn. On contest nights, they fill their time by eating a lot of food and watching hours of surf videos, but on this particular occasion they decided they needed to rent a movie, too, in case they found themselves with 10 or 20 seconds of unoccupied time. On our way to the video store, the girls told me they admired my rental car and said that they thought rental cars totally ripped and that they each wanted to get one. My car, which until then I had sort of hated, suddenly took on a glow. I asked what else they would have if they could have anything in the world. They thought for a moment, and then the girl in the backseat said, "A moped and thousands of new clothes. You know, stuff like thousands of bathing suits and thousands of new board shorts."

"I'd want a Baby-G watch and new flip-flops, and one of those cool sports bras like the one Iris just got," the other said. She was in the front passenger seat, barefoot, sand-caked, twirling her hair into a French knot. It was a half-cloudy day with weird light that made the green Hawaiian hills look black and the ocean look like zinc. It was also, in fact, a school day, but these were the luckiest of all the surfer girls because they are home-schooled so that they can surf any time at all. The girl making the French knot stopped knotting. "Oh, and also," she said, "I'd really definitely want crazy hair like Gloria's."

The girl in the backseat leaned forward and said, "Yeah, and hair like Gloria's, for sure."

A lot of the Maui surfer girls live in Hana, the little town at the end of the Hana Highway, a fraying thread of a road that winds from Kahului,

Maui's primary city, over a dozen deep gulches and dead-drop waterfalls and around the backside of the Haleakala Crater to the village. Hana is far away and feels even farther. It is only 55 miles from Kahului, but the biggest maniac in the world couldn't make the drive in less than two hours. There is nothing much to do in Hana except wander through the screw pines and the candlenut trees or go surfing. There is no mall in Hana, no Starbucks, no shoe store, no Hello Kitty store, no movie theater—just trees, bushes, flowers, and gnarly surf that breaks rough at the bottom of the rocky beach. Before women were encouraged to surf, the girls in Hana must have been unbelievably bored. Lucky for these Hana girls, surfing has changed. In the '60s, Joyce Hoffman became one of the first female surf aces, and she was followed by Rell Sunn and Jericho Poppler in the seventies and Frieda Zamba in the '80s and Lisa Andersen in this decade, and thousands of girls and women followed by example. In fact, the surfer girls of this generation have never known a time in their lives when some woman champion wasn't ripping surf.

The Hana girls dominate Maui surfing these days. Theory has it that they grow up riding such mangy waves that they're ready for anything. Also, they are exposed to few distractions and can practically live in the water. Crazy-haired Gloria is not one of the Hana girls. She grew up near the city, in Haiku, where there were high-school race riots—Samoans beating on Filipinos, Hawaiians beating on Anglos—and the mighty pull of the mall at Kaahumanu Center. By contrast, a Hana girl can have herself an almost pure surf adolescence.

One afternoon I went to Hana to meet Theresa McGregor, one of the best surfers in town. I missed our rendezvous and was despairing because Theresa lived with her mother, two brothers, and sister in a one-room shack with no phone and I couldn't think of how I'd find her. There is one store in Hana, amazingly enough called the General Store, where you can buy milk and barbecue sauce and snack bags of dried cuttlefish; once I realized I'd missed Theresa I went into the store because there was no other place to go. The cashier looked kindly, so I asked whether by any wild chance she knew a surfer girl named Theresa McGregor. I had not yet come to appreciate what a small town Hana really was. "She was just in here a minute ago," the cashier said. "Usually around this time of the day she's on her way to the beach to go surfing." She dialed the McGregors' neighbor—she knew the number by heart—to find out which beach Theresa had gone to. A customer overheard the cashier talking to me, and she came over and added that she'd just seen Theresa down at Ko'ki beach and that Theresa's mom, Angie, was there too, and that some of the other Hana surfer girls would probably be down any minute but they had a History Day project due at the end of the week so they might not be done yet at school.

I went down to Ko'ki. Angie McGregor was indeed there, and she pointed out Theresa bobbing in the swells. There were about a dozen other people in the water, kids mostly. A few other surfer parents were up on the grass with Angie—fathers with hairy chests and ponytails and saddle-leather sandals, and mothers wearing board shorts and bikini tops, passing around snacks of unpeeled carrots and whole-wheat cookies and sour cream Pringles—and even as they spoke to one another, they had their eyes fixed on the ocean, watching their kids, who seemed like they were a thousand miles away, taking quick rides on the tattered waves.

After a few minutes, Theresa appeared up on dry land. She was a big, broad-shouldered girl, 16 years old, fierce-faced, somewhat feline, and quite beautiful. Water was streaming off of her, out of her shorts, out of her long hair, which was plastered to her shoulders. The water made it look inky, but you could still tell that an inch from her scalp her hair had been stripped of all color by the sun. In Haiku, where the McGregors lived until four years ago, Theresa had been a superstar soccer player, but Hana was too small to support a soccer league, so after they moved Theresa first devoted herself to becoming something of a juvenile delinquent and then gave that up for surfing. Her first triumph came right away, in 1996, when she won the open women's division at the Maui Hana Mango competition. She was one of the few fortunate amateur surfer girls who had sponsors. She got free boards from Matt Kinoshita, her coach, who owns and designs Kazuma Surfboards; clothes from Honolua Surf Company; board leashes and bags from Da Kine Hawaii; skateboards from Flexdex. Boys who surfed got a lot more for free. Even a little bit of sponsorship made the difference between surfing and not surfing. As rich a life as it seemed, among the bougainvillea and the green hills and the passionflowers of Hana, there was hardly any money. In the past few years the Hawaiian economy had sagged terribly, and Hana had never had much of an economy to begin with. Last year, the surfer moms in town held a fund-raiser bake sale to send Theresa and two Hana boys to the national surfing competition in California.

Theresa said she was done surfing for the day. "The waves totally suck now," she said to Angie. "They're just real trash." They talked for a moment and agreed that Theresa should leave in the morning and spend the next day or two with her coach Matt at his house in Haiku, to prepare for the Hawaiian Amateur Surf Association contest that weekend at Ho'okipa Beach near Kahului. Logistics became the topic. One of the biggest riddles facing a surfer girl, especially a surfer girl in far-removed Hana, is how to get from point A to point B, particularly when carrying a large surfboard. The legal driving age in Hawaii is 15, but the probable car-ownership age, unless you're rich, is much beyond that; also, it seemed that nearly every surfer kid I met in Maui lived in a single-parent, single- or no-car household in which spare drivers and vehicles were rare. I was planning to go back around the volcano anyway to see the contest, so I said I'd take Theresa and another surfer, Lilia Boerner, with me, and someone else would make it from Hana to Haiku with their boards. That night I met Theresa, Angie, and Lilia and a few of their surfer friends at a take-out shop in town, and then I went to the room I'd rented at Joe's Rooming House. I stayed up late reading about how Christian missionaries had banned surfing when they got to Hawaii in the late 1800s, but how by 1908 general longing for the sport overrode spiritual censure and surfing resumed. I dozed off with the history book in my lap and the hotel television tuned to a Sprint ad showing a Hawaiian man and his granddaughter running hand-in-hand into the waves.

The next morning I met Lilia and Theresa at Ko'ki beach at 8:00, after they'd had a short session on the waves. When I arrived they were standing under a monkeypod tree beside a stack of backpacks. Both of them

were soaking wet, and I realized then that a surfer is always in one of two conditions: wet or about to be wet. Also, they are almost always dressed in something that can go directly into the water: halter tops, board shorts, bikini tops, jeans. Lilia was 12 and a squirt, with a sweet, powdery face and round hazel eyes and golden fuzz on her arms and legs. She was younger and much smaller than Theresa, less plainly athletic but very game. Like Theresa, she was home-schooled, so she could surf all the time. So far Lilia was sponsored by a surf shop and by Matt Kinoshita's Kazuma Surfboards. She had a twin brother who was also a crafty surfer, but a year ago the two of them came upon their grandfather after he suffered a fatal

tractor accident, and the boy hadn't competed since. Their family owned a large and prosperous organic fruit farm in Hana. I once asked Lilia if it was fun to live on a farm. "No," she said abruptly. "Too much fruit."

We took a back road from Hana to Haiku, as if the main road weren't bad enough. The road edged around the back of the volcano, through sere yellow hills. The girls talked about surfing and about one surfer girl's mom, whom they described as a full bitch, and a surfer's dad, who according to Theresa "was a freak and a half because he took too much acid and he tweaked." I wondered if they had any other hobbies besides surfing. Lilia said she used to study hula.

"Is it fun?"

"Not if you have a witch for a teacher, like I did," she said. "Just screaming and yelling at us all the time. I'll never do hula again. Surfing's cooler, anyway."

"You're the man, Lilia," Theresa said, tartly. "Hey, how close are we to Grandma's Coffee Shop? I'm starving." Surfers are always starving. They had eaten breakfast before they surfed; it was now only an hour or two later, and they were hungry again. They favor breakfast cereal, teriyaki chicken, french fries, rice, ice cream, candy, and a Hawaiian specialty called Spam Masubi, which is a rice ball topped with a hunk of Spam and seaweed. If they suffered from the typical teenage girl obsession with their weight, they didn't talk about it and they didn't act like it. They were so active that whatever they ate probably melted away.

"We love staying at Matt's," Lilia said, "because he always takes us to Taco Bell." We came around the side of a long hill and stopped at Grandma's. Lilia ordered a garden burger and Theresa had an "I'm Hungry" sandwich with turkey, ham, and avocado. It was 10:30 A.M. As she was eating, Lilia said, "You know, the Olympics are going to have surfing, either in the year 2000 or 2004, for sure."

"I'm so on that, dude," Theresa said. "If I can do well in the nationals this year, then . . ." She swallowed the last of her sandwich. She told me that eventually she wanted to become an ambulance driver, and I could picture her doing it, riding on dry land the same waves of adrenaline that she rides now. I spent a lot of time trying to picture where these girls might be in 10 years. Hardly any are likely to make it as pro surfers—even though women have made a place for themselves in pro surfing, the number who really make it is still small, and even though the Hana girls rule Maui surfing, the island's soft-shell waves and easygoing competitions have produced very few world-class surfers in recent years. It doesn't seem to matter to them. At various cultural moments, surfing has appeared as the embodiment of everything cool and wild and free; this is one of those moments. To be a girl surfer is even cooler, wilder, and more modern than being a guy surfer: Surfing has always been such a male sport that for a man to do it doesn't defy any received ideas; to be a girl surfer is to be all that surfing represents, plus the extra charge of being a girl in a tough guy's domain. To be a surfer girl in a cool place like Hawaii is perhaps the apogee of all that is cool and wild and modern and sexy and defiant. The Hana girls, therefore, exist at that highest point—the point where being brave, tan, capable, and independent, and having a real reason to wear all those surf-inspired clothes that other girls wear for fashion, is what matters completely. It is, though, just a moment. It must be hard to imagine an ordinary future and something other than a lunar calendar to consider if you've grown up in a small town in Hawaii, surfing all day and night, spending half your time on sand, thinking in terms of point breaks and barrels and roundhouse cutbacks. Or maybe they don't think about it at all. Maybe these girls are still young enough and in love enough with their lives that they have no special foreboding about their futures, no uneasy presentiment that the kind of life they are leading now might eventually have to end.

———

Matt Kinoshita lives in a fresh, sunny ranch at the top of a hill in Haiku. The house has a big living room with a fold-out couch and plenty of floor space. Often, one or two or 10 surfer girls camp in his living room because they are in a competition that starts at 7:00 the next morning, or because they are practicing intensively and it is too far to go back and forth from Hana, or because they want to plow through Matt's stacks of surfing magazines and Matt's library of surfing videos and Matt's piles of water-sports clothing catalogs. Many of the surfer girls I met didn't live with their fathers, or in some cases didn't even have relationships with their fathers, so sometimes, maybe, they stayed at Matt's just because they were in the mood to be around a concerned older male. Matt was in his late twenties. As a surfer he was talented enough to compete on the world tour but had decided to skip it in favor of an actual life with his wife, Annie, and their baby son, Chaz. Now he was one of the best surfboard shapers on Maui, a coach, and head of a construction company with his dad. He sponsored a few grown-up surfers and still competed himself, but his preoccupation was with kids. *Surfing* magazine once asked him what he liked most about being a surfboard shaper, and he answered, "Always being around stoked groms!" He coached a stoked-grom boys' team as well as a stoked-grom girls' team. The girls' team was an innovation. There had been no girls' surfing team on Maui before Matt established his three years ago. There was no money in it for him—it actually cost him many thousands of dollars each year—but he loved to do it. He thought the girls were the greatest. The girls thought he was the greatest, too. In build, Matt looked a lot like the men in those old Hawaiian surfing prints—small, chesty, gravity-bound. He had perfect features and hair as shiny as an otter's. When he listened to the girls he kept his head tilted, eyebrows slightly raised, jaw set in a grin. Not like a brother, exactly—more like the cutest, nicest teacher at school, who could say stern, urgent things without them stinging. When I pulled into the driveway with the girls, Matt was in the yard loading surfboards into a pickup. "Hey, dudes," he called to Lilia and Theresa. "Where are your boards?"

"Someone's going to bring them tonight from Hana," Theresa said. She jiggled her foot. "Matt, come on, let's go surfing already."

"Hey, Lilia," Matt said. He squeezed her shoulders. "How're you doing, champ? Is your dad going to surf in the contest this weekend?"

Lilia shrugged and looked up at him solemnly. "Come on, Matt," she said. "Let's go surfing already."

They went down to surf at Ho'okipa, to a section that is called Pavilles because it is across from the concrete picnic pavilions on the beach. Ho'okipa is not a lot like Hana. People with drinking problems like to hang out in the pavilions. Windsurfers abound. Cars park up to the edge of the sand. The landing pattern for the Kahului Airport is immediately overhead. The next break over, the beach is prettier; the water there is called Girlie Bowls, because the waves get cut down by the reef and are more manageable, presumably, for girlies. A few years ago, some of the Hana surfer girls met their idol Lisa Andersen when she was on Maui. She was very shy and hardly said a word to them, they told me, except to suggest they go surf Girlie Bowls. I thought it sounded mildly insulting, but they weren't exactly sure what she was implying and they didn't brood about it. They hardly talked about her. She was like some unassailable force.

We walked past the pavilions. "The men at this beach are so sexist," Lilia said, glaring at a guy swinging a boombox. "It's really different from Hana. Here they're always, you know, staring, and saying, 'Oh, here come the giiiirls,' and 'Oh, hello, ladies,' and stuff. For us white girls, us haoles, I think they really like to be gross. So gross. I'm serious."

"Hey, the waves look pretty sick," Theresa said. She watched a man drop in on one and then whip around against it. She whistled and said, "Whoooa, look at that sick snap! That was so rad, dude! That was the sickest snap I've seen in ages! Did you see that?"

They were gone in an instant. A moment later, two blond heads popped up in the black swells, and then they were up on their boards and away.


Dinner at Matt's: tons of barbecued chicken, loaves of garlic bread, more loaves of garlic bread. Annie Kinoshita brought four quarts of ice cream out of the freezer, lined them up on the kitchen counter, and watched them disappear. Annie was fair, fine-boned, and imperturbable. She used to be a surfer "with hair down to her frickin' butt," according to Theresa. Now she was busy with her baby and with overseeing the open-door policy she and Matt maintained in their house. That night, another surfer girl, Elise Garrigue, and a 14-year-old boy, Cheyne Magnusson, had come over for dinner and were going to sleep over, too. Cheyne was one of the best young surfers on the island. His father, Tony, was a professional skateboarder. Cheyne was the only boy who regularly crashed at Matt and Annie's. He and the girls had the Platonic ideal of a Platonic relationship. "Hell, these wenches are virgins," Annie said to me, cracking up. "These wenches don't want anything to do with that kind of nastiness."

"Shut up, haole," Theresa said.

"I was going to show these virgins a picture of Chaz's head coming out when I was in labor," Annie yelled, "and they're all, 'No, no, no, don't!'"

"Yeah, she's all, 'Look at this grossness!'" Theresa said. "And we're all, 'Shut up, fool.'"

"Duh," Lilia said. "Like we'd even want to see a picture like that."

The next day was the preliminary round of the Quiksilver HASA Competition, the fourth of eight HASA competitions on Maui leading to the state championships and then the nationals. It was a two-day competition—preliminaries on Saturday, finals on Sunday. In theory, the girls should have gone to bed early because they had to get up at five, but that was just a theory. They pillow-fought for an hour, watched *Sabrina, the Teenage Witch* and *Boy Meets World* and another episode of *Sabrina,* then watched a couple of Kelly Slater surfing videos, had another pillow fight, ate a few bowls of cereal, then watched *Fear of a Black Hat,* a movie spoofing the rap-music world that they had seen so many times that they could recite most of the dialogue by heart. Only Elise fell asleep at a decent hour. She happened to be French and perhaps had overdosed on American pop culture earlier than the rest. Elise sort of blew in to Hawaii with the trade winds: She and her mother had left France and were planning to move to Tahiti, stopped on Maui en route, and never left. It was a classic Hawaiian tale. No one comes here for ordinary reasons in ordinary ways. They run away to Maui from places like Maryland or Nevada or anyplace they picture themselves earthbound, landlocked, stuck. They live in salvaged boxcars or huts or sagging shacks just to be near the waves. Here, they can see watery boundlessness everywhere they turn, and all things are fluid and impermanent. I don't know what time it was when the kids finally went to sleep because I was on the living room floor with my jacket over my head for insulation. When I woke up a few hours later, the girls were dressed for the water, eating bowls of Cinnamon Toast Crunch and Honey Bunches of Oats, and watching *Fear of a Black Hat* again. It was a lovely morning and they were definitely ready to show Hana surfing to the world. Theresa was the first to head out the door. "Hey, losers," she yelled over her shoulder, "let's go."

The first heats of the contest had right-handed waves, three or four feet high, silky but soft on the ends so that they collapsed into whitewash as they broke. You couldn't make much of an impression riding something like that, and one after another the Hana girls came out of the water scowling. "I couldn't get any kind of footing," Theresa said to Matt. "I was, like, so on it, but I looked like some kind of kook sliding around."

"My last wave was a full-out closeout," Lilia said. She looked exasperated. "Hey, someone bust me a towel." She blotted her face. "I really blew it," she groaned. "I'm lucky if I even got five waves."

The girls were on the beach below the judges' stand, under Matt's cabana, along with Matt's boys' team and a number of kids he didn't sponsor but who liked hanging out with him more than with their own sponsors. The kids spun like atoms. They ran up and down the beach and stuffed sand in each others' shorts and fought over pieces of last night's chicken that Annie had packed for them in a cooler. During a break between heats, Gloria with the crazy hair strolled over and suddenly the incessant motion paused. This was like an imperial visitation. After all, Gloria was a seasoned-seeming 19-year-old who had just spent the year surfing the monstrous waves on Oahu's North Shore, plus she did occasional work for Rodney Kilborn, the contest promoter, plus she had a sea turtle tattooed on her ankle, and most important, according to the Hana girls, she was an absolutely dauntless bodyboarder who would paddle out into wall-size waves, even farther out than a lot of guys would go.

"Hey, haoles!" Gloria called out. She hopped into the shade of the cabana. That day, her famous hair was woven into a long red braid that hung over her left shoulder. Even with her hair tamed, Gloria was an amazing-looking person. She had a hardy build, melon-colored skin, and a wide, round face speckled with light-brown freckles. Her voice was light and tinkly, and had that arched, rising-up, quizzical inflection that made everything she said sound like a jokey, good-natured question. "Hey, Theresa?" she said. "Hey, girl, you got it going on? You've got great wave strategy? Just keep it up, yeah? Oh, Elise? You should paddle out harder? OK? You're doing great, yeah? And Christie?" She looked around for a surfer girl named Christie Wickey, who got a ride in at four that morning from Hana. "Hey, Christie?" Gloria said when she spotted her. "You should go out further, yeah? That way you'll be in better position for your wave, OK? You guys are the greatest, seriously? You rule, yeah? You totally rule, yeah?"

At last the junior women's division preliminary results were posted. Theresa, Elise, and two other girls on Matt's team made the cut, as well as a girl whom Matt knew but didn't coach. Lilia had not made it. As soon as she heard, she tucked her blond head in the crook of her elbow and cried. Matt sat with her and talked quietly for a while, and then one by one the other girls drifted up to her and murmured consoling things, but she was inconsolable. She hardly spoke for the rest of the afternoon until the open men's division, which Matt had entered. When his heat was announced, she lifted her head and brushed her hand across her swollen eyes. "Hey, Matt!" she called as he headed for the water. "Rip it for the girls!"

That night, a whole pack of them slept at Matt's—Theresa, Lilia, Christie, Elise, Monica Cardoza from Lahaina, and sisters from Hana named Iris Moon and Lily Morningstar, who had arrived too late to surf in the junior women's preliminaries. There hadn't been enough entrants in the open women's division to require preliminaries, so the competition was going to be held entirely on Sunday and Iris would be able to enter. Lily wasn't planning to surf at all, but as long as she was able to get a ride out of Hana she took it. This added up to too many girls at Matt's for Cheyne's liking, so he had fled to another boy's house for the night. Lilia was still blue. She was quiet through dinner, and then as soon as she finished she slid into her sleeping bag and pulled it over her head. The other girls stayed up for hours, watching videos and slamming each other with pillows and talking about the contest. At some point someone asked where Lilia was. Theresa shot a glance at her sleeping bag and said quietly, "Did you guys see how upset she got today? I'm like, 'Take it easy, Lilia!' and she's all 'Leave me alone, bitch.' So I'm like, 'Whatever.'"

They whispered for a while about how sensitive Lilia was, about how hard she took it if she didn't win, about how she thought one of them had wrecked a bathing suit she'd loaned her, about how funny it was that she even cared since she had so many bathing suits and for that matter always had money for snacks, which most of them did not. When I said a Hana girl could have a pure surfing adolescence, I knew it was part daydream, because no matter how sweet the position of a beautiful, groovy Hawaiian teenager might be in the world of perceptions, the mean measures of the human world don't ever go away. There would always be something else to want and be denied. More snack money, even.

Lilia hadn't been sleeping. Suddenly she bolted out of her sleeping bag and screamed, "Fuck you, I hate you stupid bitches!" and stormed toward the bathroom, slugging Theresa on the way.

The waves on Sunday came from the left, and they were stiff and smallish, with crisp, curling lips. The men's and boys' heats were narrated over the PA system, but during the girls' and women's heats the announcer was silent, and the biggest racket was the cheering of Matt's team. Lilia had toughened up since last night. Now she seemed grudgeless but remote. Her composure made her look more grown-up than 12. When I first got down to the beach she was staring out at the waves, chewing a hunk of dried papaya and sucking on a candy pacifier. A few of the girls were far off to the right of the break where the beach disappeared and lustrous black rocks stretched into the water. Christie told me later that they hated being bored more than anything in the world and between heats they were afraid they might be getting a little weary, so they decided to perk themselves up by playing on the rocks. It had worked. They charged back from the rocks shrieking and panting. "We got all dangerous," she said. "We jumped off this huge rock into the water. We almost got killed, which was great." Sometimes watching them I couldn't believe that they could head out so offhandedly into the ocean—this ocean, which had rolls of white water coming in as fast as you could count them, and had a razor-blade reef hidden just below the surface, and was full of sharks. The girls, on the other hand, couldn't believe I'd never surfed—never ridden a wave standing up or lying down, never cut back across the whitewash and sent up a lacy veil of spray, never felt a longboard slip out from under me and then felt myself pitched forward and under for that immaculate, quiet, black instant when all the weight in the world presses you down toward the ocean bottom until the moment passes and you get spat up on the beach. I explained I'd grown up in Ohio, where there is no surf, but that didn't satisfy them; what I didn't say was that I'm not sure that at 15 I had the abandon or the indomitable sense of myself that you seem to need in order to look at this wild water and think, I will glide on top of those waves. Theresa made me promise I'd try to surf at least once someday. I promised, but this Sunday was not going to be that day. I wanted to sit on the sand and watch the end of the contest, to see the Hana girls take their divisions, including Lilia, who placed third in the open women's division, and Theresa, who won the open women's and the junior women's division that day. Even if it was just a moment, it was a perfect one, and who wouldn't choose it over never having the moment at all? When I left Maui that afternoon, my plane circled over Ho'okipa, and I wanted to believe I could still see them down there and always would see them down there, snapping back and forth across the waves.

# CHARLIE RUBIN

## "SURF DUDES OF BEACH 89"

Charlie Rubin began his career as a writer for *National Lampoon, Spy,* and the *Village Voice*. He later became a staff writer for *In Living Color, Seinfeld,* and *The Jon Stewart Show,* and served as executive producer for VH1's *Hey Joel*. Rubin is also a dramatic writing instructor at New York University. "Surf Dudes of Beach 89" originally appeared in a 1997 issue of the *New York Times* magazine.

T HE DODGE VAN is making good time along the Belt Parkway. It should, because it's 8 A.M. on a Labor Day Sunday. Three Brooklyn Surfers are in the van. They all live in Manhattan, every one of them. Adam Mergan is driving. By day he delivers for a New Jersey pharmaceuticals company. He's 27. Beside him is his girlfriend, Casey M., 24, who's in real estate, and in back with six or seven surfboards is Eric Watson, 41, a hairdresser from the salon at Bergdorf's.

They are heading out to Rockaway Beach. It is in the Rockaways that these three and scores like them got their nickname, Brooklyn Surfers, even though they are obviously Manhattan Surfers, because that's what kids from Rockaway, in Queens, call anybody who isn't a Rockaway Surfer.

There are people who surf Montauk and Jones Beach. Good for them. This is a story about people who swear by beaches they can subway to, where the waves maybe don't "break steady" but satisfy an exploding population of mostly teenagers and 20-ish surfers who design their lives around wave sizes, who track "ocean temp" on the Internet's buoy map of the East Coast and who take guff from weirded-out straphangers for lugging their boards onto the A train and give it right back, sprinkling Hawaiian words into their obscenities. It's these folks who have been raising eyebrows along Rockaway's 7.5 miles of beaches, because the "Rockapulco" Surfers know that the Brooklyn Surfers are as dedicated to wave-riding as they are. Maybe more. Because where you can't see surf, you must think it. All the time. N.B.W. Nothing But Waves.

Adam and Casey are discussing a jellyfish. "The lifeguard went right into it, face first," says Casey. "She's O.K."

Adam says: "You get bit by a man-of-war like they have in Florida, it causes total paralysis. That I know for a fact."

Eric says, "I'm just going to keep my eye out for it." Adam parks a block from Beach 89, and everybody carries a couple of boards across Rockaway Beach Boulevard.

"I got a new stick," says Adam, who has taken to building boards on the roof of his Upper East Side high-rise. "It's a fast little gun."

"I can't wait to ride my Mako," Eric says. This is a tomato-red, Beach Boys–era classic longboard that Eric bought, used, last week for $175.

"It's sweet," says Adam.

"It's a *log*," Eric says. He repaired it, adding a "Jesus Saves" sticker. "Was Pretty Boy out Friday?"

"Yeah," says Casey. "With that Brooklyn kid who dropped out of school to surf."

Adam suddenly says, "I gotta catch some swell!"

Eric suddenly says, "This homeless guy wanted to go surfing, but I couldn't find him."

Beach 89 is the hot beach, but the surfers migrate as far west as 92d with the waves. The lifeguards are flexible about it, in part because the original surfers' beach, Beach 38, was overrun by hookers and dealers. There were muggings, and one Brooklyn boy is famous for surfing with a knife taped under his board. These days, surfers who brave 38th drive their cars right up onto the boardwalk so they can surf while guarding their car stereos.

The Brooklyn Surfers are studying the ocean. Two months into hurricane season (which can run through November) and so far it's a serious dud; which, after a fierce '95 and a solid '96, is just killing everybody. "The tropicals are out there, enticing us," one says, but they weren't coming near enough. Still, Adam and Casey intend to start living in a tent on the beach next week.

Now they wrap towels around their waists and change from shorts into wetsuits, pulling and fastening, done. Adam nudges Eric: "Look, that's a ridable wave. That's a nice righthanded wave." He unzips his silver board bags. Some surfers are moving into the water, to the right of the rock jetty, Adam paddles out. After 20 minutes he's back, and all the other surfers follow him to the left of the jetty. Adam has a quiet prominence here.

A kid goes by, announcing: "There's gonna be something Wednesday! Guy saw it on the Doppler!"

Eric gave away his boards when he moved to Manhattan from California 10 months ago, figuring that part of his life was over. Now he shouts, "Maiden voyage!" and rides his Mako all the way in on a nothing wave, beaming.

By noon, the sand is packed with "whoo girls"—local slang for women who get suntans until a surfer makes a good ride, then jump up and go: "Whoo! Whoo! Whoo!" Casey's different. She's usually the only female surfer on 89. "It's not really encouraged," she shrugs. "I just went in the water and did it."

Two examples of harmless surfer macho, from another day, on Beach 118: 1) Several surfers two-fingering raw soup from cans—a 15-

year-old surfer called it a "pointless local energy fad." 2) Surfing with a Jets helmet on.

And then there's "localism."

Tommy Sena, 43, owns the Rockaway Beach Surf Shop. He learned surfing in the early 60's by watching John and Tom McGonigal, who had watched Pat Reen and the Schreifels, Wally and Kenny, who may have watched a lifeguard named Mickey McManamon in the 50's. Back then, nobody resented new surfers. The more the merrier. "Today," Tommy admits, "there's a little bit of pressure down the beach."

Turfy beach fighting among surfers is way up, according to a Rockaway regular. He broke it down this way: Rockaway's predominantly Irish surfers don't like being crowded off their home waves by Brooklyn's Italian and Jewish surfers. Nobody's delighted by the Hispanics who come over from the Bronx or the Haitian and Jamaican "wave snakers" or the random gay surfqueen.

The surfer party line is that these clashes are about waves, not race, and only occur when the waves are way up, making the competitive stakes higher. (Rockaway veterans estimate great wave days at about one in six during the summer, much higher in winter, when the hardcore surf through blistering cold and nasty ice-cream headaches.) On exceptional days, surfers say, you can see the snarls on people's faces, and hear the "power surfing"—grunting and sneering while riding—out in the street.

Adam is talking about whether he's had problems on the beach with Rockaway Surfers: "No." Shrugs. "One guy, but we didn't go to fists. He backed off. Sometimes two or three people catch a good wave and no one seems to mind. He didn't want anyone on his wave. He said, 'Peek!' I said, 'You peek!' He left his board in the sand, he wouldn't come back for it. He had to be escorted off the beach by three guys." Adam adds: "I was a pretty

wild guy. I'm sure you can tell by my tattoos. I tried to change my ways and be a human being now because I met a woman I love."

An 11-year-old surfer from Brooklyn, Michael Vagle, has been run down on the water by locals. Xavier Ceniceros, 26, snorts: "All the Irish geeks out there. They're shanty Irish. Young punks who think they have something to prove. But once you show that you're as determined as they are, you kind of earn your localism."

A surfer from Beach 135 says: "You know what the Brooklyn Surfers really hate? When we call 'em Brooklyn Surfers."

Oddly, for a while in the early 1980's, there was a shabby storefront near the Brooklyn courthouses that wore its name proudly: BROOKLYN SURFERS. It was a teen-age boys' clubhouse, and inside, in the dead of winter, you could see them marching around barefoot with surfboards while their girlfriends assembled a "Have a Surf Xmas!" window display. Several of them lived upstairs in a kind of surfer flop, having quit school to be boxboys or Xerox room guys or to take night jobs to surf all day. That profile still fits a lot of (real) Brooklyn Surfers.

In contrast to Rockaway kids from strong working-class backgrounds, who tend to live at home with parents who are policemen, firemen or schoolteachers, true Brooklyn Surfers are a muttier bunch. Is it any wonder that Brooklyn Surfer is a term of derision, and probably fear?

It's 4 P.M. and the Brooklyn surfers from Manhattan are in the emergency room of Lenox Hill Hospital in the East 70's. Adam is pressing a cold soda can to his lower lip, which split open when he was bushwhacked by his own board in the water. He wanted to let the wound—which is ugly—heal on its own, but was finally convinced to let a doctor look at it.

An hour passes in the waiting room. Occasionally, Adam studies his lip in the men's room. He says: "That's the only reason I'm here. 'Cause I seen the meat hanging out." He wonders, could he just shove it back in with a Q-Tip? Eric says: "I tried to save a baby bird like that last summer. It fell out of a nest and hit its head on the pavement, and it had a piece like that sticking out, so I stuffed it back in. But it died."

Adam says, "Thanks for the story."


Famous surfers have surfed Rockaway but no famous surfer has ever come from Rockaway. Or Brooklyn or Manhattan, needless to say. Tommy Sena says, "What if one tried?" He sounds doubtful and hopeful, both.

Petey Egan, 18, from Belle Harbor in Rockaway, is considered gifted. But when asked, "Have you ever thought of going pro?" he answers, "With the winters being so cold and the summers so flat, what can I do?" Then he adds quietly, "Sure, I'd love to, but I know I don't have it."

And then there's Joe Zwick's dream, which he has nurtured since he first laid eyes on a wave that Breezy Point Surfers, at the far western tip of Rockaway, call the Avalanche. The Avalanche shows up in hurricane season. Twice. If that. A mile, maybe two, out in the heart of New York Harbor. Waves up to 25 feet high.

Nobody's ever ridden it. How would you get to it? Joe Zwick has a plan. He is going to be towed into it. By Jet Skis or boat. On a surfboard with straps. Bring him right up to it and then...he lets go. "It would be a ferocious ride." He estimates more than a minute long, over half a mile. Out in the harbor where there is no Brooklyn, no Rockaway, just the Avalanche.

"I've gotta do it before I quit," says the schoolteacher, who has surfed these waters for more than 35 years. "Every wave is ridable."

———

Eric returns from his nearby apartment with some surf videos for Adam. There is a soundless TV set with a built-in VCR on the E.R. wall and Eric wants to put a video in. Adam stops him. "No, no, no. It's not our machine."

Twenty more minutes go by. Adam: "Eric, get the tape."

They ask the room, mostly elderly patients, does anybody mind if they put a surfing video on? Nobody blinks. But the VCR's too high up. Eric says, "If I had that lady's cane I could get it in." This plan dies.

Outside the hospital, smoking, Adam talks with some people he meets on the street. They all shake hands enthusiastically. Adam returns. He seems better. "They didn't know you could surf here," he says.

Finally he's called. When he comes out, it's with six stitches and a huge smile: "The doctor was a surfer and lives in Rockaway. He thinks there's something coming up from Florida."

# FIVE

# FISH OUT OF WATER: THE LANDLOCKED SURFER

Billionaire oil baron J. Paul Getty and knockabout Southern California surf bum Edward "Pop" Proctor shared a common reverie at the end of their lives. Getty on his deathbed in 1976 allegedly claimed that the only really happy moments of his life came when he rode waves at Malibu as a young man. Proctor, who often said he'd surf until he was 100, was left more or less housebound in 1979 after the state revoked his driver's license at age 97, and he spent most of the last two years of his life quietly soaking in a bathtub and reliving better days on the beach. Sad, melancholy endings. But also kind of inspiring to think that surfing can create these kinds of Rosebud moments as we shuffle off our mortal boardshorts and begin riding the endless pointbreak of eternity.

Also illustrated here is how the real measure of someone's devotion to surfing—the purity of one's stoke, the depth of one's essential surf-being—might best be revealed *away* from the natural surf setting. Easy enough to be a surfer on the beaches and in the surf shops, among surfer friends, with surfwear spilling off department store counters and surf vibes beaming out from movie theaters, TV screens, and computer monitors. But with Getty and Proctor in mind, the question comes up: What kind of surfer would you be on your deathbed?

Dislocation of one kind or another makes up a small but rich vein in surf writing. The surfer may be removed from his beloved sport by time or geography, physical or mental duress—everything from impending death to an approaching dinner date. The terrain here is mostly psychological, not physical. In "Return of the Prodigal Surfer," middle-aged ██████████ describes coming back to the sport after a decades-long layoff, while ████████, in "Black Sea Blues," looks back twenty-five years and recalls his jangled mental state while freebooting across Eastern Europe during the cold war. ALLSTON JAMES's "Waterbed" raises the stakes, opening with an American GI laid up in a Vietnamese hospital, staring at his war-mangled right foot and wondering if he'll ever surf again. With "Surfers of Fortune," DEREK RIELLY first takes an unsentimental look at Michael, a pot-smoking, surf-obsessed quadriplegic, then swivels around to call out the surf public at large for the myriad petty grievances we inflict on each other. As Rielly presents it, the real tragedy isn't so much the unchangeable fact of a poor Aussie cripple in the wheelchair, it's about the rest of us *electing* to often

mishandle and underappreciate our relationship to surfing. Check yourself, Rielly advises. To be a healthy surfer in this day and age, in *any* day and age, is to be part of the greatest experiment in good fortune the world has ever seen.

## "WATERBED"

California's Allston James wrote *Surfer* magazine's environmental column from 1987 to 1993, and has contributed nearly a dozen fiction articles to the magazine. He's also published two collections of poetry, as well as *Attic Light*, a novella inspired by his experience in the Vietnam War. James teaches English and Literature at Monterey Peninsula College. "Waterbed," one of his first published essays, appeared in a 1972 issue of *Surfer.*

SUMMER. More precisely, first summer swell. As I paddled out past the shorebreak, the grime that my arms had picked up from the car roof gradually faded away with each new immersion in the sea. Each individual stroke of my arms was important, not because of the resulting forward progress but simply because I was doing it. The time-lapsed pregnancy of a small wave lifted my board. Paddling over the next wave of the set, thoughts of the war came to mind. Not whole thoughts, just fragments. That's the way memory shovels war to you after you've left the scene; just an occasional piece or fragment. Memory of anything is always going to be less than the whole, but with war, memory often seems less than nothing. A vacant lot in the head.

The Asian horror show had folded for me months ago. Not for everyone, but it had for me. It ended, then continued in a different way on hospital beds in Vietnam, Japan, and America. That's the main thing I think about when I think about the war and hospitals...beds. Beds upon which every man can become the island that no man is supposedly capable of becoming. Or at least that's what they used to say in Sunday school. No man is an island. That's what they said. Before I ended up in a hospital, I had always thought that when people got hurt in wars, they got hurt in the arms, legs, shoulders, or stomachs. You know, sort of categorized. Like, War Injury Type A, War Injury Type B, and so on. But it wasn't like that. After all, how would you classify the guys who were urinating and defecating through plastic tubes and bags? Or what about the 19-year-old kid who woke up at two o'clock one afternoon and asked for the lights to be

turned on? Not yelling, just asking very softly if someone would please turn the lights on. From my bed I could see blackened flesh all around the edges of his facial bandages. Where his eyes had been, there were now two big yellow gauze pads. He looked like a big fly or something. About the third or fourth time that he asked for the lights, I rolled over in my bed and cried until I urinated through my pale blue pajamas.

There were lots of people like that in the hospitals; people with burned-out eyes and people who cried and pissed all over themselves when they saw such things. I was lucky, although at the time I didn't quite see it that way. A few days after I got hurt, a doctor came to my bed and told me I might not be able to walk again for a long time. It scared me. When he left the ward, I stared at my crushed foot for a long time, several hours. It just sat there pulsating at the end of my leg. The pain told me that my foot was not right, that it wasn't really even much of a foot anymore. If a foot can't act like a foot, then it can't honestly be called a foot, can it? That's when I started thinking about the island.


Week after week I lay beneath the sheets, my body forming ridges and valleys under the whiteness. The space beyond the sides and ends of my bed constituted a great ocean, full of dragons, Vikings, and submarines. The other patients around me had no idea, but I dragged all of them into my nautical world as well. They were their own islands, complete with coasts and interiors. Knowledge of their '56 Chevys, hometown football teams, and girlfriends was translated into knowledge of their islands' mountains and valleys. Idle conversation provided me with all the charts and maps that showed me weird trails and secret caves on the islands surrounding my own. All of this was important, but not significant.

The significant thing was the surf. I began discovering surf spots all around my island. Several well placed reefs just off of my forearms provided some damn hot peaks on occasion, and there was a constant beachbreak all along the stretches of both of my legs. But the best surf on the island was found along the shores of what I had at one time considered to be my right foot. Down there, long glistening lines wrapped around a point that used to be a big toe. Perfect sets every time. On some days every spot on the island would be working, and on those days I never talked to anyone. The bed and I were an island, and we had waves breaking around us.

"Son, we're sending you home in a few days."

"Where?"

"Home. We're sending you home."

"I don't have to go back to the jungles?"

"No, you're going home. Back to the States."

"Will I be able to walk around when my foot gets well?"

"Sure, but right now don't worry about that. Just think about home."

"OK, please wake me up when the plane gets there."

My mother forwarded a surf magazine to me a few days before they flew me home. I looked at the pictures and wondered about them for a long time. They seemed unrealistic, these photographic images of two-dimensional humans stuck on the sides of billboard-like waves. The photos lacked the life of the waves that washed across the shores of my bed.

Outside. I turned to watch the last wave lay itself down on the shallow waters near the shore. A sun-speckled swell began to peak behind me. My foot ached in anticipation of what was to come. It wasn't ready for this.

THE TRADE WINDS
"New York's a Lonely Town"

*My folks moved to New York from California*
*I should have listened when my buddy said "I warn ya"*
*"There'll be no surfin' there and no one even cares"*
*(My woody's outside) covered with snow*
*(Nowhere to go now)*
*New York's a lonely town*
*When you're the only surfer boy around*
*From Central Park to Pasadena's such a long way*
*I feel so out of it walkin' down Broadway*
*I feel so bad each time I look out there and find*
*(My woody's outside) covered with snow*
*(Nowhere to go now)*
*New York's a lonely town*
*When you're the only surfer boy around*

Learning to support a body that wanted to walk was one thing, but this was different. Back in the hospital beds, the crushed foot had only been called upon to serve as a point of land around which perfect waves could break. It wasn't ready to be a part of a man on a wave. It had been ready at one time, back before Asia, but it wasn't now. It just wasn't ready. But then it had never really been ready for jungle boots and leeches either, so perhaps this was fair play after all. I'd considered a bellyboard or kneeboard but couldn't manage the fins and kicking.

I looked over my shoulder to check my position, then paddled a few yards to the right. My pale forearms and legs, suffering pangs of apprehension and doubt, protested by way of small muscle spasms, but just like small waves, they were gone in a moment. Even so, I could sense my body's disapproval, much like it had done months before when it had begun to weaken in the first of many beds—beds that had turned my entire form into the mountainous terrain of a strange island...my foot into a point of land...my arms and legs into ridges...my body into an island...the emptiness beyond into a sea. All, a stiffness.

I stroked toward shore. The sand on the beach looked like a soiled sheet, and the wave, as it lifted me, seemed like a mechanical bed. I began to slide. I stiffened my arms to raise my chest from the deck, and then, leaning instinctively, put the board on an angle across the face of the small wave. My speed doubled. The time was here. I went to stand but fell face down on the deck. The foot wouldn't work; it just went limp.

Clutching the rails for stability, I felt like crying. And the wave wasn't over yet. It wasn't over, but I didn't want to be with it anymore. The board continued to slide across the little wave out toward the shoulder. Everything felt awkward. I just lay there waiting for the inevitable wipeout, but it wasn't coming, at least not as quickly as I expected. Why should this wave continue to carry me? After all, I wasn't really surfing it. I was just lying there waiting for the dump. I just happened to be there. I should have been dumped yards ago. I may as well have been on the face of a billboard. Were people supposed to be on the faces of waves if they really didn't feel like they were there?

Just as I began to wish I was back in the military hospital ward where my foot could resume its character and role as a point of land, the lip of the wave, only a foot or so above my head, began to bounce a bit as the wave sucked itself up over the sandbar. I knew that I was about to swim. The board began to move faster in response to the increasing hollowness. The lip of the wave, done teasing, jumped out and circled down, washing the side of my face. The lip was now a roof. I lay there beneath it, head twisted around to see the watery shelter. It was then that I realized that this was no more a billboard than a bed is an island. Waves don't wrap around big toes; they wrap around people who happen to be traveling through them. The absurdity and wisdom of it all crept into my mind just in time for me to giggle as the roof caved in, washing me up on the beach in a sprawling confusion of happiness.

# WILLIAM FINNEGAN

## "BLACK SEA BLUES"

"Playing Doc's Games," William Finnegan's 40,000-word *New Yorker* essay, published in 1992, describes his agonizing decision to give up the life of a full-time surfer and become a serious author. He became a *New Yorker* staff writer, focusing mainly on international political hot spots and the underside of American culture; his books include *Cold New World: Growing Up in Harder Country* (1998) and *Crossing the Line: A Year in the Land of Apartheid* (1986). "Playing Doc's Games" will be featured in Finnegan's next book. "Black Sea Blues" first appeared in a 1999 issue of the *New Yorker.*

I COULD HAVE BEEN the first man to surf the Black Sea. I got off a bus in a coastal village somewhere in northern Turkey, and there it was: brown and misty and full of mediocre, blown-out waves, dribbling in from the general direction of Odessa. This was 1970. I was a hippie surf punk from California, dialled in to the world surf underground (if not much else), and was therefore fairly certain that the Black Sea hadn't been surfed. I didn't have a board, but I figured I'd find something to ride. The beach was deserted, but I saw in the distance a couple of decrepit cafés at the edge of the sand. One of them probably had an old German paddleboard lying around. The water would feel good. I'd have something cool to claim. Instead, I turned and trudged inland through hot, scrubby dunes, got to the middle of nowhere, and had a little nervous breakdown.

My problem, Doctor, was freedom. I was seventeen, and I had taken advantage of a certain lapse in cultural authority to declare myself a sovereign state. That summer, my girlfriend and I were bumming around Western Europe, living on crackers and fresh air, sleeping under the stars. C., also seventeen, also from California, but less callow than I, had grown tired of the merciless pace I set—the gruelling pilgrimages to rock festivals (Bath) and surf towns (Biarritz) and the old haunts (and graves) of my favorite writers—and she'd finally dug in her heels on the western Greek island of Corfu after I announced that I had a burning desire to see more "Turkish influence." I could go hunt for Ottoman minarets on my own, she said. And so I up and left her on the remote, mountain-backed beach where we'd been camping au naturel. Neither of us, I suppose, believed I would really do it, but I was adept at, if nothing else, moving quickly through strange territory at low cost, and within a week I was in Turkey itself, newly intent on travelling overland to India. Motion, new companions, new lands were my drugs in those days—I found they did wonders for addled adolescent nerves. Turkish influence had fascinated me for about half an hour. Now only Tamil influence would do.

But something about that Black Sea beach brought it all to a grinding halt. The emptiness, the silence, the familiar but unexpected sight of surf, the beckoning goofy feat. Had I really left my girl alone in the boondocks in Greece? Nubile, smart-mouthed, tenderhearted C., whose mother, once she saw that we were actually catching that rattletrap charter to London, had ordered me desperately to watch out for her baby? I looked back now and felt like Orpheus seeing Eurydice get sucked down into Hades, except that I hadn't tried to rescue her; I'd just abandoned her on the trail. My lust for new scenes, new adventures, had seemed all-important. It wasn't. At least, it vanished in a bitter puff as I lay there in the Turkish scrub and dogs barked and darkness fell and I saw myself not as the dauntless leading lad of my own shining road movie but as a hapless fuckup: deadbeat boyfriend, overgrown runaway, scared kid in need of a shower. Also far, very far, from home.

The next morning, I started back toward Europe. I got picked up by a kind journalist and his family from Ankara, who took me to a resort on the Sea of Marmara. They fed me, washed my clothes, studied me wonderingly. I was, for them, an outrider from a wild new Western tribe—children who had suddenly won, somehow, unprecedented amounts of permission. For me, the question was becoming: Permission to do what? I wrote the family a midnight thank-you note and split without saying goodbye.

Europe turned out to be harder to reenter than it had been to leave. There was a cholera scare, and the borders with Greece and Bulgaria were closed. I bounced around Istanbul, walking along the Bosporus, sleeping on roofs. I tried to go to Romania, but Ceauşescu's sentinels reckoned I was a decadent parasite and refused me a visa. Then the police raided a flophouse where I was staying. They arrested three Brits, who were convicted the next day of hashish possession and sentenced to several years each. I moved to another roof. I wrote brave, boastful postcards: hey, no photograph could do justice to the beauty of the Blue Mosque.

But I was frantic about C. Although she had said that she would find her way to Germany, where we had friends, I kept imagining the worst. I bought her a cheap purse in the Grand Bazaar. I befriended other stranded Westerners. Finally, I broke down and phoned home. It took all day to get through. Hanging around the vast old post office: an idle, scruffy foreigner, heretically long-haired, squatting like a beggar in the shadows, offending the eyes of busy clerks and shop owners running their workday errands. Then the connection was awful. My mother's voice sounded terribly frail, as though she had aged fifty years. I kept asking what was wrong. I told her I was in Istanbul, but I still hadn't asked for news of C.—nor mentioned that I hadn't seen her in weeks—when the line went dead.

In the end, I bribed some Bulgarian border guards, made my way through the Balkans and over the Alps, and found C. in a campground near Munich. She was fine. A little wary. Yes, I said, I'd got my fill of Turkish influence. She accepted the purse. We resumed our rambles: Switzerland, the Black Forest, Paris. In Amsterdam, we heard that Jimi Hendrix would be playing in Rotterdam. We planned to go. Then, suddenly, Hendrix was dead. This was a couple of weeks before Janis Joplin. (Jim Morrison was the following July.) It was slowly becoming obvious that not all of us would get out of this funhouse alive.

C. and I flew home. I started college. The structure suited me—for a year. Then I dropped out and moved to Hawaii to live in a car and surf. C., though doubtful, came along. I worked in a bookstore. She worked in an ice-cream parlor. She hung in there for quite a while, really. And then she didn't.

I later became a foreign correspondent. Sometimes, though, I feel like I'm still in Istanbul, 1970. My addiction, never conquered, to the remote leads me over some distant horizon, deep into the peculiar intellectual ecstasies of the unfamiliar, and then into nineteenth-nervous-breakdown territory, and then I'm scrambling to find my way home. Meanwhile, I've left those whom I should be looking after to fend for themselves. My freedom problem persists, Doc. But—have you noticed?—everybody surfs now. Decadent young parasites are probably carving artful S-turns in windblown dribble off Odessa as we speak.

# BOB SHACOCHIS

## "RETURN OF THE PRODIGAL SURFER"

Florida resident Bob Shacochis has written articles for *Harper's, Outside,* the *New York Times, Men's Journal,* and *GQ,* and has published four books of fiction and nonfiction, including *Swimming in the Volcano* and *The Immaculate Invasion. Easy in the Islands,* his first collection of stories, won a National Book Award in 1985. Shacochis, who learned to surf along North Carolina's Outer Banks, teaches in the graduate writing programs at Bennington College and Florida State University. "Return of the Prodigal Surfer" originally appeared in a 2001 issue of *Outside.*

KIRITIMATI, Christmas Island, erstwhile thermonuclear playground in the mid-Pacific. Neither the beginning nor the end of a journey toward the lightness of being but, for me, more of the same, surfwise, selfwise, further evidence of the cosmic truth inherent in the mocking axiom, *You should have been here yesterday.* Yesterday, in fact, is the stale cake of many an aging surfer. Yesterday is what I walked away from, determined to someday again lick the frosting from the sea-blue bowl.

Out there on the Kiritimati atoll, we were a small, neoprene-booted family of silverbacks—Mickey Muñoz, Yvon Chouinard, Chip Post—and brazen cubs—Yvon's son and daughter, her boyfriend, Chip's son. Mickey, 61, was the first maniac to surf Waimea Bay, back in 1957. Yvon, 60, founder of Patagonia Inc. and legendary climber, had surfed just about every break on earth, starting with Malibu in 1954. Chip, 60, a lawyer in L.A., had seniority in almost every lineup from Baja to San Francisco. Our

Generation Xers, in their late twenties, were already dismantling breaks all over the planet. In years (middle), condition (not splendid), experience (moderate), and ability (rusted), I was the odd watermonkey in the clan, neither out nor in, and the only one dragging an existential crisis to the beach. The only one who had opted out of The Life, the juice. Maybe I wanted back in, but maybe not. I felt like an amputee contemplating the return of his legs, but long accustomed to the stumps.

In the coral rubble of the point we stood brooding, muttering, trying to conjure what was not there. The glorious, mythical break had been crosswired by La Niña, and the deformed shoulder-high waves now advanced across the reef erratically, convulsed with spasms, closing prematurely, like grand ideas that never quite take shape or cohere to meaning. In years past at this same spot, Yvon had been graced with an endless supply of standard Christmas Island beauties—precise double-overhead rights, shining high-pocketed barrel tubes that spit you out into the post-coital calm of the harbor. We'd come all this way for Oceania's interpretation of euclidean geometry and we got this: bad poetry, illiterate verse.

Yeah, well...this was a hungry crew, and you never know what's inedible until you put it in your mouth.

The Xers flung themselves into the channel; the rip ferried them out to the reef. Chip goes. Then Yvon, but less enthusiastically. "I'm not going," said Mickey, squatting on his heels. I sat too, thunderstruck with relief. Forget that it had been more than seven or eight years since I surfed, almost 15 since I surfed steady, daily, with the seriousness and joy of a suntanned dervish. With or without its perfect waves one thing about this break horrified me: As each swell approached the reef, the trough began to boil in two sections, and when the wall steepened to its full height, thinning to emerald translucence, the two boils morphed into thick fence posts of coral.

We watched Yvon muscle onto an unreliable peak, gnarled and hurried by the onshore wind. The drop was clean, exhilarating, but without potential. He trimmed and surged past the first spike of coral, the fins of his board visible only a few scant inches above the crown before the wave sectioned and crumbled over the second spike. He exited and paddled in.

"Those coral heads really spook me," I confessed.

The stay-alive technique, Yvon assured me, was glide shallow when you left your board, protect your head, avoid disembowelment or the tearing off of your balls.

"Yeah, I guess," I said.

For a half-hour we watched the rodeo out on the reef, Chip and the Xers rocketing out of the chute, tossed and bucked into the slop. Mickey kept looking up the coast, across the scoop of bay to a reef I had named, ingloriously, Caca's, because the locals in the nearby village mined the beach with their morning turds. The tide had begun to ebb.

"Caca's going off!" Mickey cheered. Yvon and I squinted at the froth zippering in the distance.

"Yeah?" we said, unconvinced. But off we trudged to check it out.


So there is a pathology to my romance with surfing that contains a malarial rhythm; its recurrence can catch me unaware, bring fevers. For a day or two I'll wonder what's wrong with me, and then, of course, I'll know.

I would like to tell you that I remain a surfer but that would mostly be a lie, even though I grew up surfing, changed my life for surfing, lived and breathed and exhaled surfing for many years. Now I can barely address the subject without feeling that I've swallowed bitter medicine. I avoid surf shops with the same furtiveness with which I steer clear of underage girls, and I wouldn't dare flip through a surf magazine's exquisite pornography of waves, unless I had it in mind to make myself miserable with desire.

My life only started when I became infected with surfing, moonsick with surfing, a 14-year-old East Coast gremmie with his first board, a

Greg Noll slab of lumber, begging my older brothers for a ride to Ocean City. Before that, I was just some kid-form of animated protoplasm, my amphibian brain stem unconnected to any encompassing reality, skateboarding around suburbia like an orphan.

I remember the spraying rapture of the first time I got wrapped—seriously, profoundly, amniotically wrapped—by an overhead tube, an extended moment when all the pistons of the universe seemed to fire for the sole purpose of my pleasure. It was at Frisco Beach, south of the cape on Hatteras. I remember the hard vertical slash of the drop, the gravitational punch of the bottom turn and that divine sense of inevitability that comes from trimming up to find yourself in the pocket hammered into a long beautiful cliffside of feathering water. It only got better. There, pinned on the wall in front of me, entirely unexpected and smack in my face, was a magnificent wahine ass-valentine, tucked into a papery yellow bikini. For a moment I thought I was experiencing a puberty-triggered hallucination, but there she was in the flesh, whoever she was, wet as my dreams, locked on a line about two feet above me. Surgasm—can that be a word? The wave vaulted above us and came down as neat and transparent as glass and we were bottled in brilliant motion, in the racing sea. And friends, that ride never ended, unto this day. Boy, girl, wave—whew. On earth, I could ask no greater reward from heaven, nor define any other cosmology as complete as this.

The first time I declared my irreversible independence and defied my father, it was to go surfing. I joined the Peace Corps to go surfing in the Windward Islands. Later I moved my household from the ocean-lonely prairies of Iowa, where I was teaching, to the Outer Banks to go surfing. I chased spectacular waves off Long Island, New Jersey, Virginia Beach, North Carolina, Florida, Hawaii, Puerto Rico, waves that when I kicked out, through the sizzle of the whitewater I could hear hoots of astonishment on the beach, which felt like your ecstasy was shouting back at you, and beyond you, to a future where one day you might recollect that once, for a time, you had been a great lover in your affair with the world. You weren't just sniffing around.

Now, years later, on Christmas Island, I didn't know if I wanted to surf again, to become reinfected, because I knew there was a chance I would stop living one life and start living another, that I would uproot everything, and I didn't particularly think that was possible. Still, Mickey designed me a new board, which Fletcher, Yvon's son, shaped and glassed for me. Still, I flew 6,000 miles to Christmas Island, artificially mellowed by some kind of depresso's drug to make me stop smoking. Still, I gulped back the dread that the point break had induced and walked down to Caca's with Mickey and Yvon.

What we found was surfing's equivalent of a petting zoo—little giddyup waves, pony waves, knee-high and forgiving. The silverbacks made every wave they wanted; I made maybe one out of five. I felt clownish, hesitant, my judgment blurred by bad eyesight. But finally none of that mattered, finally I started hopping into the saddle, having fun. That I considered to be a mercy.

I had collided head-on with my youth and with what needed resurrection, though not in the boomer sense of never letting go. I had already let go. But the dialectic of my transformation had reached a standstill: Surf = No Surf = ??? I wanted more waves. I wanted more waves the way a priest wants miracles, the desert wants rain. Throughout my celibacy, living a counterpoint life, I had prayed hard to be welcomed home again to waves, and these tame ponies would, I hoped, serve as that invitation. I have since surfed San Onofre with limited success. Florida too, but only once. I have yet to find the equation that will spring open my life, re-arrange my freedoms. My resources are modest, my obligations many; my dreams are still the right dreams but veined with a fatty ambivalence. Maybe the season has passed, but I don't think so.

The thing about surfing, Chip told me, is that "you leave no trail." Yessir, Mickey agreed: "It's like music—you play it and it's done."

The strategy you're looking for is the one that teaches you to hold the note.

## "SURFERS OF FORTUNE"

Derek Rielly was the editor of *Australia's Surfing Life* magazine from 1995 to 1999; he later served as editor for the French-based *Surf Europe,* and contributed to *Surf Rage: A Surfer's Guide to Turning Negatives into Positives.* Rielly's work has been published in *Surfer, Waves,* and *Tracks.* "Surfers of Fortune" first appeared as the introduction column for a 1997 issue of *Australia's Surfing Life.*

M EET MICHAEL. Twenty-three. Perpetually untidy dark-brown hair. Doesn't work. Enjoys nothing more than sitting around with his mates with a lungful of pot smoke and watching the latest surf vids. Reads surf mags cover to cover and thinks all the girls in bikinis are pretty hot. An average surfer, you'd reckon.

He would be except Michael has never surfed. Never will. When he was nine he dove off a jetty into a shallow sandbar. The impact crushed the vertebrae in his neck. Hasn't felt a thing in his arms, torso, legs or penis since 1983. Lives in a Melbourne nursing home, shits and pisses in a bag that hangs over his wheelchair and that has to be emptied by the nurses he'd love to bonk if he could feel anything, and he'll probably die of the usual complications that afflict the paralyzed—infection, liver malfunction—in 20 or so years. A good bloke, but prone, understandably, to depression and drug abuse.

When he gets his hands on something like *Surfers of Fortune* or the *Billabong Challenge* vids, however, his life changes. The grim grey and metal surroundings of his ward fade away as he enters the cool blues and greens of

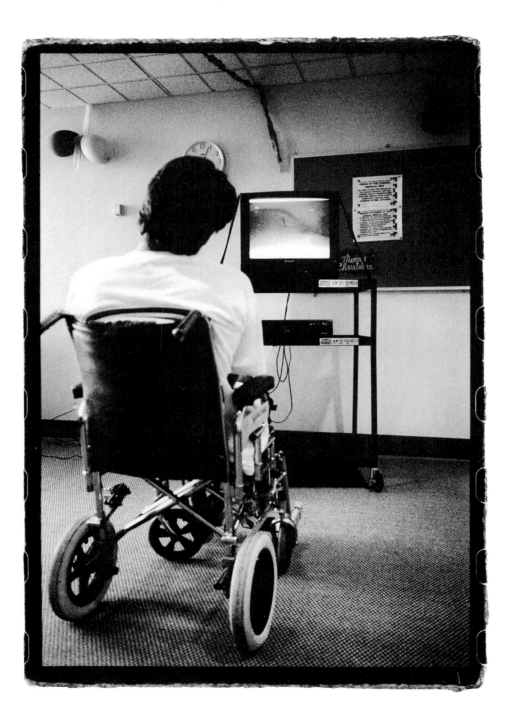

the ocean. He watches with quiet awe as surfers duckdive their boards. How incredible it must feel to have a wave pass over your back and to surface into the bright tropical sun. And how amazing it must be to view the world from inside the tube. At night he dreams that his body works. Dreams of paddling into a Grajagan boomer, the spray blinding him for a moment only to clear as his tail lifts and he drives down the face and begins his hunt for the tube. But when he wakes, he's a man in a wheelchair. No magical cures.

Along with a few new vids, I recently gave Mick a plastic surfboard for Christmas, the kind you get for free with those Headworx digital watches. Another joy. He puts it on his table and uses a pen in his mouth to move it around, banking off imaginary wave sections like a miniature Kelly Slater.

His family doesn't visit much any more. More often than not, Mick's a bit of a trial to be around. He knows that. He'll cry at the smallest thing, like his seven-year-old cousin, Lisa, giving him a drawing she did in school, and overreacts if he thinks he's being patronised. He regrets it after but it leaves everyone pretty upset.

Michael thinks about death a lot and would like to commit suicide. He is jealous that others have the luxury of being able to hold a gun or throw a rope over a rafter. He imagines dying will be like finally breaking the tape after an endurance race. He pictures a heaven—paradoxically he reckons God has to be a hoax—where his legs are strong and his arms power him and his surfboard through the water.

I write about Michael only to serve as a reminder of how completely lucky we all are to be able to go surfing. Happiness, I'll agree, is relative, but I see guys slapping the water, yelling at everybody to fuck off, flicked boards, kids getting smacked around because they ride a bodyboard, grommies throwing a fit because they lost a surf contest, punches thrown at even imagined slights, and grown men nearly in tears because the wind or the tide is wrong and I think...

Jesus, if you only knew.

# SIX

# THE NINTH WAVE: SURF NOIR

Surfing is first and foremost a joy, and this has to be the starting point for any worthwhile description of the sport. "It's much more fun than it looks," said Australian board designer Bob McTavish in 1977, "and it really looks like fun." *Gidget* and *The Endless Summer* were founded on this idea, and so were the Beach Boys. Barefoot troubadour Jack Johnson was a surfer long before he was a singer/songwriter, and his languid melodies seem to flow directly from the purring high that follows a three-hour tropical surf session.

But the sport has dark shadings as well, which is an excellent thing for surf writing, as worthwhile literature—essays, fiction writing, and journalism included—often grows best in an atmosphere of conflict, stress, tension, and tragedy. Big-wave surfers, for example, are often defined in part by their suffering: Ken Bradshaw's depression following the biggest wave of his life, or Roger Erickson's mind-warping Tet Offensive experience at Khe Sanh. Mark Foo's story goes even further. Foo was one of the world's best half-dozen big-wave riders in 1994, but otherwise lived a pretty straightforward life, writing a column for the local paper and operating a bed-and-breakfast. Killed that year during a wipeout at Maverick's, Foo not only rocketed to brief but international mainstream celebrity status, but was also transformed into a far more interesting person, with, as *Outside* magazine put it, "a life and death woven through with dark ironies."

Death has a quiet presence throughout EUGENE BURDICK's bleak debut novel *The Ninth Wave,* with the ocean first serving as a kind of incubator for predatory backroom politician Mike Freesmith, then dragging him under just before his final rise to power. KEM NUNN's *The Dogs of Winter* also builds to a fatal climax, but the bad news visited upon central character Jack Fletcher begins in the first chapter, as readers learn about his divorce, chronic back problems, and a small but growing drug dependency. JOY NICHOLSON's *The Tribes of Palos Verdes* is similar to *Dogs of Winter* in that surfing's relationship to tension and conflict cuts both ways: Steely teenager Medina Mason has a terrible family life, is verbally and physically abused at school, and finds herself in the middle of a local surf community filled with youthful perverts and thugs. But wave-riding itself provides blissful relief. "In the water," Medina says, "they can't reach me. It feels so great to walk away and go surfing."

With "Salty Dog Sam Goes Surfin'" underground cartoonist finds a discomfiting area on the far reaches of satire as he looks at racial stereotyping and environmental decay.

Undercover CIA agent and square-jawed surfer/swinger William Cartwright, hero of PATRICK MORGAN's late-'60s pulp-fiction thriller *Hang Dead Hawaiian Style,* also has problems. But nothing that can't be cured with a double belt of scotch, a curvy blond, a good swell at Waimea Bay, and a bottomless supply of hard-boiled beach patter. "My board, my woody, my style, they're all part of the same bag," Cartwright suavely explains to a new lady friend, before setting off on another high-stakes surf noir adventure. "It's my extended middle finger to the Establishment."

# THE NINTH WAVE

Iowa-born Eugene Burdick (1918–65) was an Oxford-educated Rhodes scholar teaching political theory at U.C. Berkeley in 1956 when *The Ninth Wave,* his first novel, was published. His work was also featured in *Harper's* and the *New Yorker.* Burdick's other books include *The Ugly American,* a bestseller from 1958, and 1962's cold war thriller *Fail-Safe;* both were made into movies. Two chapters from *The Ninth Wave* are included here. Mike Freesmith and Hank Moore are introduced in "The Ninth Ninth Wave," which takes place in 1937; "The Last Green Hump" is set 10 years later, after Freesmith has become a ruthless and all-powerful California backroom politico, and includes Freesmith's girlfriend, Georgia Blenner.

## THE NINTH NINTH WAVE

A BUICK DROVE UP BEHIND the circle of Model-A's that were parked at the top of the cliff. One or two of the cars had neat chrome-plated engines, powerful squat carburetors, wire wheels and twin exhausts. The others were dilapidated and broken down. All of them, however, had braces on the tops where the long surfboards were slung.

Mike opened the door of the Buick and at once passed from the smell of the woman, the odor of perfume and deodorant, into the hot odorless sunlight. He turned and looked at Miss Bell through the open window.

"I'll see you again, Mike...very soon," she said expectantly, half whispering.

"If I can get away," Mike said, hedging. "Busy this week. I have to..."

"If you have time for surfing you have time to see me," Miss Bell said sweetly, but there was the corroded edge of a whine in her voice. Mike smiled at the way the flesh around her mouth worked in tiny flat jerks. "Please now, Mike."

"O.K. I'll try. I've got some work in chemistry to catch up. Maybe by Friday."

They talked for a few more minutes. Mike could feel the sun starting to open pores on his back, through the thin cotton of his T-shirt...the tight blue jeans over his legs turned warm. He was bored, but it was pleasant to talk to her. Some angle of the car caught the sun and reflected chrome brilliance in his eyes so that all he could see of Miss Bell was a black faraway figure. She receded and as her figure grew more doll-like and remote it took on a reprimanding, hostile look. Mike squinted his eyes to keep the blue refracted light from the Pacific from blinding him entirely.

Her voice took on its piping schoolteacher's authority. "You just must be more considerate of me, Mike. You must."

"Why?" he asked idly. "Why, Miss Bell?"

At once the remote doll-like figure collapsed into a posture of apprehension. Miss Bell's voice lost its crisp quality and quavered.

"Well, don't you care, Mike? Doesn't it mean anything to you?"

It is so easy, he thought, so easy to make her drop that cool note of authority in her voice. He reached out and touched her shoulder and at once she leapt back into proper proportion, was neat and full-sized in her flowered silk dress.

"Sure I care," Mike said. "I'll call you later in the week."

"For sure?" she asked.

"For sure," he replied.

He turned away from the car and started toward the edge of the cliff. He heard the Buick start and then turn slowly. Mike smiled out at the blue

Pacific, noticed a tanker, hull-down and far at sea, smoke from her stack smearing the blue-white sky.

When he got to the path that led down the cliff he stood for a moment while his eyes cleared of the glare. At the bottom of the cliff there were two umbrellas, shabby and stringy. Anonymous legs stuck out of them. A few surfboards were scattered around. The sand was white and washed looking, picking up all the sun in the cove.

I know, Mike said to himself, that you look clean from here, but when I get down there you will be jumping with sandfleas, a regular layer of them, just off the sand . . . hopping, jumping, screwing around. Jumping into the air and rubbing their legs. But I like it. Sandfleas don't bite, they just tickle.

As he started down the narrow curving path he could see that most of the boys were far out in the cove. Very far out, as if they were waiting for the occasional big hump. Their boards rose and fell, they sat with their feet up, some of them wearing straw hats to shield their faces from the sun . . . tiny, lazy, Mexican-looking figures.

One of the boys was eating from a paper bag and Mike was sure that it was Hank Moore. It was just like Hank to take his lunch out on the board. That was what was confusing about Hank, Mike thought. He was like an old lady before he got in the water. Cleaning off his board, testing the water with his toe, edging slowly into the water and not diving sharply in like the rest of the boys. Hank would go out slowly on his board, not yelling like the other surfers, but picking his way out cautiously, watching the waves, protecting the brown paper bag which held his lunch. But once he had eaten his lunch out of the brown bag, wadded it up and thrown it out on the water, Hank changed. He sat stubbornly, endlessly waiting for the ninth ninth wave. Some of the other boys would get excited, mistake a big hump for the ninth ninth, but never Hank. He always knew when it would come; he never took a smaller wave; he always waited for the big one. They all believed that every ninth wave was bigger than the preceding eight, and every subsequent ninth wave was bigger than the one before it, until the biggest wave of all was the ninth ninth.

Mike wasn't sure if the system was accurate, but he did know that there was always one wave a day that was bigger than the rest. The other waves might be big and sometimes they were really huge and you might get excited and think that one of them was the ninth ninth. But not Hank. He always knew when to wait. He always got the biggest wave of the day.

Some days he would sit quietly, glancing over his shoulder at the humps, watching them come working up out of the ocean, not moving for three hours. Then finally, he would turn around, start to paddle, and it would be the biggest wave of the day. If he picked his board up and got out of the water that was a signal there would be no other big ones that day. Hank read the weather reports in the papers because a storm far out at sea would often mean big waves and every day, winter or summer, that a storm was reported Hank was down at the cove, looking out to sea, waiting.

As Mike came down the steep cliff he watched to see how the waves were shaping up. The coast was flat and even except for this cove which had been carved by waves into a huge U-shaped indentation. The swells rose quietly and smoothly from the flat ocean, beginning at the very edge of the horizon. In even lines each wave moved toward the shore, increasing in speed as it approached shallow water and beginning to steepen. Then as the waves reached a certain point of shoal water they turned a concave face toward the beach, reached higher and higher and began to feather with foam at the top. Along the rest of the coast they pressed powerfully against the rocks and sand without breaking, but as they came into the cove the feathering tips broke forward and the entire wave crashed over and rolled like a long, noisy, incredibly powerful cylinder toward the shore.

Mike could see that the waves were big, but no one was taking them. They were waiting for a ninth wave. When it came, swelling up big and green, sucking up all of the water in front of it, slanting sharply into the sky, the lines of surfers kicked their boards around, lay on their stomachs and began to paddle slowly, looking back over their shoulders. Only one person did not move in the line and that was Hank Moore. Monkeylike he reached down a hand, touched the water and moved his board away from the nearest person. Then he looked out toward the sea. Mike began to trot down the path, suddenly anxious to be in the water.

When the wave reached the line of surfers several of them backed water, afraid to try it. Several more skewed their boards sideways when the wave began to feather and prepared to smash forward. In the end only two or three boys actually rode the wave through its crash and only one of them was able to control his board and finally get to his feet.

As Mike rounded a boulder his view of the cove was cut off. When the ocean came in sight again Mike was much lower, walking steadily downward into the hot reflected sun, the densing odor of seaweed and iodine, the sudden streaked smell of long-burned charcoal. This descent into the odor, the heat, the smell of sand, was as pleasant as the first second when he dove into the water. He walked slowly, controlling his urge to get quickly to the beach. He felt the muscles of his legs strain with the slight effort of holding back as he descended.

When he got to the sand he took his shoes off, slid his blue jeans off and stood up with only his swimming shorts on. He walked toward the nearest umbrella.

"Hi, Mary Jane," he called to one of the girls.

The girl rolled over, shaded her eyes against the glare. Here at the bottom of the cove, cut off from the wind and picking up all the dull reflection from the sand and water, it was hot with a dead pleasant heat that pulsed rhythmically as the waves shifted the air and made it heave and swell. Mary Jane's nose had sweat on it and the edge of her bathing suit was rimmed with moisture. She stared for a moment, expectant, a smile on her lips but unable to see him. Mike stood still and waited. He knew what she was seeing. When you lifted your head suddenly and looked into this dull, glaring sun people looked like black solid shadows, faceless, formless, only the edges of their bodies glowing with an astral brightness.

Then Mary Jane recognized Mike.

"Hello, Mike," she said. The other two girls under the umbrella looked up, their faces surprised; suddenly unfocused and confused. They did not smile and the smile faded from Mary Jane's face. Their faces were bruised somehow with a hard memory; a curiosity that changed to irritation.

"Where have you been, Mike?" Mary Jane said. "Waves have been good all day. Some really big ones. Tommie said they were eighteen feet high . . . base to feather."

"I've been riding around," Mike said. He squatted down on his heels. The sandfleas started at once, a blanket of tumbling, falling, jumping, writhing black dots; falling to the sand and then springing wildly back up-ward. He felt a light, delicate itch start over his feet, reach up to his ankles.

"Riding?" Mary Jane asked. "Riding all morning?"

Now the bruised, disinterested look was gone from their faces and was replaced with curiosity. Their eyes were wide with interest, although their lips were drawn thin with some sort of disapproval. Mary Jane's lips drew back and showed moist teeth and pink soft flesh in the corners of her mouth.

"Yep, just riding," he said. "Out toward Long Beach, past the docks, then over here. Nothing but riding."

Oh, he thought, you'd like to ask, wouldn't you? You'd just like to screw up your courage to say "Who with?"

He squatted there in the sun, feeling like a roadblock in the easy flow of their serenity, sensing the curiosity well out across the sand like a physical substance. Squatted there, his knees drawn under his body, all his muscles taut, his arms dangling, he felt powerful and poised. He closed his eyes and for a few moments he dozed. When he opened his eyes the girls were pure black figures. Gradually they swam into perspective.

The girls were tense with elaborate disinterest. Mary Jane yawned, then opened her mouth as if to speak, but stopped. Mike smiled at them and quite suddenly their faces looked outraged.

"I think I'll try some waves. Can I borrow somebody's board?" Mike said.

"Board?" Mary Jane asked, her voice round with surprise. "Sure, of course, see Bill Flatter over there. He just came out."

The quick first impression of antagonism had vanished from all the girls' faces; they were tense now with curiosity. As Mike stood up the girls twitched with irritation. Mary Jane scratched at her ankles, her eyes following Mike.

"Bill, can I borrow your board?" Mike asked a long, very tanned boy.

"Sure, Mike," the boy said waving his hand, his black eyes searching Mike's face once and then falling away. "Remember, she's heavy in the tail so ride her a few inches more forward than you'd do normally."

"O.K. Thanks," Mike said.

He picked up a long narrow board, natural mahogany-colored on the body of it and trimmed with blue at the edges. His fingers unconsciously ran over the wood, measuring the smoothness, judging the quality of the board. He swung the fifty pounds of it over his head and walked toward the water. It's a good one, he thought. That Bill Flatter makes a good board, heavy in the tail or not heavy in the tail.

When he got to the water Mike stopped and stood on a rock where the water was only a few inches deep. Usually he would wait until a wave deepened the water and then with a sweep he would throw the board on the shallow water and swing himself aboard and with one movement be heading out to sea with only the tips of his toes wet. But today he waited a moment and then put the board on the dry sand.

He walked to the water up to his knees, waited for a wave and with a clean strong dive dove over it and into the water. He let his body glide, held himself straight and stiff. Then he stood up and made a curious un-premeditated gesture: he wrung his hands over his head and then threw them down to his side and at the same time looked up at the people on the beach. They were all watching him.

Mike felt a surge of surprise. The gesture was so strange. He was not sure why he had done it. It seemed vaguely propitiatory like the sign he imagined a priest would make over an animal sacrifice, or the motion that a magician makes after a trick, the jerking wave of hands as if to cleanse them; to take a curse off.

Mike looked away from the people under the umbrellas. As he walked to the board the sandfleas jumped on his legs and stuck to the moisture. He waded into the water again to drown them. Then he lay flat on the board and headed for deep water.

It took him ten minutes to work out through the waves. The waves were big and as the lines of broken surf approached he dug his hands powerfully into the water and then came up on his knees so that his weight went toward the rear of the board and shot its nose up over the foam. When the nose was over the foam the body of the wave would hit the board and smash it forward with a whipping action.

There is a point in the surf where the waves have just broken and the tons of green and white water are falling almost straight down. One must cross this point between waves or the surfboard will be thrown backward or turned over. Mike waited cautiously until there was a lull, then shot forward over the shattered hulk of one wave and slid up the side of another wave before it broke. Then he was in the clear water beyond the surf line.

There were almost a dozen boys waiting on their boards. Some of them were lying flat on their backs, others were sitting with their feet dangling in the water. Mike saw that half of the boys were from Manual Arts High and the rest he did not know. He saw Hank Moore and paddled over to him.

"Hey Hank," Mike called. "How're they humping? Been waiting long for one?"

Hank Moore swung around. He was a short, stocky, freckled-faced boy. Although his hair was blond and his eyes light blue he had a perfect Semitic face. Hank looked coolly at Mike. He's bright, Mike thought. He's got intelligence.

"They're good," Hank said. "Long wait between big ones, but when they come they're really huge. Must be some sort of funny storm out at sea. Never saw such big ones mixed up with such little ones. About every other third ninth is big and then every ninth ninth is a big baby. Pretty soon there'll be a really big one."

Mike splashed his hands gently into the water and his board skimmed over the surface, jarred against the end of Hank's board and the two boards were held together by the slight pressure. Hank was sitting neatly in the middle of his board, his knees pulled up under his chin. The top of his board was covered with intricate lines where the salt water had dried on it. Hank never dove off his board or played around in the water. For him the water was only a means of getting out to the waves and he disliked swimming. Hank was talking to a boy Mike had never met.

"Where've you been, boy?" Hank asked, looking at Mike. "You've missed some good ones. Farting away the day in L.A. when you could have been down here."

Mike grinned back.

"No. I've been for a drive. Just riding around Long Beach, Pedro, Wilmington ... just got here now. Nice day for riding."

"Riding in a Buick, I'll bet. A blue Buick," Hank said and his voice ended in the slightest burr of a snarl, so faint that only someone who knew him well would know that he was angry. "Riding in a Buick."

"Yep, in a blue Buick. And stopping and eating four hamburgers, and two Mile-Hi cones and shooting a rifle twenty-five shots at a gallery.

Doing that and riding in a Buick that'll do fifty-two miles an hour in second." Mike stopped and looked coldly at Hank for a moment. "Your ass, Moore. Right up your ass."

Deliberately Hank reached out a hand, stuck it in the water and moved his board away from Mike's. He did it as a rebuke.

Mike felt a sense of excitement; an excitement that was really a spasm of triumph. Even old Hank, he thought, even old Hank is that way. He pushed his board forward so that it touched Hank's board again and smiled at Hank.

"Look, Hank, grow up," he said. The strange boy stared in bewilderment. "You're seventeen years old. Grow up. She knows what she's doing. Don't worry about her. Just worry about yourself."

"You son of a bitch," Hank said.

Mike watched Hank's strange Semitic face, with the sharp flat planes and the odd blond, twisted hair and the light blue eyes. Hank was angry, but Mike knew that he was also confused.

But Mike was not confused. Not me, he said to himself, not me anymore. Carefully, picking the words, he phrased the meaning to himself. He was excited.

You, Hank and all of you, you think that some day you're going to stop worrying. You think that you'll get older and just by getting older some day that god damn worry and uncertainty in your guts is going to stop. You think that you're going to come in out of the worry and the fret and the doubts, like stepping out of the sun into the shade. All that has to pass is time. You think you don't have to do anything; that it will just happen. Well, it won't. Absolutely, positively, without fail, it will never happen. You'll always be the same, you'll always be miserable . . . right at the core, you'll be miserable. And you'll spend most of your time trying to escape that fact. That simple little fact.

Intuitively, on some obscure level, Mike knew he had discovered something valuable. He knew he had a tiny fragment of insight that at once made orderly and understandable a lot of things that had been chaotic. Also, and this with a kind of disappointment, he knew that he could use his special knowledge. Also he knew he would add to it. He would find other things.

Sitting on the gently heaving board, watching Hank's face, Mike spoke a law to himself: Everyone is scared.

Mike sat and stared at Hank for a moment.

"What's he so tough about?" the strange boy asked Hank.

"He's not tough," Hank replied. "He's just a cocky bastard. Not tough though."

"Well, what's he so cocky about?" the strange boy asked. He looked sideways at Mike and Mike grinned at him.

Hank lifted his head from his knees and turned toward Mike. "He screws the English teacher. That's why he's so cocky." Hank said it coldly.

"Big hump, really big hump," someone shouted.

"Big hump, big hump," everyone in the line said, taking it up like a chant. The boys who were dozing came awake and began to kick their boards around so they faced the shore. Everyone began to chatter with excitement. The strange boy was talking to Hank, but looking at Mike. Mike swung his board around and then looked over his shoulder. He could see at once that it was huge. It seemed to take something away from the two waves in front of it so that they were small and shrunken and behind them the big one humped up, already so high that it was losing the blue color of the ocean and taking on a green thinness as the sun came through it.

He looked quickly at Hank. Hank stared for a moment at the wave. He pulled his shorts up tight. He looked over at Mike and for a moment, just the slightest fraction of a second, something dark flitted across Hank's eyes and then was gone.

It's the big one for the day, Mike said to himself. And Hank is scared of it. Like he's scared of all the big ones.

Watching it, Mike felt the usual slow chill of fear. At some point the big waves were always like that, so awesome that he felt as if he would like to dig his hands in the water, shoot the board out into the safe water beyond the surf line. And then there would be the grind of satisfaction, as he made himself stay there and move his hands to put himself in the proper position to catch the wave.

Most of the skill in surfboarding depends on catching the wave at precisely the point where it has reached its highest peak, is beginning to feather at the top, and is ready to let all the tons of green water it has held in a curious rhythmic control for so many miles crash downward. A second too early and there is nothing for the board to ride. A second too late and the board is submerged in a lather of foam. Some people are never able to catch this knack, this ability to sense the precise moment when the wave will crack and let its water spill.

The wave moved from the middle distance with a rush; drew itself from a hump into a towering cliff of water and now, like strange plants frozen in old green ice, Mike could see pieces of kelp in the water, every thread of their filigreed detail caught for a moment in the sunlit water. The water was soundless at this point, but Mike felt a pressure rise in his ears and head as the wave gathered itself.

Mike felt the water fall from beneath him as the huge wave rose. He looked over his shoulder and saw its green, soft and ominous bulk take shape above him. The wave was pure and undiluted; not a trace of foam in it. He gave a couple of strokes with his arms and the board began to move ahead. He looked sideways and saw the scared white faces of the other boys. Most of them were backing with their hands, making sure that they did not catch the wave. Hank, however, was crouched on his knees on his board. With his hands he was crumpling up the brown bag which had held his lunch while he looked over his shoulder at the wave. His face was rapt with attention and something more; a sort of tough angry belligerence. Hank threw the paper bag away without looking at it and then took two strokes in the water with his hands.

Mike felt his board lift and savagely he cut the water with his hands. Midway in the fourth stroke he sensed that he had it; felt the body of the wave grip his board and he began to move forward. He looked sideways and saw that only he and Hank were still riding.

For a few seconds the wave rushed silently forward. Then a thin vein of foam gathered at the top of the wave and formed a lip which bent slowly forward. The speed of the wave increased. This was the critical second when the surfboard would not only be moving forward at great speed, but would also drop down the face of the wave as it crashed over.

Mike glanced sideways and looked at Hank. Then suddenly Mike stood up on his board, still looking at Hank as he did it. This was not the time to stand up, for usually one stood up after the wave had broken and the board had smoothed out. Mike had never stood up at this point, and

he was not sure he could keep his feet in the next few seconds. Hank looked at him without blinking and stood up also.

For a moment they stood calmly as the wave moved forward. The only noise in the vast moving green world was the hissing of the boards over the water. Then from deep in the wave came a sound like rocks rolling together and with a curious lunge it broke. A great green tunnel of roaring water was formed in front of the wave, foam gathered as high as Mike's waist and the board almost dropped away from under his feet. With a slight liquid shock the board landed on solid water and although Mike's feet slipped for a moment he remained steady. He looked sideways and saw that Hank also had survived the crash of the wave.

Mike's board chittered with speed, slapped a thousand blows against the water. They were rushing toward the blue water of the cove and the noise was enormous.

That's right, Mike howled to himself. I screw the English teacher. Just what all the rest of them would like to do. But I'm the only one that does it and I'm wiser than the rest of you because of it.

The surfboard shook with speed, the water hissed and roared, foam tossed up over his shoulders. Words rushed through his mind, piled incoherently on one another, forming impressions and all this mixed somehow with the taste of salt on his lips and the noise in his ears.

You all think you'll get better as you grow older, but I know you won't. Because I know Miss Bell who is twenty-eight, which is very old, and I know that she lies naked in a bed and cries when she calls me in. I know that right in the center she is rotten with fear and because of this I know that we will always be that way. That it won't change when you get to a certain age, but it will always be the same.

The wave was dying now and in a few seconds the board came to a halt in a few inches of water. Mike stepped off and looked over at Hank. He felt suddenly depressed, sorry that he had this piece of knowledge that none of the rest of them had. And he was sorry because he knew he would use it. It was as if he already knew how unfair was his advantage.

"That was pretty chicken, Mike, standing up before the wave broke," Hank said. "Trying to delight the girls, eh? You did it because you're chicken, that's why."

"Sure, Hank, that's why. I'm chicken," Mike said, but he laughed and Hank looked up quickly, his face confused. "You just go on believing that."

Mike picked up his board and laid it on the sand and in the hot sun the wood began to steam and the salt traced out a pattern on the board.

"Hank, can I ride home with you?" Mike said. "Don't have a car today."

"Sure. I'm going right away. Hurry up."

## THE LAST GREEN HUMP

The October storm waves came thundering in. In the far distance they were blue, heavy and innocent. But as each wave reached the shallows it turned green, its huge bulk rose into the air, it turned a concave face toward the beach. There was a moment when the wave seemed frozen, motionless. It stiffened and along its back appeared short, striated lines of power, like muscles tightened. It was sleek and smooth with force. Then a line of white spume, as solid as cream, appeared along the top of the wave and it curled forward. With a crash the whole wave broke. The green mass was gone and the wave disappeared and was replaced by a huge white seething wall of foam that roared in to the shore.

The waves piled in without pause. They were the edge of a storm that was thousands of miles away. They were huge. From the breaking point to the sand the sea was foaming white, roiled with splintered waves, twisted by undertow, streaked with clouds of sand.

Hank took one board from the rack on top of his car and walked to the edge of the cliff above the cove. The place was deserted; the beach was empty. As he walked down the path he noticed that the ice plant was dried out and brown, waiting for the winter rains. The path was drifted over where the wind had gnawed into the soft soil of the cliff and made miniature landslides. He walked slowly, feeling his way carefully over the drifts, balancing the board on his shoulder. Halfway down he stopped and rested. Then he went the rest of the way.

The storm waves had narrowed the beach. It was only fifteen or twenty feet wide. Hank put the board down. For a moment he squatted in the sand and looked out to sea. Here, with his eye almost at water level, the long sweep of ocean to the horizon was invisible. He could see to the shallows but no farther. There his vision was blocked by the slow, regular, inevitable heaving of the ocean as the newest wave was formed. The waves reached into the sky, blotted out the sky and the Channel Islands.

The waves exhausted themselves just at Hank's feet. He reached down and touched the last thin edge of the waves. They hissed softly against the sand, turned it gray, and then slid backward.

Hank stood up. He started back up the cliff.

Ten minutes later he had the second board on the beach. He brushed them both off, set them carefully on their sides. He took his pants and shirt off and stretched out on the sand in his shorts.

The early winter sun was very thin. The surface of the sand was warm, but not like the summer sand. Just below the surface the sand was chilled; slightly wet. And there were no sandfleas.

Once Hank opened his eyes and looked at the sun. It was yellow and pale. A thin corona, like a black line, traced its shape.

He thought of the summer sand; the deep swelling warmth that seemed to come from the interior of the earth. He rolled over on his stomach, laid his cheek against the sand. The grains were instantly cool. He turned again on his back.

A gull came in from the sea, kaaing as it slid down a smooth layer of wind. Hank was looking straight up into the sky and saw it for a moment. Its white shape and the pink feet scarred the blueness of the sky and the yellow light between the sky and earth. It looked very small.

He forgot how long he lay there, pulling the heat from the sky, feeling the coldness of the beach against his back. But finally he heard the sound of a car at the top of the cliff. He sat up. He saw Mike's head, and then Georgia's peer over the side of the cliff. Then they started down the path.

Hank picked up one of the boards and stepped to the edge of the water. He waded in until the water reached his ankles. In a well-remembered motion he swung the board into the water and forward and, at the same time, landed on the board while it still had motion. He squatted on the board and began to paddle.

The board chunked into the first shattered wave. It was a wall of foam only a few feet high. The board cut up through the foam, sliced through empty air and then whipped flat. Hank eased his weight onto his arms, lifted his knees slightly from the board and when the board slapped against the water began paddling again.

The next three waves were easy because they were almost spent. But between the waves the water hissed and boiled in a way Hank had never seen. The water moved in quick senseless eddies, was checked by other pressures and tossed aimlessly. The board cut across the eddies, making a slicing neat sound that came minutely to his ear, cutting through the larger sounds.

The fourth wave was difficult. It came combing down on him, four feet of foam, laced through with green strands of water. He paddled hard, with his cheek flat on the board. As the nose of the board hit the wave, he slid his weight back to raise the board, and then, instantly, pushed forward.

The board whiplashed into the foam; crashed into the wave with a motion that was arclike, but moving forward. The wave sucked at him, he lost way and then, almost as he stopped, it released him. His eyes were full of water but he was already paddling. He blinked his eyes clear and looked ahead.

This is the moment, he thought. The moment when you see the ocean's worst face; when you are most evenly matched.

Twenty yards in front of him a big wave was forming. It rose silently, steeply, without effort. The mound of water started to peak, to raise itself into the air.

Hank paddled in deep powerful strokes. His whole body was bowed into the effort. He stared at the wave, watched the line of spume suddenly thread along the top. The wave turned concave; became a huge forward-bending wall. He felt a pressure in his ears and knew the wave was about to break. He paddled savagely and just as the tons of water curled down he shot into the concave green substance. He cut through the middle of the wave; he locked his arms around the board. He felt the wave crash down on his ankles; the board shivered for a moment, was almost dragged backward and he heard a great rumbling savage noise as the wave hit the surface of the ocean. Then he was released. He slid out past the surf line.

Hank swung into a squatting position and paddled slowly out for a few more yards. Here the skin of the ocean was flat and smooth and the waves looked harmless. Hank swung the board around and looked toward the shore.

Mike and Georgia were almost at the end of the path. Mike was wearing swimming shorts and was barefooted. They were standing still, watching him. Hank waved his hand and they came the rest of the way to the beach. They stood for a moment talking. They looked out to sea and then at the surfboard. Georgia spoke once, looked again at the waves and then, it seemed to Hank, she became silent. She put her hands in the pockets of her coat and leaned against a rock.

Mike walked to the edge of the water and put a foot in the next wave. He hopped back, pounding his hands across his chest and shouting something to Georgia. She did not reply. Mike picked up the surfboard and walked into the water. With the same skillful, swinging motion that Hank had used he swung the board down and forward and while it was still moving he slid onto it. Then he disappeared as he entered the surf. Hank saw the tip of the board occasionally as it went up over a wave. Once he saw Mike clinging to the board as it whiplashed over a wave. Then as another hump of water gathered itself, heaved into the sky and narrowed out, its powerful green impeccable back was shattered as if a boulder had been thrown through it. It was Mike and his board. They shot through the body of the wave. They came like a sailfish; sharp and flashing, spray flying, cleanly slicing the wave. They slid past the surf line and out into the smooth water beyond.

Hank watched quietly, not moving from his squatting position except to straighten his board occasionally by putting his hand in the water. He felt withered, dried out. His mind was empty and blank. He was aware of the thin warmth of the sun, the swelling of the waves, the sound of the surf and unconsciously he counted the waves and waited for a ninth wave.

Mike's board slid across the water.

"You sure picked a day for surfing," Mike said. "You don't go surfing for ten years and then you pick a day like this."

"You didn't have to come. I just told them at your office that I was going and if you wanted to come I'd have a board for you," Hank said.

"Don't get touchy. I wanted to come. Haven't been surfing for ten years. But this is some surf. I never remember it like this. There must be some hell of a storm somewhere."

"They're humping all right. And they're getting bigger. There'll be a really big one along pretty soon."

"Old Hankus, the medicine man of the sea," Mike said. He brought his board close to Hank's. "Just like old days, eh?"

Hank looked down between his knees. The middle of the board was drying out, leaving a thin film of salt. It was cold. The breeze off the ocean was stronger than the sun. Hank looked up at Mike.

"Just like the old days, only a little bit different," Hank said.

"What's different?" Mike asked. He was grinning; the old, tough, confident, independent, knowing grin. "You're the same. I'm the same. Ocean's just the same; maybe the waves are bigger, but everything else is the same."

"You're not the same. You're different."

Hank did not know where his words came from. He did not think them with his mind or phrase them before he spoke. They seemed to be manufactured by his lungs and lips quite independently. In the withered, brown, desiccated interior of his head Hank felt nothing; he was blank, waiting for some signal.

"You're wrong," Mike said. "I'm just the same. Hank, I haven't changed a bit since the last day we were out here on the boards. Maybe you have, but I haven't. Not the least little bit."

The boards rose on the swell of a wave, dropped into the trough. Hank saw that Georgia had climbed up onto a rock and was sitting with her hands clasped around her knees.

"I guess you haven't changed, Mike," Hank said. "You're just the same. But I didn't really know you before. And then maybe the world changed around you."

Some old long-forgotten sensitivities came alive in Hank. Because of the depth of the trough and the shape of the waves and impulses that came through the board he knew a big hump was coming. He turned and looked over his shoulder.

They both saw it at the same time. It was a long dark blue line that blotted out the horizon. It rose so high above the other waves that it caught the wind and was laced with veins of white foam. Because of its bulk it seemed to move slowly, deliberately, reducing the waves in front of it and absorbing the waves that followed.

"My God," Mike whispered. "It's huge. It's the biggest I ever saw."

Hank backed his board toward the wave, sensing that it would break farther out than the other waves. The big hump was only four waves away when Hank stopped and waited. Mike was beside him.

They watched the color of the wave change. The deep blue faded and it became green and translucent. A delicate filigree of kelp was visible in the wave; the nodules black and solid, the strands as distinct as rope. To one side was a sting ray, caught in the wave. It was like a scarab; motionless, its wings spread, its ugly short tail straight out behind it. In the taut amber of the wave the ray was entombed, harmless.

Then all the other waves were gone and the big hump was all that was left. They lay flat on their boards, looking over their shoulders. Deep in the wave they could see the sea grass trembling, the sharp tips reaching up from the bottom of the ocean and fluttering in the base of the wave. Then they heard the rumbling noise.

They started to paddle. Hank looked over at Mike.

"Don't take it, Mike," Hank called. "Let it go. It's too big for you. You can't ride it."

And Mike grinned. His arms kept pumping. They felt the sea rise beneath them, push against the boards, lift them high. Flecks of foam shot past their boards. Then, just at the tip of the wave, the mass of water gripped them and they started to shoot forward. For a split second they slid forward and upward as the wave continued to gather itself. The roar, the grinding, tearing, rumbling, fundamental sound, grew louder. They could see the tattered surf in front of them, the smaller, minor waves that had gone before and been ruined. They rose still higher and the drop seemed incredible, unbelievable, staggering.

Hank looked down at the beach and he could see Georgia's white face turned toward them. He felt the wave start to break and he looked at Mike.

Mike was getting to his feet. He grinned over at Hank. He was going to ride down the crash.

Numbly, with relief, Hank felt that he had received the signal; been given permission. He started to stand too.

And then the wave broke. The board was hurled forward and in the same instant it slid down the front of the wave. The foam rose around Hank's knees. The board chittered under his feet and his toes worked for a better grip. He looked over his shoulder and saw the mountain of foam and green tossing water behind them.

Hank pressed with his foot and his board angled across the foam, slid toward Mike. Mike saw him coming. Mike did not angle away, he did not look down. He watched Hank's slanting. Hank sensed that Mike knew what it was about; what had to happen; what was coming. And again the relief deepened and Hank felt reassured, decisive.

When his board was a few feet from Mike's he straightened it. Hank stared at Mike for a moment and then he dove at Mike's knees. He felt his ankles slap hard on Mike's board and then they were both in the water.

The broken wave snatched at them eagerly. It was the grip of the entire ocean: ancient, massive, stern. They were swept forward, but were held so tightly they could not move even their fingers. The wave threw them to the bottom and swept them through a patch of sea grass. The tough strands whipped at their bodies. They rolled over and smashed into a great slime-covered rock. The slime was rubbed off instantly and Hank felt the sharp edge of sea rock slice the flesh from his ribs. He was held against the rock and then drawn slowly across the cutting edges.

Then the pressure was gone and they swirled through the green water. Mike reached down and twisted Hank's middle finger loose. He bent it back, almost to the breaking point. Then, quite deliberately, he let go of the finger. Hank tightened his grip.

Hank opened his eyes. Under the wave the world was filled with raging clouds of sand, the black shape of rocks, the twisting blades of sea grass. Closer, just before his eyes, was the solid muscle of Mike's leg. Digging into the flesh were his own fingers.

In the green uneven light he saw Mike's hand come down, grasp his finger and bend it. He threw his head back and there, inches away, was Mike's face. The face was softly distorted by the few inches of water. But Mike's eyes were open and the grin was clean and distinct. Hank closed his eyes.

The finger bent straight back from his hand, a sharp pain came from a great distance, sped down his arm and exploded in his brain. He screamed and bubbles slid from his mouth and floated away. Then, just before the finger broke, Mike let go.

He could have broken my grip, Hank thought. He could have gotten loose.

He made his mind blank, for this was temptation. He dug his fingers into Mike's legs and held more tightly.

They were swirled upward, almost to the surface and then whipped downward. They smashed into rocks again, swept across a layer of sand that quickly, in a few short licks, rubbed the skin from Hank's legs.

Suddenly Mike jerked his legs up and almost tore loose. Hank tightened his grip and with a peculiar distinctness felt the sharp wiry hairs of Mike's leg brush against his cheek.

The wave held them motionless for a moment and then brushed them flat against a shoal of barnacles. Hank felt the sharp, painless slice of the shells as they cut into his back. His lungs were hot and he knew that soon he would open his mouth and the salt water would pour into his throat. He opened his eyes and far away he saw the lively bouncing sunlit surface. Just above him a layer of green water was rushing swiftly past, pierced with beads of foam, flecked white. But, by some oceanic trick, they were held motionless, paralyzed by the great pressures into immobility. The shells sliced his flesh soundlessly.

It's not for you, Hank shouted in his mind. Not for all you stupid cloddish ignorant bastards, walking the face of the earth with plenty of air and sun and clouds. I'm doing it for myself. For selfish reasons. For my own reasons. Not for you.

And then the wave released them. They were lifted up and Mike jerked again, pulling them almost to the green foamy surface. It grew brighter, but at the edge of his vision a black circle was growing, narrowing the light to a contracting circle. Hank knew he was close to unconsciousness. He sobbed and took a mouthful of water down his throat. He clamped his mouth shut. The area of blackness grew.

The wave moved them forward and slammed them against a single rock. There was the sound of a crack, a dull unnatural muted crack. Mike went soft in Hank's arms, collapsed downward upon him. Mike's fingers slid down Hank's back, his head bounced limply from his shoulder. In the center of the tiny circle of vision still remaining to him Hank saw Mike's face. The eyes were open and staring.

Hank let go. He ran his hands over Mike's limp body. Hank pushed upward, very weakly.

His head broke through the surface, but only slightly. The surface was covered with leaping fleck and gobbets of foam. Hank gasped and got a mouthful of foam and some air and was pulled under again. He was pushed to his knees and swept forward. He pushed upward again and this time got more air.

He did not believe he could reach the shore and he did not want to, but he could not control his body. It fought toward the shallow water;

weakly, grotesquely, without his help. He came to the surface, snatched a breath of air and swallowed it along with bitter foam. Then he was pulled under. He crawled over rough rocks, patches of sand, the dead sharp bodies of crabs and old shells. Above him the water still rushed and tossed. He sobbed as he crawled and wondered, dully, with a black lassitude, how much his tears would salten the water. The sea rumbled at him; talked of death and oceanic peace and somehow it made him sob more. He got to his feet and found that he was in the shallows. But another wave smashed at him and he went under again. He slid along the bottom, helpless.

Then something caught him by the wrist, held firm. He staggered to his knees. The water was very shallow. He looked up. Georgia was standing in the water and holding him by the wrist. She pulled him to the edge of the water and rolled him on his back.

"Poor Hank," she whispered and her fingers ran over the cuts on his arms and chest, gently touched a long neat slice that was just starting to ooze bright red. "Poor, poor Hank."

Hank tried to speak, but salt water foamed between his lips. He spat. Then he could talk.

"He could have gotten loose," Hank said. "By breaking my fingers he could have gotten loose. But he didn't." He coughed and warm vomit and salt water spilled in a gush on his chest. He whispered, "Why didn't he, Georgia? Why didn't he break my fingers and free himself?"

"Poor, desperate Hank," she said.

His eyes blinked away the salt water. The sun now seemed bright and huge. He could see Georgia. Her face was tight with pity and despair, but also with understanding.

She put her arm around him and pulled him upright. He coughed again. She held him in a sitting position.

They sat there for a long time, waiting for Mike to drift in.

# R. CRUMB

Pennsylvania-born Robert Crumb was recognized as first among equals in the late-sixties underground comics movement, and is best known for his work in *Zap* and *Head Comix,* and as the creator of Mr. Natural and Fritz the Cat. Few artists have ever walked as fine a line between humor and outrage. Critics have described Crumb's work as sexist, pornographic, racist, and violent, and his comics were temporarily banned. Defenders view him as a satirist who exposes the particularly American forms of repressed anger and desire. "Salty Dog Sam Goes Surfin'" was originally published in a 1972 issue of *Surfer* magazine. Surfing was then still regarded as something of an underground sport, and Rick Griffin, longtime *Surfer* cartoonist (see page 132) was directly tied into the underground comics scene. "Salty Dog Sam Goes Surfin'" was the final piece in a *Surfer* comic insert that also included cartoons by Jim Evans, Robert Williams, and shock-master S. Clay Wilson.

Crumb's work has become less provocative over the years, and his cartoons now appear in the *New Yorker.* The documentary *Crumb* (1994) earned a Sundance Grand Jury Prize and was named Best Documentary by the National Society of Film Critics. Crumb lives in France and is married to cartoonist Aline Kominsky.

# KEM NUNN

EXCERPT FROM

## *THE DOGS OF WINTER*

California-born novelist Kem Nunn has been called the inventor of surf noir. *Tapping the Source,* his dark and edgy 1984 debut novel, is set in the low-rent section of Huntington Beach, and tells the story of a teenage surfing newcomer looking for his missing older sister. *Source* was nominated for an American Book Award. In 1997's *The Dogs of Winter,* the action focuses on the chilly northern California coastline, home to a mythical and terrifying big-wave break called Heart Attacks. *Tijuana Straits,* Nunn's third surfing novel, was published in 2004.

T HE FIRST BIG SWELL came early that year, a gift before Christmas, wrapped in cloud. In downtown Huntington Beach, in Southern California, Jack Fletcher did what passed for sleep in a rented studio apartment and the phone call woke him. He had been into the beer and muscle relaxants again and it took him several moments to identify the caller. When he did, he recognized the voice as that of Michael Peters, publisher and editor of *Victory at Sea,* the oldest and most successful of the half dozen or so magazines devoted exclusively to the sport of surfing.

There was a considerable amount of background noise on the line and Fletcher concluded the man was calling from the condo the magazine kept near Sunset Point on the North Shore of Oahu where it appeared a party was in progress. It occurred to him as well that it was the call he had been waiting for. The recognition was accompanied by a slight quickening of the pulse.

"Here's the situation," Peters was saying. "The pot is up to twelve hundred dollars. R.J.'s already down six. There's a deuce and a jack of hearts showing. Should he pot it or pass?"

Fletcher righted himself on a lumpy futon. He drew a hand through his hair, then used it to massage the back of his neck. "What?" he asked.

"Come on," Peters told him. "We need a little advice here, Doc. Does he pot it or pass?"

Fletcher found that he could envision the party house quite clearly— the cluttered rooms, the empty beer bottles, the spent roaches, the boards propped in every available corner, the inevitable surfing video going largely unwatched upon some big-screen television, ensuring that whatever else was happening, regardless of the hour, there would always be waves. There would always be girls and golden sand and blue skies filled with light.

Seated in the darkness of his apartment, Fletcher felt himself quite taken by a wave of nostalgia, a kind of sorrow for his fall from grace. There had been good times over there, he thought—twenty seasons of trips to the islands. Twenty years of iron men and holy goofs. In the darkness of his room, he was suddenly more lonesome for their company than he would have thought possible.

"Okay," Fletcher said. "Give it to me one more time. The cards, I mean."

"A deuce and a jack."

"What the hell," Fletcher told him. "Pot it."

He could hear Peters talking to the others. "The doctor says pot it," Peters said. The words were greeted by a chorus of voices, a moment of silence, and finally an explosion of laughter, hoots, and catcalls.

"A deuce," Peters said. "He's down eighteen hundred bucks." The man's voice was full of pleasure.

"By the way," Peters continued, as if this were somehow incidental to the game. "The Bay broke today. Close out sets."

Without really thinking much about it, Fletcher found that he had risen from the futon, that he had begun to pace. It was happening more quickly than he would have imagined. Peters had first contacted him about the trip less than two months ago in mid-September. Neither man had expected anything like this so early in the season.

"I checked the buoy readings for you," Peters continued. "They're just beginning to show. Fifteen feet. Fifteen-second intervals. It should be coming up. I'm putting Jones and Martin on the red-eye to LAX."

Fletcher drew a hand over his face, the three-day stubble. "What time is it?" he asked.

"Ten o'clock."

"Here or there?"

Fletcher could hear Peters sigh, even with the bad connection. "Here," Peters said. "You'll have to figure your end out on your own. The way it stands now, you pick up Jones and Martin at the airport and drive straight through, you should hit it just about right."

"I got you," Fletcher said.

"I hope so," Peters told him. "You should have been on this already."

There was a moment of silence between the two men, and Fletcher could hear once more the din of voices issuing from across the sea. It sounded to him as if he heard someone say, "Just tell the dude not to blow it this time."

He supposed it was Robbie Jones. The boy had been one of the contestants at last year's Pipe Masters event. Lost in the throes of a major hangover, Fletcher had gone into the water only to shoot the finals with a roll of previously exposed film. It had proved his last gig for Peter's magazine, or any other for that matter.

"That was Robbie," Peters said. "He said to tell you not to blow it."

"Maybe he should tell me something else," Fletcher said. A portion of his desire for their company had died on the vine.

"What's that?"

"Maybe he should tell me what flight he's going to be on."

Peters laughed. "Yeah," he said. "I guess cab fare to Heart Attacks would be a bitch."

When Fletcher had the information he required, he returned the cordless to his machine. He set about flipping on lights and pulling on clothes. Dressed, he made up the futon and found his way to the kitchen. Unhappily the place was a litter of soiled dishes and empty bottles. Less than a year ago he'd had a wife to aid him in such matters. Now, in the aftermath of the divorce, his wife was living across town, in the company of his daughter, in the neatly manicured little bungalow Fletcher had purchased more than a decade ago in the last Orange County beach town where such a thing was still possible on something less than a six-figure income. And Fletcher was alone, doing his own dishes in a one-room apartment. A clock above the stove told him it was 3:00 A.M. A cooler man might have used the opportunity to grab another couple hours of sleep. Fletcher was no longer cool. He mixed a protein drink in his blender and used it to wash down a pill.

As a kind addendum to his failed marriage, Fletcher had managed to get himself bent on a sandbar in Mexico, on what should have been a routine session. His back had not been right since. It was a matter of some concern. When the X-rays and MRI failed to turn up anything, his doctor had spoken in vague terms of various arthritic conditions, suggesting that Fletcher see a rheumatologist. Fletcher had declined. Arthritic conditions did not figure into his deal with the universe. He saw instead an acupuncturist where twice a week he lay listening to the taped recordings of whale songs while a dark-eyed beauty rerouted his energy channels. Between visits he relied heavily on pills and beer. That Michael Peters should have called in mid-September, in the midst of such decline, to offer a plum like

Drew Harmon and Heart Attacks had come as a bolt from the blue, a thing scarcely to be believed, for each was the stuff of legend.

One was the old lion, the holy ghost of professional surfing. The other was California's premier mysto wave, the last secret spot. They said you had to cross Indian land to get there—a rocky point somewhere south of the Oregon border where Heart Attacks was the name given to an outside reef—capable, on the right swell, of generating rideable waves in excess of thirty feet. There were no roads in. They said you risked your ass just to reach it. If the tide was wrong, or the swell of insufficient power, or not properly aligned with the coast, if there was poor visibility, due to fog or winds or heavy rains, or anything else that might prevent you from actually seeing the wave, you would never know whether you had reached it or not. If, on the other hand, one did find it, one risked one's ass all over again. The reef lay among some of the deepest offshore canyons in the northern Pacific, naked to every hateful thing above and below the water. Nor were the homeboys keen on visitors. At least one photographer Fletcher knew of had been badly beaten. Others had gotten in but come back empty, convinced it was a hoax. Still, the legend remained, kept alive by the occasional murky photograph, the tale told by someone more reliable than the average idiot, someone who claimed to have actually seen that outside reef work its cold, gray magic.

Photographs of the place were understandably rare. The ones Fletcher had seen were of a uniformly poor quality, shot from the hip, on the run, making any real estimation of wave quality difficult if not impossible. A chance for access with someone who knew the ropes would have been any surf photog's dream; that the guide should turn out to be Drew Harmon was so perfect it was almost a joke.

There was a time when you couldn't pick up a surfing magazine and not see Harmon's picture. World champ. Pipe master. One of the first to charge Hawaii's outer reefs. And then he was gone, walked on the whole deal. Some said he had run afoul of the law. Others said he had simply tired of the sport's growing commerciality, the consummate soul surfer gone off to surf big, soulful waves. A decade's worth of rumors floated in his wake. Recent photographs were as rare as those of Heart Attacks.

The last anyone in the surfing community had heard of him was that he had shown up in Costa Rica for a legends event, then pulled out before the contest. That was five years ago and he had not been heard from since. Not until September, when Michael Peters had picked up a phone to find Drew Harmon on the other end. The man was calling from Northern California and he had called to say that Heart Attacks was for real—a world-class big wave hidden among the rocks and fog banks, the recipient of Aleutian swells. He'd been surfing the place for the past two winters and he was ready for pictures. His only stipulation was that Jack Fletcher take them.

Peters had called Fletcher the following day, asking to meet at the Pier restaurant in downtown Huntington Beach. Fletcher's machine had taken the message. "Don't bother to call back," the message had said. "I'm gonna be there anyway. Just meet me in the bar. Five o'clock. I'm sure you can find the bar."

Had things been better, Fletcher might have blown the guy off. As it was, the month of September had found him beset by leering in-laws and moon-faced brides, shooting weddings as far inland as the Pomona Valley, the land of the powder blue tuxedo. He had accordingly, at precisely five o'clock on the following day, made his way to the Pier restaurant overlooking the graffitied boardwalk and polluted waters of his old hometown.

In fact, the meeting had not been especially cordial. Fletcher had found his former employer seated in the glow of a magnificently swollen sun, poised to descend behind the isthmus which bisected the northern quarter of

Catalina Island. The scene was framed by the tinted rectangles of glass which formed the bar's western wall, and the room was filled with a dusty orange light.

Peters was a tall, heavily built man, roughly the same age as Fletcher. Both were in their early forties. Peters had lost most of his hair. What was left he wore pulled into a shiny black ponytail just long enough to dangle over the collar of his shirt. Fletcher considered this something of a bullshit hairdo, more appropriate for aging Hollywood types than former big-wave riders. As Peters rose to greet him, however, Fletcher was reminded that a big-wave rider was exactly what the man before him had been, that beneath the rounded edges there was still the man who'd ridden giant Waimea—in the old days, before wave runners, leashes, or helicopter rescues—then gone on to make enough money in the drug trade to buy his way into the good life. He was still, Fletcher supposed, somebody you wouldn't want to fuck with.

"Dr. Fun," Peters said. He spoke without enthusiasm.

Fletcher seated himself at the bar, facing the beach. No one had called him Dr. Fun in a long time.

Peters sat down next to him. "How are you, Doc?"

"I'm okay."

Peters studied him for a moment. "I hate to tell you this," he said. "But you look like shit."

Fletcher had responded by ordering a drink.

"You still in the movie business?"

"Oh, you know. A snuff flick now and then."

Peters forced a laugh, leading Fletcher to conclude the man was probably a connoisseur. As for Peters's remark, it had been aimed at a recent project of Fletcher's, an off-beat little opus called *The Dogs of Winter,* a phrase generally reserved for big waves generated by winter storms. In Fletcher's movie, the doctor had trailed a pair of metal heads from one

wave pool to another across the continental United States. In fact, Fletcher had been rather fond of the film. He'd thought it prophetic and funny, in a bleak sort of way. Others seemed to miss the point entirely, particularly those in the industry. Most, Fletcher believed, were pleased that it had failed, Michael Peters among them.

"Okay," Peters said. He sighed, tapping the bar with an empty bottle, allowing Fletcher to see that he intended to come right to the point. "I didn't get you down here to bullshit with you. I've got something and I need to know if you're up for it. I should add that it's more than you deserve."

"Intriguing."

"Manna from fucking heaven, that's what it is," Peters said. At which point, Peters had told him about Drew Harmon's call.

Fletcher's first impulse was to believe that he was being fucked with in some way. It was too good.

"Don't worry," Peters assured him. "I tried to talk him out of it. I told him you were out of the loop, that you had become a fuck-up, that I had half a dozen guys could do the job."

Fletcher decided the man looked just unhappy enough to be telling him the truth. The knowledge did something to the pit of his stomach, a sensation not to be had in the wedding chapels of Santa Ana.

"Jesus. I'm surprised he even remembers."

"Come on."

"So I shot him in the islands."

"No shit."

Fletcher had smiled then, giving in to the memories. For he had been young and innovative in those days, one of the first to experiment with poles and helmet rigs. He'd backdoored a peak behind Drew Harmon at Rocky Point once. Fifteen years ago, and the shot was still radical.

Peters had looked unhappily toward the beach, where a considerable number of gulls circled in a thickening orange light. "This isn't going to be easy," he said. "You know that. We get the place on the right swell, surfing it is one thing, getting good shots is something else. You get fog up there. You get rain. You get clouds. The light is shit. Harmon knows that too. That's why he asked for you. Radical conditions, a narrow window. You better have somebody who can get the shot. His problem is, he thinks you're still the one."

"What do you think?" Fletcher had asked him.

Peters had given him a hard look. "What I think don't count, Doc. He's the man on this one. But I'll tell you this. You go, we're all going to find out. We're going to find out if you're still the one or not."

And that was how they had left it, until this morning, until the coming of the swell.


Fletcher finished his protein drink. He added the soiled blender to the mess in the sink and went outside. It was the finding out that occupied his mind just now, standing at the side of the garage, searching for the proper key in the moonlight. He had begun to swim again, marking his progress by the number of lifeguard towers he could pass as he slogged along beyond the surfline, but his progress was slow and he had counted on several more weeks of preparation.

As he slid the key into the door, it occurred to him that not long ago he had stood in almost this same spot. His daughter had come for a visit. She'd brought a friend and the girls had played at being fairies, paper wings taped to their backs, clad like gypsies in a funky array of old slips, gaudy belts, and feathers. The friend owned a dog—a small brown-and-white terrier—and as Fletcher stood on the deck, he'd become aware of the children and dog racing around him in dizzying circles, and he had felt himself at the eye of something. In its midst, he had experienced only loss, a sense of dislocation. The feeling was an unnerving one and had haunted him for several days. It suggested, he decided, a continuum from which he was set apart, a failure of purpose.

Fletcher's gear was stowed in the garage, in a metal filing cabinet to which the owner had granted him access. It was gear he had not used in some time. The Gore-Tex stuff bags were dusty and the home of spiders. He brushed them off then wiped them with a towel. He pulled out the old waterproof housing he'd made himself, examining it by the dim overhead light that filled the garage.

The housing was composed of a bright orange plastic, its seams stripped with silver duct tape. It was, by any contemporary standard, too big and too heavy, but it had served him well and he had once made something of a name for himself by losing it at the Pipe on a huge day, then staying outside to dive for it on the reef where eventually he'd found it, lodged in a crevice among the coral. It had been his second winter in the islands, and he had needed the pictures to pay his bills. To have lost the camera would have blown his entire scene. Still, diving for it had been a rash act. It was a big day and beneath the surface there was no way to see what was coming. He could easily have been caught on the reef and stuffed into a crevice himself. But later, people seemed to remember what he had done.

He took out his old Nikon and his 230 mm lens, which was the largest he still owned. They were using 600s from the beaches now, with converters and automatic focus, and the camera did half the work. Fletcher believed a man should find his own focus, should be forced to pull the trigger himself. It was also true he hadn't the money to modernize his act. His, it seems, had gone for such items as doctors' bills, an acrimonious divorce, a failed movie. He supposed he'd had it coming, for his desultory ways. For that failure of perception which had allowed him to conceive of the extended party as a suitable response to life's trials. He had meant no harm. He had failed to compensate, was all.

When he'd laid out what he intended to take, he went back to the apartment. He took his heaviest wetsuit from the closet. He took booties and gloves as well, then discovered that he had lost his hood. It was while he was looking for the hood that he found the book, a battered paperback with the ludicrous title: *A Wave Hunter's Guide to the Golden State.* He'd picked it up years ago, thinking it might be good for a laugh, only to discover its authors had, in fact, worked their way from Oregon to the Mexican border with a thoroughness Fletcher had been compelled to admire. He sat with the book now on his futon, suddenly curious to see if the authors had managed any photographs of something that might pass for a world-class big wave in the northern reaches of the state.

The appropriate section was filled with small black-and-white photographs and Fletcher was treated to a monotonous parade of murky slate gray humps marching over slate gray seas toward slate gray rocks, set before slate gray skies. Disappointed, he turned to the text where, to his sharp delight, he found something of interest—a rumor, even then it seems, but the elements were accounted for.

"In a place where Northern California's most pristine and remote public lands meet with the reservations of the Yurok and Hupa Indians," the authors had written, they had picked up word of a long point capped by grasslands, around which huge waves had been known to wrap, exploding finally upon a deep, natural bay. The place was known to the locals as the Devil's Hoof, and they had gone in search of it.

They had approached from a campground to the north. Access was difficult. Fletcher could imagine them out there, a pair of hippies slogging through creek beds in baggy shorts and huarache sandals, coming at last to the coast only to find themselves nearly trapped upon a huge boulder field without exits.

A medium tide and small surf had permitted a northbound crossing where they had huddled for the night on a sandy beach at the base of steep cliffs. They had awakened to spectacular scenery and a flat ocean but had looked with a surfer's eye upon the configuration of land and sea, permitting their imaginations to run wild with what might have transpired there, had they hit it on another day. For they had indeed seen the grasslands capping an arm of land which formed the northern end of a great bay and around which a northern swell of sufficient size and power might push. "As yet unconfirmed," they admitted. "Definitely unridden and likely to remain so. Too big. Too cold. And too lonely."

"Still," they had crooned, in a riff appropriate to the age, "this is sacred wilderness. The path is treacherous and at times unmakeable. But if one perseveres, the magic of this land will be yours to appreciate. It is a place where native Americans lived in harmony with the land, long before the white men came. It is a land of the Great Spirit—the place where the wilderness meets the sea."

They had concluded with a last item of interest. It had to do with the nearest town, a small, logging community where they had stopped long enough to buy a tire for their bus. The name of the town was Sweet Home. It was the town Peters had named as their destination, the place from which Drew Harmon had made his call.

Fletcher had added the book to his gear and gone back to looking for his hood when the phone rang once more.

It was Michael Peters.

"They're off," Peters told him. "I put them on the plane myself."

"That goes without saying," Fletcher said. "You wanted them on the right plane."

"Lighten up," Peters told him. "Make believe you're still Dr. Fun."

"You know what Robbie Jones was doing the last time I saw him? He was head-butting some guy's car."

"I remember that. The Op Pro. The guy was checking out R.J.'s girlfriend, man. What do you want? He's an excitable boy."

"He's a moron. The only guy on the tour any dumber is Sonny Martin."

"You're just sore, 'cause he was needling you about blowing the finals last year. Anyway, I should point out to you that Mr. Jones has gotten religion. He's a new man."

"No."

"Born again."

"Christ, Martin too?"

"Are you kidding?"

"You're doing this to me," Fletcher said. "It's punishment for getting the gig."

"Forget it," Peters told him. "These guys are going. Besides, that's not why I called."

There was a moment of silence on the line. It occurred to Fletcher that Peters was probably on his car phone, alone upon that great red plateau of pineapples in the first light of a tropic sunrise.

"You know what they say about this place," Peters said. "It's not just the drop. They say it's got that old magic, the way the Bay had it, in the old days, before they turned it into a theme park."

"Maybe it's all that Indian land," Fletcher suggested. It suddenly felt to him as if some offering of peace was about to descend.

"Maybe so," Peters said. "Harmon's married now. You know that?"

"I hadn't heard. Who's the lucky girl?"

"Don't know. No one does, as near as I can tell. Last I heard the guy was living in Costa Rica. He calls from Northern California. Tells me he's married, that he's gotten himself a chunk of land..."

"That was probably how he got the land," Fletcher said. "He found himself an heiress."

"Half his age no doubt."

"With a large trust fund."

The men allowed themselves a moment of laughter.

"I ever tell you about that time in Biarritz? We're camping on the beach for two days, waiting on a swell. Finally we get it. I get up at dawn, look out. There it is, corduroy to the horizon. The sun is out. The wind is offshore. I hear something and I look up. A Mercedes wagon pulls up and stops. Door swings open. Out steps Drew Harmon. Man's wearing shades and an ankle-length fur coat. I can see this blonde sitting in the seat behind him. He's got at least four boards racked to the roof. He pulls one out. Pulls on a wetsuit. Walks down. And rips. For about three hours. Never says a word. Just rips. He leaves and the wind turns around, starts blowing on shore. Half an hour later and the place is shit."

In fact, Fletcher had heard the Biarritz tale before. But then surfers did love their stories. Big waves and outlaws. Anybody who could grow old and stay in the life. Drew Harmon was all of those things.

"You remember when I took over the magazine?" Peters asked. "You remember what it looked like then? We changed all of that, Doc. You changed it. All that shit you shot from the water. That was heavy stuff. You set the standard, man. You upped the stakes..." The man paused, moved perhaps by his own rhetoric.

"What I'm trying to tell you," Peters said finally, "is that I'm pulling for you on this one. Sonny Martin's nothing new. But R.J. is. He's the real thing. You get Jones and Harmon, passing the torch in mysto California surf..." The man paused once more. "You can tell the newlyweds to go fuck themselves."

Fletcher had been off the phone for a full five minutes before it occurred to him that Michael Peters had just made reference to the weddings. He paused at that point in his packing. He looked with some wonder upon the first light. You lost your money. You fucked up your back. In the end, it was hard even to maintain one's front. In the end, they knew. In the end, they had you. He glanced at his watch. He stuffed the last of his gear into his bags and went with it into the alley where he had parked the old Dodge. As he did so, he was just in time to see a pair of egrets as they swept up from the remains of the Bolsa Chica wetlands where once his great-grandfather had come on horseback from Los Angeles to hunt with his friends. The birds passed almost directly above him, wing to wing, sleek prehistoric shadows before a tarnished silver sky.

# PATRICK MORGAN

## EXCERPT FROM
## *HANG DEAD HAWAIIAN STYLE*

Patrick Morgan is one of several pen names used by durable pulp-fiction novelist George Snyder. *The Surfer Killers,* his debut, was released in 1963. *Hang Dead Hawaiian Style* was the first novel in the nine-book Operation Hang Ten series, published from 1969 to 1973, featuring surfer/swinger/undercover CIA agent Bill Cartwright. Snyder has written twenty-seven books altogether; his latest, *Bleeding Sisters,* was released in 2003.

J IM DANA, head of West Coast Headquarters of Operation Hang Ten, leaned back in his battered desk chair, swung his feet up to the window sill, and peeled the second of his two breakfast oranges. The poorly-lit office was toward the rear of a slim, obscure building on Pico Boulevard, in downtown Los Angeles. Behind Dana was a knife-marred, dark desk, with one black phone. His chair was blond-turned-to-yellow, armless, resting on three casters.

In his late forties, Dana had at one time or another worked for them all, including the CIA and the FBI. But he didn't stay too long because his methods, although they got results, were a little too unorthodox for the paper pushers in Washington.

When Operation Hang Ten was created, Washington decided they needed someone unorthodox. They handed it to Dana, told him to operate it any way he wanted. The standard methods just hadn't cut any ice when it came to teen-agers. Operators trying to infiltrate the teen-age ranks to learn something were quickly spotted and avoided. Hang Ten had succeeded so far because Dana had reversed the usual method. Instead of trying to get someone inside, he pulled young people out of that world and made operatives out of them. They knew the world and they were trusted. His operatives were mini-skirted girls as well as surfers and beach bums. Hang Ten was getting results. But to Washington it was still a stepchild agency. Money came lean and seldom.

Dana separated the triangles of orange and popped them one at a time into his mouth. His operatives were working on four minor cases right now. He had two agents in the San Francisco area and one in Australia.

The black phone behind him almost startled him with its ring. Dana dropped his legs from the sill, set the unfinished orange on the desk, and picked up the phone.

"Dana here," he said.

"Dana? McGraw, CIA. I think I've got something here I can throw your way, you know, kind of help you out. Interested?"

Dana didn't try to hold his smile. "Well, I don't know. We're kind of busy right now. Maybe if you call me next month some time—"

"Okay, okay, so you'll make me say it. We've got something we're having a little trouble with."

"Come again?"

McGraw's voice rose. "All right, dammit! So we've got one we can't handle! They spot our agents and there's nothing we can do about it! Satisfied?"

"You want us to take over, right?"

"I don't think you'll do any better, but orders are orders."

Dana reached out, took another section of orange, leaned back in the chair. "I'm listening," he said.

"We got a call from old Mike Ho, a twenty-year cop who came up the hard way. He's now Chief of Police in Honolulu. It seems he's having problems with some surfers—"

"At Waimea Bay," Dana cut in.

"How the hell did you know?"

"Waimea Bay is where the surf is. That's where the surfers are. That's where the action is."

"Well, right now we got more action than we need. Anyway, these surfers have got something new going for them now, smoking opium."

"McGraw, you're judging the many by a few. You're not trying to tell me every surfer at Waimea Bay is hooked on opium?"

"Okay, okay! So *some* of them are smoking the stuff. The point is, Ho has himself a king-size problem. He's sent a couple of his younger officers over there to see what they could learn. But they were spotted and edged out. Some person or persons are supplying the stuff."

Dana was jotting notes on a slip of paper. "All right," he said. "What else?"

"What do you mean, what else?"

"Come on, McGraw. Dope pushing is small stuff for the CIA. You've got something else, something bigger."

McGraw sighed deeply. "Okay. It was weird that Ho should call when he did. We had an agent over there. Hell, we had more than one, but the others were spotted like Ho's men. This agent, Rettig, had one hundred thousand dollars on him. He was supposed to contact a Chinese agent and pay the money for a micro dot which supposedly contained specifications on a new and powerful laser beam the Chinese are working on. Evidently this Chinese agent double-crossed the Reds. We *do* know the Russians were bidding on the micro dot too. We were informed that since our offer was higher, we'd get it."

"Did you?"

"We got something all right. We got Rettig killed along with the beach bum he was supposed to contact. It looked like a shoot-out with each of them killing the other. The bum was using a Russian gun and we found some Russian documents in his pockets. Maybe it was a big put-on, I don't know. Could be the Russians actually *were* behind it. When we got the bum to the lab, they found him loaded with opium. Get the connection?"

"Way ahead of you, McGraw. What about the micro dot? Did you find it on the bum?"

"Missing, right along with the hundred thousand."

Dana finished jotting, popped another section of orange in his mouth.

"Well?" McGraw asked. "What do you think?"

Chomping, Dana said, "I'd say you had a hell of a problem."

McGraw raised his voice again. "Come off it, Dana! You're itching to get your hands on this one! You know if you can pull it off you might rattle some more funds out of Washington. Don't try to con me, Dana!"

"Wouldn't do that for the world. But like I said, we're kind of busy right now." He sighed deeply making sure McGraw could hear. "I guess if you really *can't* handle it, we could try to squeeze it in someplace."

"Damn you, Dana! If I hadn't been ordered, I never would have contacted you!"

"Bye now," Dana said softly. "Thanks for calling."

McGraw was still cursing when Dana dropped the receiver on its cradle.

He pushed the last piece of orange into his mouth then leaned back, making a tent out of his fingers under his chin. A fan buzzed loudly from the corner. Outside the window, a hazy sun tried to break through the smog. That was California, still hot in November.

Dana slapped both palms on the desk and pushed himself on the chair casters to the gray, three-drawer filing cabinet. He pulled out the middle drawer, fingered through a row of manila envelopes, pulled out one simply marked in large block letters—Cartwright. He pushed himself back to the desk and opened the folder. There was a large photo with specifications on a sheet next to it.

It was the face of a young man, somewhere in his early twenties, long, straight blond hair with sideburns extending along the bottom of his ear lobes, bushy eyebrows that looked almost white in the photo, hovering over deep-set, smiling eyes. The cheekbones were high, separated by a straight nose with just a trace of Indian hook at the end. The lips were full, and the chin looked squared off at the end like somebody had been at it with a hammer and chisel.

And next to the photo:

Cartwright, William. Born November 8, 1945. Works as a private investigator. U.S.C. graduate. Entered Hang Ten September, 1966. Childhood spent on coast cities along California, Hawaii, and Australia. Surfing main childhood activity. Won several championships as a teen-ager. Parents killed in auto accident leaving Cartwright an estimated ten million. Private eye work is cover for Operation Hang Ten. Home is the same as office, a thirty-six foot trailer with the latest equipment, license number HAY699.

And under Record:

Four paternity suits filed from 1961–1964. Cartwright acquitted for lack of evidence. Three breach of promise suits filed from 1963–1966. Acquitted again for lack of evidence. Also acquitted from assaulting an officer, charge filed June 8, 1967, for lack of evidence. All records available only through Operation Hang Ten Headquarters, Washington, D.C.

Dana closed the folder, picked up the notes he had jotted, reached for the phone. He dialed the special operator.

"Number please?" the cooing voice asked.

Dana said, "Give me six-oh-dash-six-nine."

The trailer was tucked away in a far corner of the Manhattan Beach court. It was as loud a canary yellow as the old wood-sided station wagon parked in front of it. Both had four-inch stripes laying over the top. Both had exposed chrome wheels. The blood-red surfboard with black swirls causing a marbled effect leaned against the trailer just under the sign: William Cartwright, and under that, Private Investigations. To the right of the board, just above the doorbell, another sign, fiberglassed into the side of the trailer, stated: If You Don't Swing, Don't Ring. And on the wooden tail gate, just under the rear window of the station wagon, in bold, one-inch black letters, a sign read: Indoor-Sports Car.

Inside the trailer, thermostat controlled to a constant seventy-one degrees, Bill Cartwright had shoulders and head completely entwined in the white sheet. He was lying sideways on the bed, his lanky legs dangling over the edge. The bed vibrator had been shut off some time during the night. He wasn't sure when. He was awake, his eyes were open looking at the inside of his sheet hood. The sheet turned green. The multi-colored, swirling lights were still on. And he could hear violin music coming from the hi-fi speakers located everywhere in the trailer. His temple was pressed against Connie's ankle bone. With his legs stuck out he felt like a man coming backward off a roof, searching with his feet for the ladder. He couldn't figure how he got so twisted around, so wrapped up in the sheet. It had been some night all right, one of the better ones. And the way things had been going with Connie lately, there weren't too many better ones. He still wasn't fully awake.

Coffee! For the Cartwright machine to function, it needed coffee. He pulled at the sheet, finally getting it over his head, and wiggled his knees to the floor on the side of the bed. He glanced at Connie's sleeping naked body, then switched off the colored lights. It was then that he noticed the small winking red light on the side board of the bed.

Pushing on the bed with his hands, he got to his feet, bumped into the door, opened it, and closed it behind him. He moved silently, bare feet on thick carpet, past the bathroom door on the right, through the kitchen with sink and stove on the left, dining table on the right. Just past the kitchen to the left was the computer. He dialed "Liquid," switched to "Coffee," and pressed the button. The phone in the living room, sitting on top of the short-wave set, kept buzzing. Bill stumbled back into the kitchen, pulled a cup out of the cupboard, and on the way back to the computer almost tripped on a pair of black, lacy panties with a tiny pink bow at belly-button level.

"All right, all right," he mumbled to the buzzing phone. His voice was still thick with sleep. He pointed his finger at the phone. "Cartwright gets his coffee first, see?" He picked up the panties and dropped them on the dining table. At the computer, he pulled the small lever and smiled as the black liquid tumbled into the cup. The coffee temperature was perfect, as always. He slurped noisily at the cup. The dry rags around his tonsils were washed away, the cotton candy was fanned out of his head. He patted the computer lovingly.

In the small living room, he stumbled to the Danish Modern couch, brushed aside one sweater, one sleeveless blouse, two skirts, two pairs of panties with Wednesday and Thursday patches sewn on them, and two foam padded bras. When couch cushion was visible, he sat on it, sipped some more out of the cup. He leaned forward to the coffee table and swept away one pink nail polish bottle, one white cold cream jar, one blonde hair net, three brass lipstick tubes, and four earrings, two with pearls, two with glass diamonds. When white marble was showing, he pulled the buzzing phone off the short-wave, set it on the coffee table and lifted the receiver to his ear.

"Yeah."

"Cartwright?"

"Hell no, man. This is your friendly neighborhood burglar. I'm cleaning out the joint. You interrupted me."

"How about cleaning yourself onto a plane for Honolulu?"

"When?"

"No rush," Dana said. "Any time within the next hour."

Bill groaned. "You got to be joshing me."

"Not joshing, sweetheart. You'll just have to kiss her goodbye, pat her on the rear, and shove her out the door."

"Who?"

"You sound like an owl. The little whatever you happen to be playing with right now, that's who."

"But Christ, an hour!"

"Right. You ready to be briefed?"

"You mean you already made the arrangements for the flight?"

"Make your own damned arrangements."

"But man! You're not talking about a twenty-pound suit case. You're talking about a thirty-six foot trailer, a full-size Woody automobile, and one Cartwright-size body! You just don't get them ready to fly across an ocean in an hour!"

"You'll muddle through in your usual fashion. So maybe I'm pushing it a little. Take an hour and twenty minutes. Are you ready?"

"Okay," Bill sighed. "Let's hear it." He sipped his coffee and nodded occasionally while Dana told him everything he had learned from Mc-Graw. The coffee was gone when Dana had finished.

"You shouldn't have any trouble getting in with the crowd over there," Dana added.

"So how do you want me to work it?" Bill asked.

"You know better than that."

"All right, so I'll play it by ear as it comes along. Anybody hire me?"

"No, you're on vacation. Just over there to have a ball."

"Oh, I plan to."

"Yeah, well give the job a thought now and then, will you?"

"Get out of my life, Dana."

"Gladly."

A short drenching tropical rain passed over the north shore of Oahu Saturday night. And Bill sat in the trailer drinking one Scotch and soda after another, listening to the downpour. By midnight he was so plastered he couldn't make it to bed. He slept on the couch. It was almost noon Sunday before he awoke.

And the word was out. Another storm was brewing a thousand miles off the coast of Japan, moving toward Oahu, due to hit the Islands Monday or Tuesday. But before the storm came the waves. And from Sunset Beach, Waikiki, and other parts of the island, the wave hunters came searching. They had checked the scary ones, Kaena, Avalanche, Himalayas, and had decided to head for the churchtower. They came in battered Fords, long Packard hearses, wood-covered station wagons. Boards stuck out of car windows, were hastily tied to rooftops. The surf was up at Waimea Bay.

Bill was nursing a large head when the first of them came. He watched them and the others that followed with mixed emotions. Time would stop because the only life, the only action, was the sets of man-killing waves that rolled in from the north. They blotted out the hazy sun when they rose, and as they broke they sounded like huge trains thundering by. And each breaking wave brought an earthquake to Waimea. The ground rumbled and the sound was like the big guns on destroyers. They ranged in size from fifteen to twenty-five feet, and it was good sense to look at them in fear.

Bill sat in his patio chair and noticed many of the wave hunters were from California. He also knew what was running through their minds. The California surf was tricky. There were rip tides and jutting rocks to slow or speed the wave as it rolled in. But California waves were small, and those who grew up with them conquered them easily. They were a tricky bunch, those Californians, they could hotdog it, skim sideways across the crest, walk the board, hang ten, and smile to the approval of the gallery. They were performers, and they were good, and some were even cocky. But when they gazed at, and later tried, the giant size waves on the north shore of Oahu, they realized how lousy they actually were. One sweet ride on those watery mountains was an accomplishment all itself. The sets were unpredictable. One set could contain both the smallest and the largest wave of the day. So you tried to ride the fifteen foot and under ones, and hoped to survive the twenty to thirty footers. To wipe-out in California meant sand in the waistband of your baggies, maybe in your ears, and hopefully, to retrieve your board before it killed someone. But to wipe-out on the north shore meant being pounded by millions of tons of water grinding your flesh into coral rock and lava. And if you recovered, it meant being sucked far out to sea as the next gigantic wave built itself up. If one wave didn't get you, the next one would. But Bill knew that once you were up there, once you had the speed of the wave judged right, had your board placed just so, the ride in was the sweetest, most powerful feeling there was.

But fearing the wave was only part of it. The surfer's biggest enemy was himself. Wipe-outs were dangerous. Loose boards were like floating knives, the fins could gut a man like a fresh-caught fish being cleaned. To have a board slam into you could start a job that the next wave would easily finish. With nobody on them those boards were lethal weapons.

So Bill sat in his patio chair drinking coffee, and watched as the wave hunters came. The awning poles shivered each time a gigantic wave crashed down. Crowds stood on the rocks and on the beach. Small groups mumbled about the wind, about a growing chop. They looked and judged from the beach, but as yet none had tried the big waves.

Bill drained the last of the coffee. Surfing was good therapy. There was a time for shock, a time for grief, a time for anger. There was the drowning of sorrow and the watermelon-size head. The butterfly of love had touched him and moved on. Now it was time to jump back into the stream that flowed from womb to tomb. A killer was loose, a thing, an it, a he, a she, and he had to find the whatever. He had seen the galloping ghost of death on a sweet girl who blessed the air she breathed.

And there was Operation Hang Ten. The opium thing. Emotion had run its course through him. Now he had to become, once again, the hunter, the cold analyzing calculating machine. And there was no room for emotion.

But first there was the therapy. The big waves.


A few had already tried when Bill, in the early afternoon's hazy sun, trudged across the short span of beach to where wave afterbirth boiled like soap suds. He was dressed in his bright yellow baggies. The blood-red board with its black marble swirls was tucked under his arm. The earth shuddered with the thunder of each breaking wave. The swells started far out in the bay. He could almost feel the suction as the waves gathered, pulling in, rising, and still rising, blotting out sky, sun, clouds. Then they crashed along the reefs, boiling and churning. And Bill felt the quickness of his heartbeat. Puny man on his fragile overgrown ice-cream stick facing the one thing over which he had no control. The sea. Man always challenged but never conquered.

The few who were out there looked scared, and with good reason. The wind had grown, there was a chop, and the suction of the building waves exposed ugly jagged heads of coral.

As Bill watched, one of the surfers caught a beautiful wave. He was riding it in, looking like a dark Quasimodo. Bill smiled. Onyx color and style and grace, that was how John Fast Black Washington rode it in. He had a dangerous position just below the crest, but the board was angled sideways and he slid along twisting and arching his body to compensate for the changes in wave speed. A good fifteen feet below him, clutches of jagged coral rock waited. The rear half of his board was hidden by churning white water snapping at his ankles like a pack of albino wolves. It was a sweet fast ride, and when the wave started to break up, he turned out.

Bill had seen it coming but there was no way of warning John. The set was close. A twenty footer was building just behind the wave John rode in. When he turned out, the second wave started sucking him out into the bay. He knew he was in trouble. He lay prone on the board, his thick muscles bulging with the power of his paddling strokes. But the current was too strong. As the wave built it pulled him into its curl. And it was going to go more than twenty feet. Bill had his board in the soup. He didn't want to start paddling out until he was sure what was going to happen. A crowd had gathered on the beach. John grew smaller as the wave pulled him out to sea. But still he paddled, as though he hoped it would break behind him and push him in. But even the strength of his strokes couldn't fight that current. Then he was a mere speck in the curl. The top of the wave leaned over. John stopped paddling. He hooked his arms and legs around the board. A girl on the beach screamed. The sun was blotted out, then the mountain crashed down. John disappeared. When the thunder subsided and the wave was rolling white water coming in, John's board zipped into the air, high, twisting and twirling. It came down then bounced up again, not quite so high. There was no sign of John. A third wave was building.

Bill started paddling with all his strength straight for the current he knew would suck him into the wave. He saw a dark ball bob up and down far ahead of him. But the ball was moving out to sea faster than Bill could get to it. Then Bill was in the current. He was being pulled and he helped by paddling. The gap closed. John was swimming toward him, getting nowhere against that strong current. The third swell was building higher. Bill was beyond the reef, well into the bay. He was close enough to see fatigue on John's face. His swimming strokes were lifeless, without strength. There was a nasty gash above his left eyebrow. Bill got beside him and twisted the board around nose to the beach. He felt John's hands on his legs. There was no time for talk. John climbed up on the back of the board. A shadow loomed behind them. When Bill felt John's head against the small of his back, he started paddling. John seemed to get his second wind. He paddled too. With both of them working they slowly made their way against the current. The shadow above them darkened. But they weren't in the curl, they were ahead of it. The current stopped and Bill knew any second the wave would come down on them. He felt the eerie split-second of silence just before the wave thundered down. He shut his eyes and hung on.

It came down with a deafening explosion, right at the arches of their feet. The board shot ahead like a bullet out of a gun. The wave churned behind them, pushing them ahead, faster and faster. They skimmed over the reef. Bill opened his eyes. He could see the jagged rocks to his left, and above them, the Waimea Churchtower. Directly in front of him the beach drew closer. They slowed and started paddling again. When they felt a new current start to pull them back, they rolled off the board and touched bottom. With one on each side they pushed the board between them. Bill's breath came in short pants. He could hear John's quick breathing. When they got to the beach, they staggered a few steps, let the board fall, and dropped to their knees. They entwined arms around each others' shoulders, put their heads together panting.

Then grinning in John's face, Bill said, "A funny thing happened on the way to the beach today."

John shook his head. "Man, there I was, old Fast Black hisself, out there in that nasty ocean. My arms felt like wet macaroni, and I says to myself, Fast Black you just ain't going to make it. And then here comes that loose-jointed Grand Duke of the Surf paddling out to me for all he's worth, and I says to myself, That damn fool's on a suicide mission. But still you came, and you got me, and bless you with your foolishness."

They slapped each other and laughed. But it was a nervous laugh for Bill, and he knew it was for John too. They had been touched by the Finger, but the Hand had moved on.

EXCERPT FROM

# THE TRIBES OF PALOS VERDES

Novelist Joy Nicholson grew up in the luxurious Southern California waterfront community of Palos Verdes, and *The Tribes of Palos Verdes,* her jagged 1997 debut novel, is partly an indictment of the upper class. *Tribes* tells the story of fourteen-year-old Palos Verdes newcomer Medina Mason, who learns to surf as an escape from family, school, and the gorgeous but cruel "towel girls." Nicholson lives in Los Angeles, and has published articles in *Westways* and *L.A. Weekly. Flack,* her second novel, was released in 2004.

IT's MY FIRST MONTH in Palos Verdes. The moon is full and gigantic; cloud strands float by in the night sky like silvery ribbons. I keep erasing my French homework until the paper is such a mess I can't see anything but smudges. Frustrated, I look out my bedroom window hoping to see sea lions and sea cows. My father says Palos Verdes used to be full of sea lions, but they don't like cars and noise so they've gone away. But sometimes they come secretly in the night, he says, so if I look hard I might see some.

Suddenly I hear a quiet splash. I crawl out on the window ledge, teetering as the wind puffs my pajama bottoms into big pontoons.

That's when I see them.

Eight or ten surfers cut smoothly through the black water, shiny in their rubber wetsuits. They move quickly, silently, flashing their cigarette lighters in code as they take their places in the lineup. The first surfer stands up and pushes off. The wave arcs high and topples; I see a shadow race down its face, faster and faster, until it disappears from sight into the black water. I suck in my breath as the wave crashes and an explosion of silver light is thrown up against the moon. Other surfers follow, one after the next, shimmering with speed, melting into the liquid. I hear them laughing in the dark, then taking off again.

The air is wet as I hold my arms out against the salty breeze, imagining, cold air hitting my teeth.

As their lighters get doused, the surfers begin to scream to each other across the waves. Their voices carry clearly to my window.

*"I'm fuckin' next."*

*"You're such a friggin' wave whore."*

*"Whooooooooooo!"*

All order breaks down in the dark. They start to take off two and three to a wave, yelling, badgering each other. They race, paddling fast, laughing and cursing. There's a sharp crack as two boards collide, then silence.

A woman is standing on the edge of the stairs, searching with a powerful flashlight, shining it on each of the surfers, aiming for their eyes, telling them to keep their voices down or she'll call the police.

Immediately I hide from my mother.


My father is a heart surgeon to the stars in Beverly Hills. He removes fatty deposits from famous comedians and handsome-but-aging television stars.

As long as I can remember, he wanted to live in Southern California—the Golden State. The day he told us we'd be leaving Michigan he picked me up, swinging me around and around, almost knocking over the coffee table. He said soon we'd have orange trees, a big pool, and a pretty view of the ocean. There would be clean beaches, dolphins, and whales, and best of all it would never, ever get cold. My mother wasn't convinced. She said California was full of divorced people, murderers, and earthquakes.

In Palos Verdes, if you are close enough to the shore that the waves keep you awake at night, you are admitted to the tennis club, where you can play a set with the Mad Servers and complain about the water.

"It's just so loud. So incessant. I can't sleep."

My mother has plenty to say to the ladies of the Mad Servers.

"The surfers. They destroy all the ice plant. They drag their boards across the ice plant and ruin everything."

The Mad Servers look at each other. A few nod their heads politely. Until she continues.

"What's wrong with this place? How come the children roam around in packs? Why do they gather like mantises on the cliffs?"

This is my mother's first faux pas. The ladies of P.V. don't want to hear complaints about their children. The drinking, the smoking, the violence. No one wants to think about *that*. A kiss on both cheeks, a bibb lettuce luncheon: that is friendship.

"I know you want it," my neighbor Danny says.

He is fifteen and superweird. He says he'll give me a surprise if I lift up my shirt, let him see. We're sitting in his tree house above the eucalyptus grove in his backyard. Pot is puffing out the sides of his mouth, choking him like an amateur. He stares at my flat chest, choking.

His eyes are red and filmy, his hands tightly clenched over the nose of the vanilla surfboard he offers. The board is smooth and pale white, with a single flame of orange down the left side. It has two fins. Two. Danny strokes the board cockily and tells me I have to hold up my shirt for ten seconds if I want it—he'll count.

I think about the ocean outside my window, how I see the guys glide on it. I imagine myself free.

"That's all," I tell Danny. "One—one thousand, two—one thousand, like that. And you have to stay over there."

He eyes the board, then my shirt, squeezing his palms together, stoned, fanning his ugly face in the warm air. He nods, he gestures for me to lift it up.

"First put that board over here," I say.

I watch him put the board in the crook of his arm, carrying it to the place I decree. A place just beneath my feet.

"Now go back there, to where you were."

The whole ten seconds, I look at his eyes, at his dull expression. He stares at my bare, flat chest, saying nothing, blowing air on the inside of his cheeks like a stupid puffer fish.

When it's done, he doesn't look at me. He lies down on the wooden floor, breathing hard, dizzy. He motions for me to come to him, but I run, putting the vanilla board in the crook of my arm, dragging it down the rope ladder, smelling its coating of coconut wax and resin. All night I think about it, sitting in the garage, waiting for me to hold it.

After breakfast the next day, I avoid my mother and her dark sunglasses and heavy silences, but I sneak my brother Jim out to the garage and show him the vanilla board. I run my fingers over its nose, talking about water. I promise I can get him one. I cross my heart.

Then I go to Danny in his tree house, climb right up the ladder as if it's mine.

"I want another," I insist. "I want another board."

He doesn't look at me, but he says he will talk to his friend.

The next day I go to Adam Frankel's house. Adam Frankel is sweaty, nervous, clammy. He tells me three times that his mother is coming home soon. His giant Adam's apple strikes me as funny, so I laugh and laugh. Then lift up my shirt, still laughing.

My brother's new board is green like his eyes.


The next day is free-dress day. The popular girls are all comparing their pretty outfits, doing a mock fashion show under the awning. I smile secretly, thinking of my surfboard as I sneak past them in the concrete hallway. But the girls come to hover around me, laughing, trying to trip me with their feet. I walk past, float even, as Cami Miller shouts out, "Five dollars!" eyeing my favorite brown pants.

Adelle Braverman follows suit, yelling, "Six ninety-nine!" and spitting at my pretty leatherette thongs.

I flinch only when Cami almost hits me with a heavy science book. As I jump back, Cami says, "Don't worry, we aren't gonna hit you. We wouldn't touch such a dirty girl."


I feel clean later, lying in the pool on my board for the first time. Cami is on the beach, a million miles away. I curse her as I float through the deep end, scanning the stairs for Jim, so he can hold my ankles if I try to stand up.

As I wait, I paddle slowly, back and forth in a line, maneuvering through the flat water on my belly, humming to myself.

I'm going to be the only girl to surf Palos Verdes.

Sometimes I dream I'm a boy.


The next day I carry my board, balancing it on my head down the cliff stairs to the bay. Jim follows, embarrassed, dragging his board under his arm like a suitcase. The water is calm and flat like the circle in a turquoise ring, but Jim bites his lip, scanning the horizon.

"People will laugh, maybe we should learn somewhere else."

"Oh Jim, don't be such a pussy, just close your eyes and go in."

For a minute I think he is going to punch me, but instead he smiles.

"You're insane, you crazy girl."

He slaps me hard with a frond of seaweed. Together we fight, kicking water into each other's nostrils, struggling to push each other into the whitewash. I jump in and climb on the board, holding its rail down with one hand the way pro surfers do. Jim jumps in, too, and pushes me off. I flounder in the water angrily, spinning and defeated.

"You surf like a girl," he says.

"You suck," I say, "like a troll."

He puts his right foot forward, and then his left, and says, "Which way are you supposed to stand?"

As I think about this, I forget how mad I am.

"Whichever way feels better," I tell him.


I'm lucky it isn't winter yet, that's when the waves get big in Palos Verdes. The waves are small and swashy now, two feet, perfect to practice on. For the first hour, I concentrate on pushing myself upward as the wave is in motion. Only the third time I try, I stand up and ride the wave to the shore, wobbling but not falling. When the wave ends I know I'll always be a surfer. I know I'll be trying to catch that feeling for the rest of my life.

Jim is stronger, he pushes his body easily upward. But my balance is a little better, I stand up faster, and stay up longer once I catch a ride. I practice every day, even when the local guys paddle out but Jim goes back to shore, embarrassed, swimming fast.

My plan is to be good by December. It's hard to imagine riding big winter waves that tower over my head, but I try to see myself dwarfed by water, zooming across on the diagonal, the lip closing down behind me.

My father gave me a magazine article about a famous woman surfer in Florida, Frieda Zane. She says the only way to get good is to forget you're a girl, and surf like a man, aggressive and fierce. She says to hang around with better surfers as much as possible, study the way they stand and move, and ignore them if they laugh.

"Don't limit yourself to being a lame chick in the water," she says. "Use your mind—and your arms."

I cut out a picture of Frieda surfing a big, green, velvety wave in Hawaii and hang it over my bed, where I look at it every night before I go to sleep.

Frieda doesn't explain exactly what to do when other surfers laugh. Sometimes they catcall across the water, imitating me when I push off. *"It's a UFO,"* they yell, *"an unidentified flailing object."*

I pretend I don't hear them, but I do.


I'm on my stomach in the bay, on my surfboard, experimenting with ways to paddle out faster. The waves are getting bigger now. It seems impossible to get out to the wavebreak because the whitewash keeps pushing me back.

"It's harder for a girl," Jim tells me. "Your arms aren't strong enough."

Even though I get mad, I know it's true. When I try calling a surf shop to ask if there's a secret trick to good paddling, the guy who answers laughs. "Pretend there's a great white comin' at you, girlie." Then he laughs again and hangs up.

First I try pushing water through my fingers like I'm doing the breaststroke, but the board keeps going sideways. Next I try using my hands like scoops, feeling salt stinging the scabby spots near my bitten nails. Finally, I try pushing the water with my hands and kicking my legs, but my knees keep banging on the hard resin.

Soon I'm sweating in the rubber, but I can't take my wetsuit off, because there's nowhere to put it. Sweat and salt water start dripping in my eyes, and I punch the water as hard as I can. The rubber is suffocating me so I unzip the top of my wetsuit and balance it on my head, wearing only a cotton T-shirt now.

Then I get an idea: I imagine I'm a machine—a paddling machine that never gets tired. I plunge my arms about a foot into the water and propel myself forward, counting out loud, "One, two, one, two." I paddle across the entire bay faster than I've ever done it before. The only thing that stops me is a gulp of sea water I breathe in by mistake.


The other girls have small purses or backpacks, but I carry a silver plastic shopping bag, big enough to hold my wetsuit, so I can change in the bushes on the way to the cliffs.

The girls laugh, they point, they titter. As we all wait for the bus after school they cup their hands in perfect unison, together in tribes, planning pranks to play.

"Can I sit here?" Cami Miller is gesturing to a place beside me at the bus stop. A place that is always empty. I ignore her grandly, picking at my nails, humming.

"Well, can I sit here?" Cami repeats, looking at the other girls, smiling, winking.

"Sure," I finally say, "do whatever you want."

"But I don't want to sit here," Cami says, giggling, then laughing tiny silvery bells. *"I don't want to catch anything."*

The other girls laugh, in a gaggle. I think of them washing away. I throw my hands out in a wave.

"Die," I tell them. "Whatever."

Cami is five times as pretty as me now, but she wasn't always. She only got beautiful when she went to Dr. Rosen for a nose job. All the towel girls go to Dr. Rosen. They tape their chins and ears, sometimes they even get their eyelids ripped open and reshaped into half moons. Tara Pugh had her lips enlarged with fat from her own butt.

There are horror stories of plastic surgery gone wrong, like Mrs. Ambrose, whose face caved in from too many reductions, or poor Steph Stone who chose a nose too small for her face and ended up looking like a devious elf.

*"But that's because Dr. Rosen didn't do the surgery."* The towel girls agree, *"You get what you pay for."*

*"I mean, he was like a doctor from Afghanistan or something—from, like, a Third World country or something."*

"Why don't you wear your new dress to your French lesson?" my father asks me later.

"Yeah, why don't you?" Jim says, trying not to laugh.

"You'll look like a princess in it," my father says, grinning.

"She's not filled out enough for that dress," my mother cuts in. "It'll make her look like a scarecrow."

"I'll wear it," I say quickly. "I like it, Dad."

My mother says, "She's a good liar, like someone else I know." She looks directly at my father.

"I'll *wear* it," I say, again.

I wear the dress out of the house, but I sneak into the garage to change into shorts. Even though I feel guilty, I hide the dress inside the teeth of the lawnmower, next to the Goodwill pile.

I look best in my new wetsuit, anyway. Jim tells me I look like a pro.

If I couldn't surf, I'd just die.

*Surf or Die.* I have a sticker on my notebook that says this.


"Fuckin' ole," Skeezer Laughlin, the biggest and meanest of the Bayboys, says to Jim at the cliffs. "There's gotta be a storm from Mexico pretty soon."

The Bayboys are the popular surfer clique in Palos Verdes. They're the only ones who can surf Lunada Bay, the bay in front of our house, without getting hassled. Jim's always nervous when he sees the Bayboys paddle out; he doesn't know if it's okay for us to surf with them, even though we're locals. As soon as they paddle out, he comes in, trying to make me follow.

Jim nods to Skeezer, acting nonchalant. His fingers pick at the skin around his nails.

"Have a toke?" Skeezer offers Jim a joint, ignoring me. Jim drags hard, and looks out at the water. I see the veins pop out on his neck, but his expression is neutral. Both of them sit there, saying nothing. Skeezer passes the joint to Jim again. I hear a sucking sound, then a high squeal as a massive intake of smoke causes Jim to choke. Skeezer laughs, and starts to choke, too.

"See you at the bay one of these mornings," Skeezer says, walking away. "And by the way, it would be cool if you let us use your cliff stairs."

On the way home Jim is flushed, quiet. The bitten skin around his nails is bleeding. He wipes his fingers on his shorts.

"We can surf with the Bayboys now," I say. "If Skeezer says we can."

"I heard," he says sharply.

"So do you think we should go out with them tomorrow?" I ask, very excited, poking him in the ribs.

"Maybe we're not good enough to surf with them yet," he answers nervously.

But he's flexing in the mirror when I spy on him later.


This is how to be a wavegetter in the morning lineup. Set the alarm for 5:30 A.M. in order to do a wave check by six. If you're late, you'll have to take the last spots with the other sleepyheads, and you probably won't get a turn.

If you try to sneak a ride, the Bayboys will get mad and careen their boards at you like big, dull arrows.

Our first morning out with the Bayboys, the waves are flat and unrideable. Jim and I paddle toward the lineup, sweating in our rubber jackets. Skeezer gives my brother the secret handshake and nods to me. He tells me to get in line behind all the guys.

"Ladies don't go first here," he says.

I clear my throat. "I guess you don't get special privileges then."

No one laughs. Nervous, I look at Jim. He keeps his eyes on the horizon, frowning just the tiniest bit. Finally one of the older guys cracks up and motions for me to line up next to him.

"She got you, Skeez," the guy says.

As I paddle past, Skeezer grumbles, "Hell, from the waist up she could pass for a guy anyway—a real ugly one, though."

Because there's no waves, the guys spend the morning telling their best surf stories—like the time when Skeezer's cousin's friend saw a great white shark at Angel Point, or the day Jim Dayton surfed with Jimmie Ho, the legendary Hawaiian. No one talks to me much. Still, I feel pretty great.

When the waves start to pick up after the school bell rings, Jim and I swim to the shore, hesitating on the shallow sand. Then I decide what to do. I close my eyes and turn quickly back into the water, forgetting about school, even though I'll have to spend a week in Mr. Gross's tardy detention.

I get one junk wave, closing my eyes when I fall. I stay underwater as long as I can so I don't have to hear Skeezer laugh.

I'm going fast, flying through air, unstoppable. It's 4:30 after school and there's a freak small swell at Angel Point. It's two to three feet and round, not very mushy. The waves are softly capped, pushing against the bottom of my board, rocking me from side to side.

I'm about to wipe out, but I pretend I'm the wing of a plane, soaring through the air, above trees and rocks and grass. I don't fall off even after I've counted to five. Then I hit whitewash, and the board bounces hard under my feet, as if hitting pavement. There's a thud and I jerk to the left without warning, falling headfirst.

The water slaps my face and chest as I fall, stinging until I land in a soft nest of seaweed. Slippery fronds envelop my legs and stomach as I gasp for breath. My hands are windmilling wildly until I stop going under.

Before I can reach my board, it's spinning high in the air, pushed by a wave back to the edge of the shore, eddying on the sand in the shallow water.

A piece of hair wraps itself tightly around my neck. Another wave slaps me in the back, tumbling over my head, pushing my face into the water. When I finally come up again, I'm shaking.

Jim is watching me. He gives me the thumbs-up.

Jim never laughs when I fall.

The sand rises up on a crest in the middle of P.V. beach, making a throne for the popular kids. Everyone else sits in the furrows and cracks along the cliffs.

ANONYMOUS

# "HAOLE GO HOME"

The following article was written by an anonymous Hawaiian, and originally published in a 1969 issue of *Surfer* magazine. Long-simmering tensions between Hawaiians and *haoles* (whites, or in this case visiting white surfers mostly from mainland America) had taken a turn for the worse; local surfers, with some regularity, were punching out visitors. The violence often seemed like simple thuggery. The Hawaiians had a different perspective.

WHY DO I FEEL like stomping the haole? Well, look at my side of things. Suppose I came over to your house and said you weren't dressing right, and you weren't living right and this and that. You'd get mad and sock me, too. It's a lot deeper than that I guess, but that's the way we feel. You Mainlanders come over here and try to run the show, and we are supposed to be your servants. The trouble is, we are slaves to your system. You've taught us to need your money and your conveniences, but we'll never respect you. I get plenty burned up when I think of what's happening to my brothers and our Island. But we still have our pride.

A long time ago, our Islands were beautiful and our traditions of life were simple and honest. Then Captain Cook and the missionaries that followed taught us that we were sinners. They taught us shame, and they encouraged us to change our carefree ways. They brought the word of God, but I don't think God had this in mind. It makes my blood boil when I see all the hotels, stores, ships in our harbors, servicemen on our streets and tourists jamming up everything. Until a few years ago, we could still get away from all of this by going surfing. Now even that's been taken over by the haole. Long-haired, hippie-type, drug-taking surfers infest our best and most beautiful surfing spots. Why do those folks come to Hawaii? Why don't they go home and take their drugs and pretend they are in Hawaii? They have ruined some of my friends who never thought of any more than a little beer now and then.

So once in a while when I get a few good blasts of beer going, I get to thinking of all these things, and some haole acts up; well, I just bust him a good one, and I feel a little better.

The girls of Palos Verdes sit around in little groups. The towel girls, the Jews, the Chinese girls, the softball players. Each is a clique of seven to fifteen members who sit together in designated areas and talk only to each other. The members of each group dress alike. They wear the same lipstick colors and have similar bathing suits. Their parents have roughly the same amount of money.

The ones you notice are the towel girls, beautiful creatures who lie on Bill Blass towels, developing dark tans, sitting in their own circle on the high sand, reading fashion magazines with dark Vuarnet sunglasses perched on their upturned noses. They arch their perfect brown backs and adjust their pearls while they wait for their boyfriends to reemerge from the water. Showing the boyfriends how lucky they are.

The towel girls affect terribly bored facial expressions and eat chilled apple slices out of delicate Japanese coolers. They also keep beer cold in these coolers, beer for the boys who gesture for it later, after a few sets of waves. The girls learn from their mothers, towel mothers who pour perfectly chilled martinis for their husbands after a hard day at work. They learn serving and pouring early.

There are only a few ways to greet the towel girls. You can walk quickly past them, holding up an index finger as if testing the wind. Or you can nod your head in their general direction without nodding to any specific girl as a mark.

Nothing that insinuates friendship with a towel girl is acceptable, such as walking clear into the middle of their group and saying, "Hi, Heidi, what's up?"

If this etiquette is breached, if you dare address one of these girls in person, she will lean over to her friends, giggle prettily, and say, "Oh my God! Did you hear something?"

———

Surfing is many things. Sometimes it's a religious experience, sometimes pure domination. I tame a patch of milky waves, ride on them as if they were beautiful horses. The girls taunt me at school, chanting, *"Fatty Mom. Elephant Mom. Big as a whale. Gross as a snail."* But in the water, they can't reach me.

I love stepping into my wetsuit, tightening the zipper slowly up my back, feeling my naked skin against rubber. As I begin to paddle, long strands of wet hair tickle my neck, cashmere soft in the salty water, making me shiver and giggle out loud. Sometimes I lie in the sun for a few moments, hair fanning out, face to the sky, feeling exotic and beautiful.

It's a frank sexual pleasure to be wet and warm, lying alone on my stomach near the mouth of the sea, relaxing completely, then pushing my body upward while taming the liquid motion.

After school, I love to be in the safe, warm curl of a tube.


The winter surf is kicking up. Mountains of water are moving toward our house, carrying more and more abalone shells to the beach. There is a storm off Mexico, Hurricane Alex; the waves are five feet high.

Jim and I have been surfing for nearly seven months, but we've never tried waves bigger than three and a half feet. We huddle together in the yard, deliberating. Jim says we should tell Skeezer we're sick.

"Both of us?" I ask. "They'll never believe it. They'll say we're scared."

"We'll say you gave me the flu. I feel sick, I swear."

We take our boards to the pool and lay them belly down in the blue, calm water. For a while, we paddle from end to end, discussing different kinds of flu and their symptoms. There's the Chinese kind that makes you barf for seven days and the Taiwanese kind that gives you the runs. Jim says we can pull off the Taiwanese kind if we take six Ex-Lax pills each.

"Ex-Lax is disgusting," I say. "Besides, we're good enough to go out now."

I remind him that he never falls off. "You're just afraid the older guys will laugh and call you a grommet-fag."

"Maybe," Jim admits, picking at his fingers. "So what?"

Then I thrash around in the water, making the biggest waves I can, and tell Jim to stand up. He stands up, and laughs.

"See, you're not gonna die," I say, and I slap him a high five.

We suit up on top of the cliff stairs. I rub Jim's back before I pull up the big zipper in the back of his wetsuit. By mistake I catch a piece of his skin in the fold. I put my hand over my mouth, sucking in my breath.

"Oh my God," I say, "I'm sorry."

"What?" he says absently, leaning out to took at the waves. Then, "Damn, I don't think I can do it."

I tell him my secret strategy. "Pretend you're a barnacle on the back of a whale—stuck on forever. Pretend there's no way the water can throw you."

He shrugs, telling me to forget it. "You always imagine crazy stuff. When I get scared, my mind goes blank and I don't even know what I'm doing."

We smoke an entire joint on the way down. But Jim lights another one at the bottom.

"Forget it," he says when we get to the rocks. Looking at the towers of water, he stands still and white, holding his board stiff, like a wax statue.

I push him toward the water.

"You're gonna rule the waves," I say.

A few of the guys are watching us. Jim gives them the thumbs-up. When he turns, his eyes are raging.

"Stop poking at me!" he says. "Don't treat me like a baby in front of everyone."

The waves are a translucent emerald green, highlighted by sparks of light thrown by the setting sun. I've been paddling for fifteen minutes, but I haven't reached the wavebreak yet.

The waves are far more powerful than I thought. I can hear stones and heavy shells rumbling against the bottom.

First I try to go around the break, through to the left, but the current is too forceful, so I throw my board down and fight the whitewash in front of me. My arms are heavy with fatigue, and I'm swallowing mouthful after mouthful of spray. I can't see the sets that are coming because my eyes are slitted against the sting of salt. Finally there's a small lull, and I paddle.

Jim is nearly out. He jumped in at the jetty and started stroking, smooth and fast, riding up and over the wave faces, his powerful shoulders pushing him much quicker than I could follow. At first he tries to wait for me, but I motion him to go ahead. Now I see him with the guys, lined up, ready to go for a turn, astride his board with his legs deep in the water.

I see Skeezer being spit forward. He dances from right to left, swaying before gaining balance, leaning forward then lurching to the left, perfect. Another set comes. Another lull.

I paddle ferociously and make a lot of ground. I'm almost there, ten feet away, when the next set comes. Aaron lines up, ready to go, but I see my chance. I scream "Mine! Mine!" and turn around to catch the swell. It's late, already breaking when I catch it. The wave throws me sideways, but I hang on, stand up, and whip around in the force. Hair slaps over my eyes so I'm blinded. The roar of the water comes down as I slide over the wave, fishtailing back and forth like a sewing needle gone awry. Somehow I stay up, leaning forward, almost retching, ready to fall. But suddenly I'm riding instead, falling from the sky, watching the horizon surge upward. Then I'm kicking out just before the tube closes. I get slapped by the next wave, and the next. I'm holding on to my board with one hand, dog paddling with my other, turning my face away as the current pushes me back and forth.

*"I got it,"* I yell to the guys. *"I got a wave."* I paddle close to Jim in the next lull. Everyone is amped. Skeezer smiles at me. Tad gives me the thumbs-up.

"Hey, don't snake any more waves, Medina," Aaron says. "There's a fucking lineup, you know."

"Give spaghetti arms a break," Skeezer calls out. "It took her long enough to find us out here."

Jim joins in. "Yeah, mellow out."

He smiles at me and takes off on the next wave. All I can see is his muscled back, almost black in the semi-darkness. He stands straight, tall, maneuvering back and forth, graceful and powerful. His hands are low at his side, his left foot barely raised.

When he kicks out, the board flows sweet and steady, spinning in the water overhead. Even when he goes under, he's smooth, controlled. He comes up laughing, holding his arm up in the air in triumph. He swims right up next to me, and winks, telling me how perfect I was.

Walking home later, Jim kicks the dead brush aside for me. He doesn't say much, but he comes to my room later to say goodnight.

"Goodnight yourself," I say, grinning.

He hangs around for a while, picking through my records and magazines, then he sits down on the floor, putting his big, smelly feet up on the bed. He turns off the lamp. "That was fun today," he says in the dark, "maybe one of the most fun days I've ever had."

I nod, smiling, starting to fall asleep.

"Do you think the best times we'll ever have are happening now?" he asks softly.

"Don't think like that," I say sleepily. "It's bad luck."


Some of the Bayboys tease me about my flat chest and skinny neck, but a few of them are pretty nice. Once when I step on a sea urchin, Charlie Becker, an eighteen-year-old, helps me pull the slender spines out of my feet. I pretend it doesn't hurt, even when he digs around with a needle to find the broken-off pieces of the quills. As he dips my foot in water to clean off the blood, he tells me to wear surf booties next time—watertight slippers made of thick rubber.

"You'll have better grip; they stick really good to surfwax. And the urchins won't get you as bad."

Then he tells me to keep it up, to forget what the guys say.

"I've been watching you out there. I think you could get pretty good, *if* you get serious about it."

Then he laughs and tells me I better practice a lot, because perfect balance takes years to attain.

The next day I go to Mrs. Ornage's house, the old French piano teacher, and tell her I've decided to surf more, so I won't be coming to any more lessons. She sits with her back very straight, playing a small song on the piano, smiling faintly.

"Yes," she says, "maybe you will be better at this surfing than you are in piano. It is important to do something that you are good at."

That week I also quit flute and tennis.


There's a lot of things you have to know if you don't want to be x'd out with the Bayboys. Your hair has to be a plain crewcut, or long and feathered like Skeezer's. You have to wear tan or black boardshorts, the extra-large kind that come to your knees. I wear boy's boardshorts, because most girl's bathing suits are weird, either too lacy or very skimpy. Some of the guys think it's funny that I wear trunks.

One time Andy Aaron is reading *Surfer* magazine at the cliffs, when he holds up a full-page ad of a busty girl in a bikini kneeling on the sand.

"How about them apples," he says, waving the magazine around, howling like a dog. Suddenly the rest of the guys are howling, too, panting and beating their chests like gorillas.

Skeezer calls out to me, "Hey, Medina, why don't you ever wear a bikini like that?"

Blood rises to my face, but I laugh and pretend to go along with the joke. He asks again, walking over to me, "Why not, Medina? A nice yellow string bikini?"

"Bikinis are stupid," I say. "Besides, it would fall down in the first big wave."

"It would fall down anyway," Skeezer says, running his hand up and down in front of my chest, indicating a flat board.

When I don't say anything, he draws up his shoulders and smirks.

"Oh, you'd look all right in a bikini." He slaps me on the back. "Don't be so sensitive."

I smile but don't look at him. Later I cut him off and snare his beautiful ride on a good three-footer.

"Don't be so sensitive," I say when he shakes his fist at me.

But it's not just hair and swim trunks, there're other unspoken rules. P.V. surfers never wear colored wetsuits, or anything bright or modern, no neon. They only wear black wetsuits, holes patched with duct tape, discolored with resin stains. They have one- or two-fin boards. They don't ride squirrelly, stupid, tricky tri-fins, and don't like anyone who does.

Secretly, I don't care that much what anyone wears. I don't even care if they surf in sopping wet Levis like some Vals do. For me, the only thing that's sad is watching people go to work in their suits and ties.

It feels so great to walk away and go surfing.

# SEVEN

# VOICE OF THE WAVE: WHY WE SURF

"While inside the tube," Hawaiian pro Jock Sutherland explained in "What Is Surfing?" a 1970 *Surfer* magazine cover story, "I do not receive a giant exudence of the senses, but rather a non-feeling, as it were, of some of the prismatic auras and shimmering spectrums of bright death." Okay. Two points. First, *that's* what it sounds like when you mix irony with high-grade LSD; Sutherland loved both. Second, by whatever combination of drugs and intuition, Sutherland neatly parries the whole "why surf?" topic—and all credit to him, because the question just about always leads straight into a rhetorical double-suck closeout. Why surf? The flip answers—"It's the funnest thing ever," "To get a tan and impress the ladies"—leave out the deeper, meatier aspects. The solemn answers—"Self-expression," "To touch nature," "To see God"—ignore the happy clatter of everyday surfing: the coffee-to-go morning check, the flat-spell commiserating, the in-house jokes and hoots and whistles.

Surfing is loaded with beauty and good humor, and has a near bipolar ability to thrill and soothe. Does this mean surfers have deeper or more profound reasons for doing what they do than fly fishermen, or cyclists, or bird-watchers? Maybe not. "You're just another person who's found an outlet for making yourself feel good," Australia's Barton Lynch acknowledged with a shrug after winning the 1988 pro tour championship. "The world is full of enjoyable, fruitful pastimes."

You could leave it at that, if only to counterbalance surfing's intolerably high self-regard (Lynch further notes that surfers tend to be "more cocky and judgmental than any group of people in the world"), except the ocean itself will quietly rest its trillion-gallon thumb on the scale, to separate and then elevate surfing from the larger world of sports and recreation. The surfing environment is without equal. Bird-watching is no doubt an enjoyable, fruitful pastime. But gliding across a breaking wave you can in fact get a tan, impress the ladies, *and* see God. Of course surfers are smug.

DANIEL DUANE and PHIL EDWARDS, in their respective autobiographical books *Caught Inside* and *You Should Have Been Here an Hour Ago,* both pay tribute to this expansive view of the sport from comfortable positions just off the surf line—Edwards while sitting with his back against the warm seawall of a friend's Capistrano Beach home, Duane while changing out of his wetsuit at the base of a cliff in Santa Cruz as the sun throws a blood-red frieze against the western sky. There's a quiet pride when Duane thinks to himself, "I am more a part of this life than most Americans are of any life anywhere."

THOMAS FARBER approaches the ocean from nearly every conceivable angle in *On Water,* his book of essays, but he also returns to the shoreline. Farber at one point watches a loud, happy, interwoven group of Makaha Beach surfers, longboarders and shortboarders, kids and adults, and wonders, "Just how much of your life would you give to be in such a medium in such a way?" Waves, Farber notes elsewhere, are "the pulse of the planet." You might give up a lot to live in that pulse. And played right, you'd get everything back, with interest.

# *YOU SHOULD HAVE BEEN HERE AN HOUR AGO*

California's Phil Edwards was regarded as the world's top surfer in the late 1950s and early 1960s. *You Should Have Been Here an Hour Ago,* his autobiography, was coauthored by *Sports Illustrated* writer Bob Ottum and published by Harper & Row in 1967, just a few months after Edwards had been featured on a *Sports Illustrated* cover. Edwards has worked as a boat-maker for over thirty years.

M Y HOUSE AT DANA POINT is a lot like my life. It is actually two houses—two small, white wooden shacks, really—with the living room and kitchen in one of them and the bedroom and bathroom in the other. There is a little cement walkway between them where we set our hibachi; we cook on it in the evening and stumble over it a lot at night. I live with Heidi, my 97-pound wife; and Chassa, our jumpy Siamese cat, who is the only member of the family with a complex and that is because she is a used cat. The place smells richly of the sea, which is 150 feet straight down the cliff. I am 28 years old, California umber in color and have all of my fingers and toes. I have always wanted to live this way. I have thirty-eight pairs of surfing trunks.

In the mornings, in bed at Edwards-East, we awaken to the sounds of the ocean. (In fact, with just the right kind of quake, we could awaken some morning *in* the ocean.) By just raising my head slightly from the pillows I can look out into the Pacific. It is a moment of big, Executive Decision: If the surf is up, I can go surfing. If the surf is not right—but the wind is up—I can go sailing in my catamaran. Or, if it is one of those terrible, grim, zilch days, I can always go to work. The way we live, which you can call Stoked Casual, the costume is the same for any of these three activities. Shoes are not required.

Down the cliff from where we live, at Dana Point sea level, Capistrano Beach, I design surfboards for a living. Which is exactly what I want to do for a living; I am resigned to the fact that it is not the kind of activity that is going to get me named Industrialist of the Year by *Fortune* magazine.

Yet, this is the good life. I have this old Volkswagen, the mother of all Volkswagens, that is so beat up you wouldn't believe it. The lining is all out of it so that its beautiful West German skeleton shows and I knocked out the back window so that I can slide a surfboard into it. This creates a great visual effect as I drive down to the beach with a board sticking out the back window. It looks like the board and the car are making love.

On our surfing days, when the wind and waves are right, we assemble at the Poche Point Club, which is so exclusive you can't stand it. Exclusive: It is the little strip of beach in front of Wayne Shafer's house on Beach Road at Capistrano Beach. And exclusive means that Wayne has two refrigerators: one in the garage for beer and one in the kitchen for more beer and a little bit of food. Heidi calls it the Poche Point Club because these rickety old railroad tracks come along the other side of the road—once the tracks carried trains full of harried-looking commuters. And there is a beat-up, salty gray railroad sign there that says "Poche Point," calling attention to something none of us can see—because there is no real point there. And certainly no *Poche.*

Houses are all like this along the beaches in Southern California. They look out into the Pacific through salty windows and turn their backsides to the road. Shafer's house is at the end of Beach Road. There is this narrow, blacktopped street with "Go Slow" signs painted in white all over it. There are special bumps planted right into the blacktop, like little bar-ricades, to make certain you *do* drive slowly. With just the right kind of hangover, undulating slowly over these bumps, you can be seasick by the time you get to Wayne's house.

The club is a pickup affair: Anyone who happens to be there at the time is a member. No cards. No dues. No minutes of the last meeting. There is nearly always Wayne, who is slowly perfecting a real estate busi-ness where you never have to be anywhere; Heidi and I, our friends Mickey Muñoz and Harrison Ealy and Flippy Hoffman and Joe Lancor

and Dick Barrymore, who makes skiing movies. Barrymore also gives us special reports on *people* movies that he sees, playing all the parts himself. He is particularly good on *The Sound of Music,* singing all the Trapp family choral parts, a sort of hairy Julie Andrews.

And there we are: A real estate specialist, a moviemaker, a student of architecture, a Los Angeles hustler, a surfboard designer—and their various bikinied women—all riding those waves in front of Shafer's house. As disparate a group as you can find.

The surf at Poche Point is often jolting—it comes pounding in short and fast on most days, not exactly the sort of surf you will see in Hamm's Beer ads or on book jackets. Rather, it is the kind of ocean that disciplines you, trains you for the better stuff. It also breaks down your kidneys, tests your pelvic structures and shakes all the fillings out of your teeth.

Girl surfing champion Joyce Hoffman lives next door. We call her Boo. And one of the reasons Boo Hoffman is a champion is that she rides that surf out in front of her house—the short, pounding rides, with one wave locked in tightly behind another; where, once you make a tight turn, you are committed to your course. She rides and rides, even in blue knee and knuckle weather, wearing a pair of old plaid Bermuda shorts. And when the good days come along—those rare times when the water glasses over—there she is, standing suddenly gracefully and at ease, cutting swinging patterns back and forth on the shoulders of the waves.

Barrymore rides a short, stubby, villainous-looking black board. He has enough kitchen paraffin dappled on top of it to can thirty quarts of tomatoes. He will hack around at Poche for days, falling off, fighting his way back up in quiet desperation, working, training. Finally he will put the board on his car, drive over to Doheny State Park, which is the beach next door, and ride the Beginner's surf and hot-dog around for the benefit of all the kids and the short-stokers. Then he will come back to the Poche Club and announce to us all, "Hot damn. I've finally got my confidence back. I've been over riding those Ego-Builders. Makes you feel like the greatest surfer in the world."

Tough as it is, this is Mood surfing. We like it. Every ride is guaranteed to be a wild one; the long rides are rare and the over-all effect is wonderful exhaustion.

And every day we surf, good or bad, there is this magic time. We sit on the beach, still warm from the day's sun, and lean our backs against Wayne's sea wall, and look out at the ocean. We drink beer from the garage refrigerator (until it runs out, then we switch to the indoor refrigerator) and we dig our bare feet into the sand and we look into the Pacific and the Pacific looks into us.

We are stoked. Six, eight, nine, ten people lined up against a wall, all jazzed by the water we have just conquered. There is this feeling of vast accomplishment. It is like, say, having gone off the big jump at Holmenkollen in Norway. And you turn at the bottom and look back up at that glazed ice platform and think, "Hot damn!"

There is nothing mystical about this. There is a need in all of us for controlled danger; that is, a need for an activity that puts us—however briefly—on the *edge* of life. Civilization is breeding it out of us, or breeding it *down* in us, this go-to-hell trait. Gradually, the day-to-day people, the hackers, are taking over. There are, as you read this, uncounted millions of people who now go through life without any sort of real, vibrant kick. The legions of the unjazzed.

But surfers have found one way. God knows, there are other ways. Each to his special danger. Skiing is not enough. Sailing is near. Ski jumping is almost. Automobile racing has got it. Bullfighting makes you dead. The answer is surfing.

# DANIEL DUANE

# CAUGHT INSIDE

*Caught Inside: A Surfer's Year on the California Coast,* Daniel Duane's autobiographical second book, published in 1996, describes the joys and difficulties of learning to surf along the temperamental beaches and reefs of north Santa Cruz County. The California-raised Duane has a Ph.D. in American Literature from U.C. Santa Cruz; he's written three other fiction and nonfiction books, and his surfing articles have appeared in the *New York Times, Outside, Men's Journal, Surfer,* and the *Surfer's Journal.*

VINCE, FORTY-FIVE, a math lecturer at the university, was notorious among his many close friends for two things: first, a voracious appetite for waves. He'd compete relentlessly for every wave, even resort to aggressive and dirty tricks among friends; it kept you scrambling for your share. Second, he had an almost pathological tendency to swear that wherever he'd just been surfing (without you) had been perfect. Definitely better than wherever you'd been at the same time. Even if you showed up only an hour after he did, you could count on hearing how that hour had been the best hour in years. This all meant more to Vince than just having fun; it was a barometer of the very quality of his life. If you got more waves than he, or made a better choice of breaks, he seemed to feel he was losing what little power he had left in the world. Still, it would've taken me a lifetime to learn on my own what I learned from Vince in a year, his exhaustive knowledge of the tide, wind, and swell matrix for every local scrap of reef and sandbar that had ever been known to produce ridable surf. And in spite of his fierceness in the water, Vince was wonderful company: very wry and quite sensitive to the feelings and opinions of others. He knew when he was stepping on toes, and often seemed embarrassed about it. But he never stopped—surfing was the one part of life in which he was giving no ground.

He scheduled only morning classes in winter so he'd be free for evening glass-offs, afternoon classes in spring so he could work while the northwesterly winds blew. Office hours and appointments were always timed to leave outgoing tides available. Vince had even failed to deliver a final exam once because of a good surf session, but I suppose he hadn't exactly walked away from it. Nor had there been any friends along. He'd just stopped at the beach for a surf check on his way to campus, got a little mesmerized by the empty perfection before his eyes, and forgot all about the exam. Not until he'd left the water a few hours later did he get that nagging feeling. Walking aimlessly around campus, hair wet and sinuses draining, he was suddenly confronted by a very concerned department chair. But that was a rare lapse: Vince had held the same job for fifteen years and had been married to the same woman for longer. While he might have left her in the lurch for the off lunch date, he certainly wasn't walking away.

Still, there wasn't a surf-crazed teenager in the county who got more waves than Vince; he surfed every day without fail, and often surfed twice a day, even in the smallest, coldest, rainiest, most all-around miserable conditions, when even guys with the day off were inside watching videos. I loved being with him, loved our endless conversations and the unshakable sense that this unlikely use of time *mattered*.

Unless you're a strolling naturalist by nature, or a farmer or commercial fisherman or ranger, you need a medium, a game, a pleasure principle that turns knowing your home into passionate scholarship. City dwellers know nothing about neap tides or the topography of local reefs for the same reason few Americans know a second language: not out of moral or personal weakness but because *it doesn't matter.* For six months I'd been living just a few hundred feet off the beach in Santa Cruz. I didn't move there to perfect my backside aerial attack (or even just to learn what the hell a backside aerial attack *is,* for that matter); I moved because my need to be in the clear, alive water of my California's Pacific, on a real, honest-to-God surfboard, on a daily basis, had been a source of nagging angst since the first time I'd ridden a wave. And Monterey Bay was all the watery home I could ask for—a big dent in California's coast about seventy miles south of San Francisco Bay. Santa Cruz, an unpretentious college and resort town, crowds the cliffs of its northern lip and ends abruptly at the fields and hills of the open coast. South of Santa Cruz, small towns dot the sheltered bay shore for ten or twelve miles before Salinas Valley farmland stretches clear to the fishing and tourist town of Monterey at the bay's southern lip. As a teaching assistant at the university two days a week, I made enough to rent a room smack in the middle of all that coastline in a two-story shingled house with big gables, green trim, bits of student sculpture strewn among pear and palm trees in the front yard, and a surfboard shed so old it was held together by hand-forged nails. Built as a summer cottage when fields still ran along these cliffs, the house had old-growth redwood interior paneling, making the inside warm and woodsy and pretty off-level here and there. Most of the floors sloped one way or another, none of the doors sat quite right in their jambs, and the whole upstairs swayed gently in high winds. That house could also have used some work: the chimney just a pile of bricks from a recent earthquake, pine floors scuffed bare, black mildew spotting the bathroom ceilings, countless thumbtack holes in the door frames, sluggish drains, no hot water upstairs, and spiders in most of the ceiling corners. But in spite of very low rent, my bedroom had a clear view of the water (the outer bay in one direction, shore break in another) and windows that opened outward like double doors; and with deep reddish-brown walls, floor, ceiling, and even window frames, it felt like a stateroom on an old sailing ship.

I'd lived for the last few years in a town full of familiar faces, near great bookstores, within a few blocks of Thai, Mexican, Tuscan, and Mediterranean restaurants, next door to world-class coffee, and, like I said, in an apartment building also inhabited by eight of my oldest friends. (Nearby ran an interstate commute artery, and in the middle of the night with the city's ambient din quiet the highway made a roaring hiss much like surf.) And those friends mostly nodded with forced enthusiasm when I declared my intention to move to the water; the kind of move everyone will acknowledge *sounds* great, but in a way that lets you know they'd never make such a mistake themselves.

Vince had picked me up just after dawn, and we'd already surveyed nearly thirty miles of beach south of Santa Cruz; hadn't found a single sandbar to his liking, and were now speeding toward Willie's place up on the coast.

"By the way," I said to Vince, as we approached the farm on which Willie lived, "what does Willie do for a living?" The question had been nagging somewhat: decent car, nice clothes, more good dentistry, no apparent obligations.

Vince actually laughed out loud at the question, as though he'd been wondering when I'd ask. "Unclear," he said, looking sideways at me and raising his eyebrows. A big trailer truck passed in the other direction, laden with crates of sprouts.

"You don't have any idea?" I got a twinge that Willie wouldn't appreciate this conversation if he could hear it. Vince had also mentioned that Willie might not like our barging in on him without a phone call, but since he screened all calls, it was hard to make plans on the fly.

"He claims to work on the farm up there," Vince said, "but I have

# "WHY DO YOU SURF?"
## FROM *SURFER* MAGAZINE, 1995

"Because that's all there is. It's all surfing. Everything! Name something that isn't surfing. In the New York Stock Exchange, you check it out, you pull in, and you try to figure out when to kick out safely. Surfing in the ocean just happens to be the purest form of surfing."
—Tom Morey, 60, California

"Because my dad wouldn't let me play football."
—Richie Collins, 26, California

"I love everything about it, especially the colors made by the mixing of sun and water. I guess you could say that I go to the ocean in order to see God."
—Skip Frye, 53, California

"To escape. I detach myself from land and separate from my troubles every time I go surf. Unless it's crowded, surfing is a very private time for me."
—Chris Brown, 24, California

"There's no laws in surfing. I can go as fast as I want, get as radical as I want, get creative, with no speed limits, no stop signs, and no one telling me what to do."
—Shawn Briley, 20, Hawaii

"I surf to get tan."
—Shane Dorian, 22, Hawaii

"There are a lot of factions in surfing, but the overriding and universal draw for all surfers is that addiction to being immersed in sea water."
—Dave Parmenter, 33, California

"I can't wear my hearing aid in the water, so every time I surf I'm almost totally deaf. The only time I've ever heard anything out there was three years ago at Pipeline. I got 10 perfect stand-up pits in a row before getting the wave that changed my life. I dropped in and traveled for a long time in the tube before the thing spit. Kaboom! It sounded like dynamite. That was the first time I ever heard the sound of a wave breaking. I came out of the barrel with so much speed that I just kept going into the channel while I screamed 'I heard the tube! I heard the tube!'"
—Cody Graham, 21, Hawaii

never, in ten years, *ever* known him to miss a swell. And hey, travel? No problem. Six weeks in Chile last summer, Costa Rica this summer . . . You know he lived in Indo, don't you?"

"Where?"

Vince slowed to a stop as another car signaled to turn left across the highway. "Indonesia," Vince said. "This is the part I'm not totally clear on. He apparently dropped out of Harvard in the seventies, but other than that . . . *misterioso.*" He turned right onto a dirt road and followed it for almost a mile up the hillside beneath dense oak trees; the road made several turns before opening onto a broad dirt lot full of rusting cars. I saw no house, and the two long, windowless brown buildings bordering the lot looked like boarded-up barracks or toolsheds. A once-yellow cultivator rusted near a chicken-wire cage full of household garbage; a few white T-shirts and a pink pair of women's underwear hung from a line. Behind, open fields gave an unbroken view across the hills, over the muted green of the artichoke fields on the other side of the highway, and out to a broad expanse of glaring white sea. The whole place felt as if perched on some airy, flying plane of green-and-brown earth, a speck of land soaring among all that windswept water and sweeping sky, and away from town and the highway a palpable calm reigned in the silence. A big Labrador slept in the grass by a white Plymouth with no tires, and a silver-haired man with bright brown eyes and smooth, rosy skin smiled hello from a chair by one of the sheds—at peace in a small patch of sunshine. "World expert on basil," Vince said softly to me: one life devoted to play, another to pesto. Vince mentioned that the property belonged to the basil guy, and that Willie apparently paid no rent.

We left the truck near Willie's El Camino and walked under the shade of an oak tree to a door in a shed. Vince knocked lightly on the peeling plywood, and soon the door opened.

"*Coño,*" Vince said with a smile.

"*Yeah, now,*" Willie responded. He said that he was, in point of fact, more than delighted to pursue waves; had been just about to head out himself. He welcomed us inside while he went for his board and wetsuit, and what a revelation! Waxed cedar floors and cabinets, a huge case of books, three classical guitars, and the entire west-facing wall a series of floor-to-ceiling windows—outside, beyond a weathered deck and a small garden crowded with culinary herbs and salad greens (squalor renovated to unpretentious splendor), the Pacific Ocean beamed its overwhelming calm into every square inch of Willie's domestic life. Willie's beautiful wife, Pascale, sat at a handmade dining table, drinking espresso and reading *The New York Times*. A warm blend of Old World femme fatale and good-humored New Age feminist, Pascale seemed at once irritated and amused by the mustering of the troops, tickled by a life associated with such adult dereliction.

"Four days off I have," she said in a mock-Brooklyn accent to Vincent, whom she clearly knew well. "Four days! Any mention of plans? Any, like, 'Gee, honey, why don't we get away together?' No way! It's just like"—here her voice took on a flawlessly modulated, unexaggerated surfer accent—"'Sorry, can't say what the waves'll be doing.'" Then she turned back to her paper, muttering, "It's pathetic." Something wonderfully good-humored about the complaint, though, in spite of that element of seriousness present in every joke. I looked over the books while she and Vince talked: mostly American poetry and minority women novelists; a few stretching manuals and a book on women's health. Willie came back inside with his board and asked Pascale for a few bucks. Pascale pointed to her purse and grinned to herself as she read the sports section—turned out she had a thing for baseball—and she seemed to have been only playing the carping wife for Vince and me, as if perfectly conscious of all these little male independence fantasies, and comfortable tweaking them.

Crowded together in Vince's truck, we drove back down to the highway, then farther north, stopping at a series of watersheds; where each creek emptied into the sea, we climbed up berms or out to cliff edges, surveyed the water. None of the reefs were catching the swell quite right, so we kept pushing north, talking back and forth in an endless fiddling with variables: this spot's taking the swell bigger, but the tide's going to get too low soon, Point might be better in a little while, but the wind's only going to worsen, crowds'll probably show up pretty soon, could wait for the lower tide and try another spot, but what about the storm front coming down?

"Chummies?" Vince suggested, referring to a break in which a dive operator had begun dumping tons of chum—pig blood and animal parts—to attract great whites.

"Feeling chummy?" Willie asked.

"Could be perfect."

"No guarantees in this life, but, *hey now.* We're on the road, the road's a fine place to be, you boys are good company...Might behoove a fellow to have a look. But, of course, might behoove us to just get wet, too."

"Wetness," Vince responded. "The old hand-in-the-bush theory." Where Willie tended to advocate picking a spot and deciding to be happy with it, Vince always deferred to the greener grass that might be elsewhere. He also claimed an indisputable authority on every variable affecting nearly every break in the county, which made negotiation difficult. But after nearly an hour more of haggling and contributing to the greenhouse effect, we— *they,* really—agreed upon "Chums," much to my dismay. So we stopped where yet another creek emptied across a beach, scrambled among detritus from what must have been a spectacular wreck—a twisted car body, a crank shaft, a radiator—then walked out past white ranch buildings, knobcone and Monterey pine and a strip of chaparral hunted by a black-shouldered kite.

A band of clouds stretched from horizon to horizon with ribs forming a vaporous spinal cord; pulverized shells mixed with black pebbles gave a shimmer to the beach's crunching surface. Carnage, too: a big elephant seal with its bottom half bitten off and a bright red organ swelling out of the hole, flaps of muscle hanging pale pink and white. Two flippers lay against its side like mortified hands, and a gull stood serenely nearby, looking away from the object of interest—as those birds do—into the middle distance. Patient and unafraid, the gull let us pass by before plucking out the seal's eyes. A little farther along in the kind of daily excursus for which I'd begun to live, the wave almost a chimera to justify day after day of wandering obscure stretches of sand, analyzing the relationships of a reef's bottom contours to prevailing winds and various swell directions, we crossed yet another creek coming down from the mountains, spilling into a cobble of stones that had whorls like wood grain. And there, still more carnage: a decapitated otter, broken bones jutting through stiffened skin and the truncated spine sticking like a broken flag pole into the air. Great whites apparently didn't eat otters, just beheaded them. Two very large vultures attended the corpse, perched nearby on a log as we approached under the low cloud; in all their black patience, their feather rufflings matched the pace of our amble and their bony nostrils breathed the same kelpy breeze as our fleshy ones. And when we got close, they showed due respect for us apex predators and flapped their wide, heavy wings up to perches on the crumbling cliff.

Vince told Willie about a very successful travel photographer they both knew and whom he'd just seen at a dinner party. Quite powerful, Vince said of her, a woman of real force and ambition. Picking up stones and skipping them in the tidal film, he explained how she had traveled all over the world, through Nepal, Tibet, remote spots in the South Pacific, all over Africa. Apparently she always chided Vince for his endless returns to a group of islands off the west coast of Africa, for his failure to ever go anywhere interesting, like Africa itself. He'd been flying to that little Atlantic archipelago for twenty years now; loved the population's blend of old Moorish pirate stock, African slave castaways, and Spanish sailors. "I don't *want* to go to Africa," he said to us. "That's why. Generations of people have survived without ever going to Africa, right?" He seemed quite bothered by the suggestion, by the challenge it offered to his sense of these daily walks themselves as all the travel a person should ever need. Of course I agreed, and assumed Willie did too; but Vince seemed embattled nonetheless.

When we finally got a good view of the reef, Willie saw Vince scrutinizing it. "Let me guess," Willie said, "it was five times better yesterday."

Vince smiled and didn't answer. We took off our clothes where a few big chunks of sandstone protruded from the beach, pulled on wetsuits, and paddled out to a wave formed by the submerged underside of some vanished point. Breaks usually reflect the very outline of the continent or the flow of watersheds—tide-scalloped sandbars, the underwater projection of a cove's curve—but these waves broke straight into the beach, their reefs remnants of a coastline that no longer existed. The word *reef* is also used in mining to mean a lode or vein of ore, and in sailing as a verb for reducing sail surface—certainly a rock reef does, in a sense, "reef" in a wave. The name Chums just added to an already heavy aura around the place: a shark mauled a guy here a few years ago, and all that chumming for high-paying "eco-touring" clients had stirred huge local controversy; the dive master received anonymous notes swearing that the next time he dumped chum they'd hack off both of his legs, performing upon him, in essence, the core of their own shark fears. I applauded the intent if not the means. After all, the chum flowed with the currents, made a blood slick that sharks followed for days afterwards with their appetites aroused but not sated. And we found out later that a boat chartered by a television science show was offshore chumming that very day.

Diffuse sunlight penetrated the high clouds and rippled across the sea like a streetlamp shining on a river. The waves were surprisingly powerful: coming out of very deep water, they were no more than three or four feet high until they caught the reef. Then they stood up to twice that height, and even as the lip feathered, a second lip formed about a quarter of the way down the face, so the whole top of the wave lurched over in a phenomenon known as doubling up. After the steep drop, which I could barely make, you had to charge to make the hollow wall; the new board felt fast and loose, oddly alive under my feet. Willie and Vince got repeatedly tubed, then came flying onto the shoulder grinning from ear to ear.

"*Formidable, non?*" Vince said, turning to go on yet another great wave.

"Shrackable bowls," Willie added, referring to the hollow bowls forming where the wave heaved over.

"Yolla bowly," Vince yelled back. "The Bowlshoi ballet!"

I couldn't find my way into the tube, and Willie explained that you had to take off on the far side of the bowl, then race across it as the lip pitched overhead—in a phrase, "You gotta backdoor it to get your coverage." The problem was that if you mistimed it, you became one with the lip and participated wholly in its contact with the shallow reef. But we settled into a cycle, taking turns, not talking much, riding in and paddling out, and there was something about the still water surface that let you feel fine gradations of density and resistance. Vince was in heaven, not being the climber who lived for the biggest wall, the surfer who yearns for the ultimate, huge wave; he just sought reasonable, daily perfection, took pleasure in a simple afternoon on a good wave. There were no dragons out there he dreamed of slaying. There's a wonderful way in which surfing falls outside the narratives of death and change—makes, in fact, no story. In all its talk and writing, one rarely hears of the act itself. Three hours of the greatest surf of your life amounts to just that—no yarn. One goes out, comes in, surfs in circles, and spends the vast bulk of the time floating, waiting, driving around. One can declare the rush of the drop, but will be hard-pressed to describe how much water is moving, the feel of different motion vectors, the wild vitality of it all. One can talk of carving deep, then gouging the lip, but even if the listener *can* visualize the living pulse of the wave, imagine the thrill of responding to a supranatural flux and pulling out as it booms onto an inside reef, it still doesn't make a story. The broken truck axle and six-hour hike through the Baja desert for help are far more likely to be repeated years later than how "I made this super-late drop, and then the wave hit that inside bowl and just throated me."

A surf session is, then, a small occurrence outside the linear march of time; sure you can catch your last wave, but rather than a natural conclusion to a well-lived tale, it will simply be the point at which the circle was snipped. So one hears instead of conditions—like a good west swell and light offshore breeze—solid overhead peaks wrapping through the inside. No conflict, no crisis and resolution; no difficult goal obtained or struggle between teams or even with oneself. No obstacle surmounted against great odds—in fact, the hardest part in surfing happens before you get to your feet. Talking about it to nonsurfers becomes much like saying, "I went out and masturbated today, and it felt great." Who cares? The rich tradition of surf storytelling has more to do with what guys did before and after surfing than with the surfing itself, except, perhaps in the case of enormous, dangerous waves. Certainly, anyone can relate to the joy of clean water—birds, fish, dolphins, seals and otters and maybe sharks, kelp drifting with the swells, popping its sea-hag heads up here and there—and perhaps one can picture the crystal curtain falling all around or the wild freedom of gliding into the golden ball of a dawning sun, but still, no yarn. Thus, the tendency toward an "If you have to ask..." smugness, inarticulation as elitism: "Only a surfer knows the feeling." One often hears surfing compared to sex; quite a stretch, except perhaps in the unself-conscious participation in a pattern of energy, in a constant physical response to a changing medium—at its best, emptying your mind of past and future. Willie later described it to me as having the quality of Japanese dancing on rice paper, in which the dancer steps so delicately that the paper never tears, and pointed out how each wave washes away all that has come before. And that day at Chums, while paddling back out from a wave and feeling the glow of a glorious ride, I noticed that I couldn't remember anything specific about the wave, couldn't even picture the unbroken wall as it rolled in.

At dusk, all of us exhausted and sloppy, the sun rippled and curved behind the clouds like a bloody clamshell in a gray pool. North over the offshore island, a first patch of blue framed a chunk of rainbow, and then the sky cleared overhead and a huge bulwark of white mist glowed pastel rose. Willie caught a last wave, and as I waited for mine, I thought how awful it would be to be bitten in half after deciding to leave—like a cop getting shot the day of his retirement. But my last wave appeared as a quiet gift, shimmering and silver-smooth, with no roar, bellow, or bite; I soared for a hundred yards on a wall I could barely see. A warm breeze drifted off the cliffs as we stood on a platform of shale taking off clammy wetsuits, pulling at wet rubber and thrashing to get each limb free, and I had a pang of guilt, though for what, I had no idea. Not moving forward? Losing time? Missing life's train? "We going to get penalized at Heaven's Gate, you think?"

"Nah," Willie said, "God doesn't care about stuff like this." Unfortunately, his age rendered the assurance less than convincing; whatever it was he'd needed to prove in life, he'd apparently already proven it.

I looked anxiously at Vince. He just blew air through his lips as if to say, No Fucking Way. Declaring an unequivocal right to enjoy his chosen life. Above us on the cliff, a big, gold-breasted hawk sat perched on a knob of rock. It had grounded for the sun's final setting, coming out of the arboreal for a moment terrestrial, staring out to sea where that gentle blue faded into the very edge of the world. Hard to blame the hawk for such rapture; void being, after all, a function of one's (in)ability to make order of the space in question. And later, as we drove home, the full, purple moon rose over a bay fading like a Japanese mountainscape of misty, forested shores. The color and very face of water seeming no more nor less than wind: some winds are gorgeous, others, aggressive, chaotic, or sickly,

but that evening's offshore was pure art. And as Vince and Willie talked about camping up here twenty years ago, when only a handful of surfers knew these breaks, I decided there was something of the New Englander's affection for autumn in the Californian's for surfing—an American sense of place and region. Old-timers always recalled the sheer number of boyhood summers spent under a now-befouled pier, the teenage nights on beaches now buried in condos, the way they truly *grew up* at a now-famous break; as if to say, I am more a part of this life than most Americans are of any life anywhere. A profound insistence on authenticity, a way of believing in an identity our culture does not reward and—as of the climber still in Yosemite twenty years later—asking understanding of values and disciplines that don't answer our sense of what one does with a life.

# THOMAS FARBER

## EXCERPTS FROM
## *ON WATER*

Thomas Farber's 1994 book, *On Water,* is filled with short, poetic, nonlinear essays on a range of water-related subjects, including dolphins, drowning, sex, rain, baptism, sharks, water beds, and surfing. The Boston-raised Farber was a Fulbright Scholar and recipient of a Guggenheim Endowment, and has been a dedicated surfer since the early 1970s. He's written eighteen fiction and nonfiction books, including *A Lover's Quarrel: On Writing and the Writing Life* (2003) and *The Face of the Deep* (1998). He teaches writing at U.C. Berkeley and the University of Hawaii.

G*LASSY,* **THAT STATE OF GRACE:** no wind, no noise, board shooting along, waves perfectly defined, absolutely themselves, their shape not affected by any other force, a realm of clarity and ease. Water thick as milk, as cream. As porridge.

A windless winter day, after a month of cold. Very heavy rain, each drop making a small crater on the ocean surface, but despite the cumulative impact of so many minute explosions the net effect is to calm the water, to eliminate all other normal movement or pattern—ripple, chip, groove, rill. In the torrential downpour, each successive incoming wave seems smooth, sheer, immaculate, pure as the formula of the textbook curve.

Poet Philip Larkin: "If I were called in / To construct a religion / I should make use of water." Not to think of believing in the Almighty or not believing in the Almighty one way or the other, but then to hear the words on one's lips after two hours in the surf: "Thank you, God."

For what? Oh, for this pulsing, undulating, shimmering, sighing, breathing plasma of an ocean. For the miracle of warm water. For rideable waves and no wind.

Reaching the water again, one smiles. A smile of recognition, quick, a reflex flash. As when encountering a close friend again. Like a baby's smile, without apparent reference to externals perceived by adult eyes. To come back down to the ocean is to reexperience an essential memory trace, something once known well, to recall that one has been trying to remember.

Water music at Sandy Beach. Boomboxes in every pickup and van, vibration of the bass audible, palpable in the solar plexus, for hundreds of yards. Jawaiian music, Jamaican-Hawaiian, Rasta T-shirts popular here. All this as locals sit watching incoming waves—and the bodysurfers risking paralysis in the shore break—for hours at a time. As at a drive-in movie. As on the Fourth of July.

What's to show for all this watching...such fishing with nothing caught? John Keats urged those whose eyeballs are "vex'd and tired" to "Feast them upon the wideness of the Sea." Farmer/curmudgeon Robert Frost, however, chided those who thus "turn their back on the land":

> *They cannot look out far.*
> *They cannot look in deep.*
> *But when was that ever a bar*
> *To any watch they keep?*

Herman Melville, on the other hand, asked, "Were Niagara but a cataract of sand, would you travel your thousand miles to see it?" (Charles Darwin, a seasick sailor who had perhaps voyaged too long, wrote that though it "is well once to behold a squall with its rising arch and coming fury," a storm is in fact "an incomparably finer spectacle when beheld on shore, where the waving trees, the wild flight of the birds, the dark shadows and bright lights, the rushing of the torrents, all proclaim the strife of the unloosed elements. At sea the albatross and little petrel fly as if the storm were their proper sphere, the water rises and sinks as if fulfilling its usual task.")

As for reaching the ocean again after having been away, often one marvels that it was possible to be gone so long, ever to have left. "How did I get so far from water?" asks poet Elizabeth Bishop's Strayed Crab. And there is the response of those who, having struggled to reach the sea, finally achieve it. Keats's "stout Cortez" (Balboa, actually), who "with eagle eyes . . . star'd at the Pacific—and all his men / Look'd at each other with a wild surmise— / Silent, upon a peak in Darien." Or the experience of the Greek mercenaries after Cyrus failed in his attempt on the Persian throne. As Xenophon writes, pushing north, the Greeks fought their way toward home, their goal the Euxine Sea. One day, "as the vanguard got to the top of a mountain, a great shout went up. And when Xenophon and the soldiers heard it, they imagined that other enemies were attacking in front. . . . But as the shout kept getting louder and nearer, as the successive ranks that came up all began to run at full speed toward the ranks ahead that were one after another joining in the shout, and as the shout kept growing and louder as the number of men grew steadily greater, it became quite clear to Xenophon that here was something of unusual importance; so he . . . pushed ahead to lend aid; and in a moment they heard the soldiers shouting, '*Thalassa! thalassa!* The sea, the sea!'"

Too many surfers at the surf line, relentlessly moving toward the rising swell, forestalling competitors. Predators, feeding on waves. Seen from below, surfers on their boards may appear—to sharks—like turtles. On whom they, the sharks, prey. Nonetheless, the pleasure of a friend's company out on the water: sharing both exhilaration and risk, sharing the reading of a given moment's options, imperatives. The hoot of triumph. The dolphin that leapt right in front of both of you as the wave formed.

And yet... "dawn patrol," paddling out by oneself at first light, most of the intense and layered lives of the city's highrises not quite conscious, morning papers not yet in the boxes, a few joggers circling Kapi'olani Park, sky rouged above Diamond Head, crescent moon up there riding its own waves. There can be at times the threat of too much solitude—what if one were always so alone in the face of such a wilderness?—but there is also the joy of responding to no other human ego, surfing with no look to the side to process the hungers—aggressions, affectations, dreams—of others, only swell becoming wave as it approaches the reef, sucking up, sucking up,

higher, higher. Of course the correct—sane—response is to flee, but, since it is too late to run for shore, wave looming, the thing to do is paddle for your life *toward* it to get up and over. Then a momentary respite, with, sadly, the regrettable downside that you are now further out to sea. In such a quandary, instead of avoidance you might try this unnatural act: as the next vortex forms, move laterally, for position in what you divine will be the cup of the approaching force, the sweet spot, they call it, *turn your back* just before the looming mass begins to break, paddle several times for momentum, and, leaping to your feet... take the drop, for a moment free or almost free of gravity, and then drive, *accelerate* down the face of the wave.

With—on solitary dawn patrol—no one there to see it, despite the tiers and tiers of windows on shore, no one at all.

No one, it turns out, except Bob, who's fixing up someone's water view apartment in lieu of rent. I bump into him at midday. "Hey, man, saw you out there this morning," Bob says, noncommittal as always.


Jack the surfer. Surfing for him something about hunting the waves, or, occasionally, being hunted by them. Turning forty, still living right across from the beach in Carlsbad, in the water on dawn patrol nearly every morning. Not a beach bum, however: he has a job selling fine mountain gear, a good job as jobs go—flexible workdays, ample vacation time. Work chosen to allow him to continue to surf. Work long since pleasant, boring, unfulfilling.

When his wife accuses him yet again of being a Peter Pan, he finally goes to see his wife's psychologist, a woman. A compulsive triathlete, the therapist concludes that Jack's responsible enough, says his wife is lucky to have someone so physically fit with a passion for nature. Pleased, relieved, Jack nonetheless wonders. At a meeting of the sales force at his company, one of the managers notices that Jack's monthly calendar is also a tide chart, and teases him. Jack can read the component of envy, of course, but still . . . is surfing enough to define—to defend—a life?

Jack at forty, remembering surfing as a way to leave behind an overworked mother and an absent father. Being out on the water, thinking only of the waves. Remembering Tavarua, in Fiji, bunking with surf nazis from the States and Australia, riding almost perfect sets day after day. Being the only one there reading a book. Reading anything. And, now, turning forty, wondering why it should be more strange to know the time of the next high tide than to know, say, that the network news will be on at seven.


The painter. Raised in the home of quite secular middle class Jews, comfortably assimilated, in a southern California beach town in the fifties (his father a Bolshevik who fought in the Russian revolution before emigrating). Down to Argentina as an exchange student during high school—so many former Nazis there!—and on after college to Poland, a fellowship to study the origins of Polish abstract art (Warsaw in the early twentieth century somewhere on the road between Moscow's "Suprem50atists" and the European cultural center of Berlin). Then pursuing his own art as modernist and incipient postmodernist. Cardboard furniture, tables and benches, he fabricated for his house—oh transience! oh detritus! Also constructions, glass boxes containing images and objects to isolate and enclose meaning. Spare, this work, an approach to purity, getting at essence, if also not exactly teeming with life. At risk of being a bit clinical. For one painting, he built a wall in his studio and gridded off a canvas something like five by nine feet, the result being 21,012 squares which he painted by hand—gray—using a translucent medium with graphite as the pigment. Romantic minimalism, it could have been termed, a longing for an image anyone from any culture would be able to come to without impediment, the creation of an all-encompassing field, absolutely continuous, but each aspect articulated, so that the sum of all its moments could be the sum of . . . all possible moments, or . . . the world, you might say. The painter only years later beginning both to teach himself Hebrew and to study Torah, in the process, as if by an obvious corollary, approaching the essential vastness he aspired to in art by a quite specific source, by taking the measure of the Polish Yiddishkeit he'd arrived too late to see, painting elegies to the memories and ghosts of the Jews who'd lived in Poland for one thousand years, his oils shifting toward both warm and cool from the mix of deep and resonant reds and blues and dark browns, evoking the spirit of rolling fields, autumn haystacks, acrid coal smoke, Chopin and swans, winter's slush, "and the people themselves . . . a nation gone, vanished, not even buried."

What seems so remarkable about the painter, beyond the depth and range of his talents, is that unlike so many converts to no matter what faith, he has not needed to repudiate the life before conversion. Rather, it is as if the painter in him was waiting for him to find . . . God. (Jews, however, avoid saying the actual name of the ineffable out loud. Instead, one employs various indirections: *eheye asber ebeye,* I-am-that-I-am [or, I-am-the-one-that-has-always-been-who-is-and-who-always-will-be]; *ha-shem* [the name]; or, *maienei mayim haim,* the wellspring of living waters.)

The painter at forty-five: At home on the Sabbath, Old Testament beard, black yarmulke, having read the day's portion of Torah and some commentary in the Talmud, now talking about . . . *surfing,* about how as a child on the beach north of San Diego he started with an air mattress and, by age eleven, had a balsa board, single fin, redwood strip down the middle, purchased up the coast in Huntington Beach from Velzy/Jacobs—was Jacobs a Jew? the painter now wonders. By the time the painter finished high school the new foam boards were coming in, technology emanating from aerospace people at Convair. Before departing, the painter built an eighteen-foot outrigger, the great Phil Edwards—the first man to surf Pipeline!—a familiar figure around town and the painter's mentor for the boat. The painter smiling to remember the grace with which Phil Edwards could shape—construct—a surfboard.

Sitting in his living room, thinking of those days, the painter, full beard now very gray, suddenly jumps on to the coffee table, lands on his knees, yarmulke holding steady, and begins to paddle. Then, spotting the wave, he grasps the rails of the coffee table and, quick as a cat, springs to his feet, landing in a crouch without any discernible impact, goofy foot (right foot) forward, arms out for balance, now taking the drop, laughing, hooting. ("Straight-off Adolph," they'd call each other—incapable of making turns.) And then, moving forward on the coffee table, the painter extends his sandaled feet over the edge, hanging ten, accepts the applause, and, stepping back, hunches over in a Quasimoto (sic: surfspeak). More applause. Finally stalling the coffee table, pushing the nose up in the air by standing on the edge of the near end, and dismounting.

"Torah is water," they say (and people come to drink). They also say that the Talmud is like the sea. And, they say, "Come swim with us in the sea of the Talmud."


Older surfer in the south swell, driving left. An unmistakable stance, to anyone who has seen photos of the great surfers of the sixties, pictures of this man and others when they were eighteen/twenty/twenty-five. The good news is that this fellow is still in shape, still out there. And the other news? Oh, that he is no longer the young man he once was, whatever wisdom he's achieved along the way. *Où sont les vagues d'antan...* In the morning paper, four weekend water deaths are reported, one of them a man on the Big Island who "disappeared in the ocean."

Funeral of a surfer in Honolulu, canoes heading out off Sans Souci Beach to strew his ashes on the waves. Story of one of the last Micronesian master navigators, who not long ago apparently took his small sailing craft

JOHN KILROY
"wave for Mickey Dora"

surfed Killer Dana
before the marina
surfed Doheny
till the river made me sick
shot the pier at Newport
back when it was legal
surfed Salt Creek
before the Ritz
surfed Rincon
before the oil wells
surfed San Onofre
before the power plant
surfed Baja
before the toll road
surfed loaded
up in Malibu
surfed tired
down by Carlsbad
surfed Santa Cruz
till i nearly drowned
surfed Huntington
the day it took the pier
surfed Ventura
at midnight, naked
surfed Oak Street
the day eight kids
stomped a fag

surfed T street
when my father died
and now i can't go back

surfed a war that had no reason
surfed the politics of crime
surfed the vandals' way with money
surfed relentless loss of hope
surfed 25 years of falling down
surfed drunkenness and dope
surfed failure as only i could make it
surfed the fear in my children's eyes
surfed women strong as tides
surfing with everything i know
surfed the day that i will die

now, they want to take Trestles
turn doe-skinned bluffs to stucco
and make an ocean view
well, i surfed waves big as buildings
and i've been tunneled for a week
the only thing that can't be surfed
is this wave rolling from the east
a wave too big, a tube too black
even for Da Cat
except we all know Dora
never thinks like that

out for a last voyage and failed to return. All this evoking Queequeg, who one gray morning told Ishmael "that while in Nantucket he had chanced to see certain little canoes of dark wood, like the rich warwood of his native isle; and upon enquiry he had learned that all whalemen who died in Nantucket were laid in those same dark canoes, and that the fancy of being so laid had much pleased him; for it was not unlike the custom of his own race, who, after embalming a dead warrior, stretched him out in his canoe, and so left him to be floated away to the starry archipelagoes; for not only do they believe that the stars are isles, but that far beyond all visible horizons, their own mild, uncontinented seas interflow with the blue heavens, and so form the white breakers of the milky way. He added, that he shuddered at the thought of being buried in his hammock, according to the usual sea custom, tossed like something vile to the death-devouring sharks. No: he desired a canoe like those of Nantucket, all the more congenial to him, being a whaleman, that like a whale-boat these coffin-canoes were without a keel; though that involved but uncertain steering, and much leeway adown the dim ages."

Once washed, Ivan Illich writes, the dead in traditional Indo-Germanic cultures journeyed until they waded or were ferried across a body of water which took away the memories of all who crossed. These memories were then carried to a well of remembrance named for Mnemosyne, mother of the Muses. Drinking from her waters, living mortals, coming back from a dream or vision, could recount what they had learned. "Philo says that by taking the place of a shadow the poet recollects the deeds which a dead man has forgotten. In this way the world of the living is constantly nourished by the flow from Mnemosyne's lap through which dream water ferries to the living those deeds that the shadows no longer need." (Solitary drinker in the bar drowning his sorrows: drowning in memories.) (Souse: to plunge into water or other liquid, to steep, to pickle. Slang: to intoxicate.)

In early 1991, a seventy-two-year-old retired electrical engineer died while surfing off Spanish Beach in northern California. "That's what he did," his widow said. "He surfed. He'd just go out there and wait for the waves. If he had a profession, I guess that was it."

What a way to go, no? Right on the face of the waters. ("In the beginning God created the heavens and the earth. The earth was without form and void, and darkness was upon the face of the deep; and the Spirit of God was moving over the face of the waters.") When *I* die, please, scatter my ashes on the face of the waters. *Warm* waters, too, as I head off. Let me cycle and recycle in the tropics forever and ever, lest the residue of my flesh and bone cry out—ashes that were my teeth now chattering, ashes that were my lips now turning blue—lest the residue that was me haunt the living by crying out from the briny deep for . . . something like a wetsuit against the dreadful chill, against the dreaded chill factor. No. Make it easy on all of us: let the waters be warm.

And don't mourn for me. I'll be in touch . . . when it rains. When it pours!


"The wind speaks the message of the sun to the sea," writes Drew Kampion, "and the sea transmits it on through waves. The wave is the messenger, water the medium."

On the east side of the Big Island of Hawai'i, rain endless, 400 inches a year, soft, quiet, calming. Falling, dropping. Just north of Hilo at Honoli'i park in the afternoon humidity, mosquitoes swarming, the surfers jump into the cold water of Honoli'i Stream—a river, really—and are carried out right to the break. Conservation of energy.

Surfers as centaurs, as matadors. Teenage girl springing to her feet up off the board: Minoan dancer vaulting the horns of a bull. The ideal of the great waterman, the master surfer who has no commercial ties, surfs for the thing itself, who does not search for the waves but is, rather, found by them. Syncopation of the surfer, against the beat of the wave. Surfing is carving, they say; surfing is shredding. Surfers and time, slowing the wave down, speeding it up. The recurring mystery of moving toward the approaching wave instead of fleeing from it. Then taking the drop, trying not to wipe out. Impact zone. Boneyard.

At Mākaha on O'ahu, several older surfers on long boards sweep back and forth, elegantly, deliberately, like dinosaur herons or cranes from the Pleistocene, kids on short boards playing like porpoises, doing 360's as they hit the backwash from the shorebreak off the steep beach, and then, unbelievably, not stopping but surfing the backwash out against the flow, weaving through the incoming human traffic. Such artistry eliciting more and more and more from the waves until, in from so unutterably far away, the waves finally *expire*. As they would have anyway, this exuberant grace a gain without sacrifice of anyone or anything, a rare—impossible?—interaction of humans and the environment. Beyond the laws of physics: nothing lost.

These children at play, singing the song of the sea. What Whitman called the "inbound urge" of the waves. Pulse of the planet. This light, this air. As Keats wrote, "The moving waters at their priestlike task of pure ablution."

One's life passes before one's eyes. That is, just how much of your life would you give to be in such a medium in such a way?

# ACKNOWLEDGMENTS

THANKS, FIRST OFF, to the erudite and incredibly helpful Patrick Moser, who turned me on to the Melville piece and answered all my questions about pre-twentieth-century surf writing. Except for the ones that Daved Marsh answered. Thanks also to Parkside hacker Merlin Mann, who knows jack about surfing, but can build supercool Web sites, speed-burn the hippest CDs, and hotrod the living crap out of a five-year-old iMac—all of which he did for me during the making of this book. Thanks to Sue Antonick for all the cheerful notes and the magnificent knit cap. My gratitude to all surf industry friends and coworkers who contributed to this book one way or another, including Sam George, Marcus Sanders, Jeff Hall, Steve Pezman, Grant Ellis, Tom Servais, and Jeff Divine. Thanks also to editors Kati Hesford and Liz Parker, and to the rest of the Harcourt all-stars, including copyeditor Dan Janeck, designer Linda Lockowitz, managing editor Gayle Feallock, and production manager Fabian Clarke. As for Wendy Burton-Brouws, my ass-kicking, gold-hearted agent, will you legally become my big sister, or do we leave it informal, or what? Lots of love, as always, to my family: Michael Warshaw, Mimi Kalland, and Chris Warshaw. Shout-outs to Susie, Katie, and Jo. Thanks, finally, to all the contributing writers, photographers, and artists; it's been a pleasure and privilege to be surrounded by your work these last few months.

# PERMISSIONS ACKNOWLEDGMENTS

# ILLUSTRATION CREDITS

**Page ii–iii:** Courtesy of *Surfer* magazine; **xxii–2:** Courtesy of Bishop Museum; **7:** Courtesy of Daved Marsh; **8:** Courtesy of Daved Marsh; **11:** Courtesy of Sandow Birk; **19:** Jack and Charmain London, Waikiki, 1915; photograph by Ray Jerome Baker, courtesy of Mark Blackburn; **33:** Kathy "Gidget" Kohner, 1957; courtesy of Ernst Lenart; **46–48:** Jock Sutherland, Pipeline, 1969; courtesy of Art Brewer; **56–57:** Mickey Dora, Malibu; courtesy of Brad Barrett; **69:** Mickey Dora, courtesy of Pat Darrin; **74:** Doonesbury © 2002 G. B. Trudeau. Reprinted with permission of Universal Press Syndicate. All rights reserved; **84–85:** *Apocalypse Now* movie still, courtesy of John Milius; **88:** Jock Sutherland, courtesy of Art Brewer; **91:** Waimea Bay, courtesy of Jeff Divine; **94–96:** Mark Foo, Todos Santos, 1992; courtesy of Jeff Divine; **103:** Alaska, courtesy of Tom Servais; **110–111:** Alaska, courtesy of Tom Servais; **122–123:** Waimea Bay, early 1960s; courtesy of Val Valentine; **132–133:** "Murphy" by Rick Griffin, courtesy of Ida Griffin; **144:** Maverick's, courtesy of Scott Winer; **154–156:** Courtesy of Tom Servais; **162–163:** Courtesy of Tom Servais; **175:** Windansea surfers, 1957; courtesy of John Villarin; **182:** "Peanuts" reprinted by permission of United Feature Syndicate, Inc.; **194–195:** courtesy of Tom Servais; **210:** "N.Y.D.P." by Peter Spacek, courtesy of Peter Spacek; **214–216:** John Kelly, Yokahama Bay, 2001; courtesy of Art Brewer; **218:** courtesy of Scott Aichner; **231:** Christmas Island, 1994; courtesy of Bernie Baker; **236:** courtesy of Lee Pegus; **238–240:** Ken Collins,

Maverick's; courtesy of Patrick Trefz; **253:** Windansea, mid-1940s; courtesy of Woody Ekstrom; **267:** "Salty Dog Sam Goes Surfin'" by R. Crumb, courtesy of R. Crumb; **275:** "The Media Miracle" by Kevin Ancell, 2000; courtesy of Kevin Ancell; **291:** Courtesy of Sandow Birk; **309:** courtesy of Jeff Divine; **320–322:** Shaun Tomson, Off the Wall, 1976; courtesy of Steve Wilkings; **325:** Phil Edwards, Makaha, 1958; courtesy of Bud Browne; **341:** "Untitled" by Wolfgang Bloch, courtesy of Wolfgang Bloch; **346:** Trestles, courtesy of Jeff Divine